A STRAIGHTFORWARD GUIDE TO BUSINESS LAW

Robert Franks

Editor: Roger Sproston

Straightforward Publishing
www.straightforwardbooks.co.uk

Straightforward Guides

publisher: Straightforward Publishing, Derby, United Kingdom
EU Authorised Representative: Easy Access System Europe-Mustamaetee 5010621 Tallin, Estonia, gpsr.requests@easproject.com

British Cataloguing in Publication data. A catalogue record is available for this book from the British Library.

ISBN

978-1-80236-512-2

Printed in the United Kingdom by 4Edge www.4edge.co.uk

Cover Design by BW Studio Derby

CONTENTS

****

Introduction

This Revised edition of a Straightforward Guide to Business Law is a wide-ranging introduction to the law and practice as it affects and influences the environment that regulates business in the United Kingdom. The law is updated to 2026.

Following on from BREXIT and the pandemic, Britain is now in the grip of a cost-of-living crisis which is having a devastating effect on the way businesses operate and the subsequent survival. It is very important indeed that both professionals and practitioners have a grip on the main tenets of business law.

The book is intended for both the student and layperson and will also be suitable for the professional. Each chapter has relevant case law throughout which provides a suitable backdrop to the subject matter. However, it has to be noted that a book of this nature, whilst covering key areas, can't hope to be totally comprehensive therefore reference is made to professional bodies and websites to supplement information.

The book begins with contract law, covering the general principles, consideration and contracts, terms of contract, errors and contracts, contracts and illegality, duress and undue influence, discharge of a contract and remedies for breach of contract..

Negligence and duty of care is then discussed, covering causation, the liability of the employer and liability for dangerous products. Remedies for negligence are also covered. Employment law is covered, providing a general outline of law plus discrimination and termination of employment. In addition, company law is covered in depth.

We then go onto discuss the main areas of company law and how this affects those who operate in business.

Finally, we discuss the all-important area of intellectual property. Patents, trademarks, copyright, infringement of copyright plus design law are covered.

All the main areas that relate to business law in the United Kingdom are covered in as much depth as is possible within this brief introduction.

The book should prove ideal to all of those who wish to enhance their knowledge of business law.

****

Chapter 1

The Law of Contract-General Principles

The following chapters cover key changes to contract law that have arisen since the introduction of the Consumer Rights Act 2015.

Many people, either knowingly or unknowingly, enter into contracts without fully understanding the implications of what they are doing. Contracts can cover a number of areas, from hire purchase agreements to more complex finance agreements, contracts for construction of buildings, contracts for work around the house or contracts to supply goods. Notwithstanding the type of contract or what area of life it relates to, there is a comprehensive framework of law, both in statute and also common law, which covers parties to a contract. This book will enable the reader, whether layperson or professional, to obtain the basic facts about contract law and also to see clearly where they stand in relation to their rights and obligations. Throughout the book there is reference to relevant court cases.

The necessity of contract law

Contract law is necessary because the law only enforces certain types of promises, basically those promises that involve some sort of exchange. A promise for which nothing is given in return is called a gratuitous promise and is not usually enforceable in law (the exception being where the promise is put into some sort of document, usually a deed).

The main reason that we need contract law is because of the complex society we live in, a capitalist society. In capitalist society people trade freely on many different levels. There are many complex interactions, from small business endeavors to massive projects, such as construction projects where binding agreements are essential. Contract law is there to provide a framework to regulate activities. Contract law will rarely force an individual or company to fulfill contractual promises. What it does do is to try to compensate innocent parties financially, usually by attempting to put them in a position that they would have been in if the contract had been performed as agreed.

Contract law-a brief history

Contract law, or the origins of contract law, goes back more than three hundred years. However, because of the very fast innovations in technology and the industrial revolution generally, the main body of contract law was established in the nineteenth century. Before that, contract law barely existed as a separate area of law. Before the nineteenth century there were many areas of life where free negotiation was not an issue. Activities such as buying goods and then selling them on in the same market were illegal and were criminal offences. There was a basic right to a reasonable standard of living and no one was expected to negotiate that standard for them selves.

A similar, though less humane approach was taken to relationships between employer and employee, or master and servant as they were then called.

Today, we all expect to have an employment contract detailing hours of work, duties and pay. This is the most basic of perceived rights. We may, in most cases, not be able to negotiate the terms, but at least it is a contract. In a status society (as it was called), employment obligations were quite simply derived from whether you were a master or a servant: masters were entitled to ask servants to do more or less anything, and an employee who refused would or could face criminal sanctions. Employers had less onerous obligations that could sometimes include supplying food or medical care. Both sets of obligations were seen as fixed and non-negotiable.

Along with the development of contract law within a rapidly changing laissez faire society, came a rapidly changing political consciousness. The view arose that society was no more than a collection of self-interested individuals, each of whom was the best judge of their own interests and should as far as possible be left alone to pursue those interests. This laissez faire approach gave birth to the law of contract, as we know it, in that, as we have seen, where people make their own transactions, unregulated by the state, it is important that they keep their promises.

Freedom of contract

Its origins in the laissez faire doctrine of the nineteenth century have had enormous influence on the development of contract law. The most striking reflection of this is the importance traditionally placed on freedom of contract. This doctrine promotes the idea that since parties are the best judges of their own interests, they should be free to make contracts on any terms they choose-on the most basic assumption that no one would choose unfavorable terms.

The court's role is to act as umpire holding the parties to their promises, not to ask whether the bargain made was a fair one. However, there are many problems with the freedom of contract:

- Inequality of bargaining strength between the two parties
- The acceptance of implied terms
- The use of standard form contracts
- Statutory intervention to protect consumers; and
- The obligation to implement EU law.

Over the years, courts have moved away from their reluctance to intervene, sometimes through their own making sometimes through parliament, notably the Unfair Contract Terms Act 1997.

Contracts and the notion of fairness

Traditional contract law lays down rules that are designed to apply in any contractual situation, regardless of who the parties are, their relationships to each other and the subject matter of a contract. The basis for this approach is derived from the *laissez-fa*ire belief that parties should be left alone to make their own bargains. It was thought that the law should be required simply to provide a framework, allowing parties to know what they had to do to make their agreements binding. This framework was intended to treat everyone equally, since to make different rules for one type of contracting party than for another would be to intervene in the fairness of the bargain. As a result, the same rules were applied to contracts in which both parties had equal bargaining power as to those where one party had significantly less economic power, or legal or technical knowledge, such as a consumer contract.

This approach, often called procedural fairness, or formal justice, was judged to be fair because it treats everyone equally, favoring no one. There are, however, big problems inherent in this approach in that, if people are unequal to begin with, treating them equally simply maintains the inequality.

Over the last century the law has, to some extent at least, moved away from procedural fairness, and an element of substantive fairness, or distributive justice, has developed. Substantive fairness aims to redress the imbalance of power between parties, giving some protection to the weaker one. For example, terms are now implied into employment contracts so that employers cannot simply dismiss employees without reasonable grounds for doing so. Similar protections have been given to others, such as tenants and consumers.

The objective approach

Contract law claims to be about enforcing obligations that the parties have voluntarily assumed. Bearing in mind that contracts do not have to be in writing, it is clear that enforcing contract law might be a problem. Even where contracts are in writing important areas may be left out. Contract law's approach to this problem is to look for the appearance of consent. This approach was explained by Blackburn J *in Smith v Hughes (1871).*

"If, whatever a man's real intentions may be, he so conducts himself that a reasonable man would believe he was assenting to the terms proposed by the other party and that other party upon that belief enters into the contract with him, the man thus conducting himself would be equally bound as if he had intended to agree to the other party's terms".

It can be seen that the area of contract law is complex and yet is governed by basic principles. In this book we cover, amongst other areas:

- Contracts and the law generally
- The formation of a contract
- The terms of a contract
- Implied terms
- Misrepresentation
- Remedies if a contract is breached.

Forming a contract

Underpinning all contracts are four main principles:

1) A contract is an agreement between the parties to that contract-one

person makes an offer and the other accepts that offer
2) Both parties have an intention to be legally bound by the agreement-this is usually known as an intention to create legal relations
3) Parties to the agreement need to be absolutely clear as to the terms of the agreement – this is the main area of contention with contracts, as we will see later
4) There must be consideration provided by each of the parties to the contract – this means that one person promises to give or deliver and the other promises to pay. The offer and the payment – either monetary or in kind - is the consideration.

When making a contract or entering into a contract all parties to the contract must have the legal capacity to enter into a contract. Very importantly, a contract, in most cases, does not have to be in writing – a piece of paper is not necessary, the agreement and evidence of that agreement forms the basis of contract. There are a few important exceptions, including contracts relating to interests in land (Law of property (Miscellaneous Provisions) Act 1989), s 2(1) and consumer credit (Consumer Credit Act 1974). We will outline those contracts that do need to be in writing later in this chapter. Other factors affecting formation include:

- Form-the way the contract is created (e.g., the sale of land can only be made in the form of a deed). Form is an issue with specialty contracts but not with simple contracts.
- Privity of contract and the rights of third parties-generally a contract is only enforceable by or against a party to it, subject to exceptions and certain third party rights are now protected in the Contracts (Rights of Third Parties) Act 1999.

The nature of contracts – unilateral and bilateral contracts

The majority of contracts entered into are known as bilateral contracts. This quite simply means that each party to a contract agrees to take on an obligation. This obligation is underpinned by a promise to give something to the other party. A unilateral contract will arise where one party to the contract will make a promise to do something (usually to pay a sum of money) if the other party carries out a certain task. Examples of this are where you might undertake to pay someone a sum of money if they shave off their hair for charity or give up smoking. Estate agents enter into unilateral contracts whereby a percentage of sales go to the agent if they sell the property. However, the agent is not legally bound to sell the property, just to try to sell it.

The notion of offer and acceptance

As we have seen, for a contract to have legal status, usually one of the parties to the contract must have made an offer and the other party must have accepted the offer. Once the contract is accepted the agreement will be legally binding. However, it should be noted that case law has cast doubt on the notion that the courts will strive to uphold the parties' bargain where possible. Two important cases highlighting this are *Walford v Miles (1992)*, also *Petromec inc v Petroleo Brasiliiero SA (2005).*

The person making the offer is called the offeror and the person to whom the offer is made is known as the offeree. An offer may be express or implied. Express means that there is an express intention to offer goods and for X to pay an amount for the goods. Implied may mean, for example, when purchasing something from a store. The act of taking goods to a checkout means that there is an implied offer to buy those goods.

When dealing with contracts, or the formation of a contract, most offers are made to specific parties. However, offers can also be made to a group of people or to the public at large. One such example is where a reward is offered for information following a crime. One famous case dealing with offers to the public at large is *Carlill v Carbolic Smokeball (1893)* the defendants in this case were the manufacturers of 'smokeballs' popular at the time, which they claimed could prevent flu. They published adverts to this effect stating that anyone using their smoke balls and not being cured of flu would receive £100.

One person buying their smokeballs was Mrs. Carlill. It did not work and she claimed £100. The manufacturers' argument was to claim that their advert did not constitute a contract, since it was impossible to contract with the whole wide world. They claimed that they were not legally bound to pay the money. The court, needless to say, rejected this argument, which held that the advert did contract with the world. Mrs. Carlill accepted the offer and duly claimed £100. A contract such as the one above is usually a unilateral contract.

The invitation to treat

Certain kinds of transactions between parties might involve a preliminary stage where one party to the contract invites the other party to make an offer. This preliminary stage is known as 'invitation to treat'.

One such case that demonstrates this is that of *Gibson v Manchester City Council (1979)*. In this case, a council tenant of Manchester City Council expressed an interest in buying their house. The application was duly completed and sent to the council. A letter was received from the council stating that it may be prepared to sell the house to the tenant for £2180. The tenant, Mr. Gibson, queried the purchase price, pointing out that the path to the house was in bad condition. The council refused to alter the price, stating that the valuation reflected the condition of the property and the current property market. Mr. Gibson then wrote asking the council to continue with the sale. Following a change in the control of the council, and a new political approach, it was decided to stop the sale of houses to tenants. Mr. Gibson was informed that his application had been declined, notwithstanding the initial offer. Legal proceedings were brought against the council claiming that the letter received by Mr. Gibson, with the offer of sale at a price, constituted a contract, and was an offer which he duly accepted.

The House of Lords, however, ruled that the council had not made an offer, the letter stating the purchase price was merely one step in the negotiations for a contract and amounted only to an invitation to treat. Its purpose in the first instance was quite simply to invite the making of a formal application, amounting to an offer, from the tenant.

Retailers' websites

These are probably invitations to treat, although this has no clear definition at the moment. Regulation 12 of the E-Commerce (EC Directives) Regulations 2002 suggests that the customers order may well be the offer so that the website is an invitation to treat. *However, be aware that this no longer applies to the UK since Brexit. See* The eCommerce Directive and the UK - GOV.UK (www.gov.uk).

Offers of sale in shops

Goods in shop windows marked with a price are generally regarded as invitations to treat, rather than offers to actually sell the goods at the price displayed. One such case highlighting this is *Fisher v Bell (1961)* where a shopkeeper was prosecuted under the Offensive Weapons Act 1959 for 'offering for sale' an offensive weapon. The shopkeeper was displaying a flick knife with a price attached in the window. It was held that the display of the flick knife was an invitation to treat, rather than an offer, thus the shopkeeper was found not guilty of the offence. Where goods are sold on a self-service basis, the customer will make an offer to purchase on presenting the goods at the till and the shopkeeper may reject or accept that offer. One case which highlights this is *Pharmaceutical Society of Great Britain v Boots Cash Chemists (Southern) Limited 1953.* Boots were charged with an offence concerning the sale of items, medicines that could only be sold under the supervision of a qualified pharmacist. Two customers in a self-service shop selected the items, which were marked with a price from a shelf in the shop. The shelves were not supervised by a pharmacist, but the pharmacist was instructed to supervise at the cash desk. The issue was whether the sale had taken place at the shelf or the cash desk.

The Court of Appeal decided that the shelf display was like an advertisement and was therefore an invitation to treat. The offer was made by the customer when the items were placed in a basket and was only accepted when the goods were taken to the cash desk. A pharmacist was supervising at that point so no offence was committed. Following on from this principle, shops do not have to sell goods at the marked price and a customer cannot insist on buying a particular good on display. Displaying the goods is not an offer so a customer cannot accept it making a binding contract. (In reality, if shops do display goods at a price they generally sell it at that price although, as we have seen, they do not have to).

Contracts and advertisements

A distinction is generally made between advertisements for unilateral contracts and advertisements for bilateral contracts. Advertisements for unilateral contracts will include those such as described in the case of Carlill and Carbolic Smokeball Co or those offering a reward for information or for lost property. They are usually treated as offers on the basis that no further negotiations are needed between the parties to the offer and the person making the offer will usually be bound by it. One case is that of *Bowerman v Association of British Travel Agents Ltd (1996)* in which a school had booked a skiing holiday with a travel agent, which was a member of ABTA. Any member of ABTA must display a notice as follows:

Where holidays or other travel arrangements have not yet commenced at the time of failure of the tour operator, ABTA arranges for you to be reimbursed the money you have paid for your holiday.

In this case the tour operator became insolvent and all holidays were cancelled. The school was refunded the money paid for the holiday but not the cost of the travel insurance taken out, which was significant. The case was taken to court and ABTA lost because the notice constituted an offer which the school accepted by contracting with the ABTA member.

Bilateral contracts

Bilateral contracts are the types that advertise specified goods at a certain price such as those found in shop windows and in magazines. They are usually considered invitations to treat on the grounds that they may lead to further bargaining. One such case that highlights this is *Partridge v Crittendon (1968)*. An advertisement in a magazine stated 'Bramblefinch cocks and hens 25shillings each'. As the Bramblefinch was a protected species, the person who placed the advert was charged with unlawfully offering for sale a wild bird which was against the Protection of Birds Act 1954, but the conviction was quashed on the grounds that the advertisement was not an offer but an invitation to treat. Another important case here is *Byrne v Tienhoven (1880).*

Communication of offers

A valid offer must be communicated to the offeree. It would be unfair for a person to be bound by an offer of which he had no knowledge. This is reflected in *Taylor v Laird 1856*. The offeree must have clear knowledge of the existence of an offer for it to be enforceable. This is reflected in *Inland Revenue Commissioners v Fry 2001.* An offer can be made to one individual or to the whole world, when the offer can be accepted by any party who had genuine notice of it. In addition, the terms of the contract must be certain. The parties must know in advance what they are contracting over, so any vague words may invalidate the agreement. This is reflected in *Guthing v Lynn 1831*.

The length of time an offer should last

An offer may cease to exist in any of the following circumstances:

-Where an offeror states that an offer will be open for a specified time

-Where the offeror has not specified how long the offer will remain open, the offer will lapse after a reasonable length of time has passed. How much time can be deemed reasonable will depend on whether the offer was communicated quickly and also on the subject matter.

Some offers are made subject to certain specified conditions, and if these conditions are not in place, the offer may lapse. An offer may lapse if and when the offeree rejects it. For example, if A offers to sell B a car on Tuesday, and B says no, B cannot come back on Wednesday and insist on accepting the offer.

A counteroffer can terminate the original offer. One case that highlights this is *Hyde v Wrench (1840)* where the defendant offered to sell his farm for £1000 and the plaintiff responded by offering to buy it at £950-this is termed making a counteroffer. The farm owner refused to sell at that price and when the plaintiff later tried to buy the farm at £1000, the original asking price, it was held that this offer was no longer available. The counteroffer had terminated the original offer.

The death of the offeror can affect the offer. If the offeree knows of the death of the offeror, then the offer is terminated. If they did not, the offer still stands, although this is one area of law that is still unclear. It very much depends on the circumstances at the time.

An offer may be revoked, withdrawn, at any time until it has been accepted. This is the basic rule, although there are a number of other principles. It is not enough for an offeror simply to change his or her mind about an offer. The offeror must notify the offeree that the offer has been revoked. Revocation does not specifically have to be communicated by the offeror; it can be by another reliable party.

Acceptance of an offer

For acceptance to be valid the following conditions must be met:

- Acceptance must be communicated to the seller: the buyer must receive the acceptance to be effective (*Entorres v Miles Far East* (1955)); silence will not suffice (*Felthouse v Bindley* (1862)); acceptance can be made through conduct (*Butler Machine Tool v Ex-cell-o Corporation* (1979)).
- The terms of the acceptance must exactly match the terms of the offer: if the terms are not the same, this will actually be a counteroffer and no contract will have arisen (*Hyde v Wrench* (1840).
- The agreement must be certain (see below).

Consideration is something of legal value which is given in exchange for something else. It can be anything of value (e.g., money, property, or a service), which each party to a legally binding contract must agree to exchange if the contract is to be valid. In *Currie v Misa* (1875), Lush J referred to consideration as consisting of a detriment to the promisee or a benefit to the promisor. He described it as: '...some right, interest, profit or benefit accruing to one party, or some forbearance, detriment, loss or responsibility given, suffered or undertaken by the other.'

Certainty of agreement

Even though the parties may have appeared to make an agreement by the exchange of a matching offer and acceptance, the courts may refuse to enforce it if there appears to be uncertainty about what has been agreed, or if some important aspect of the agreement is left open to be decided later.

In *Scammell v Ouston* (1941), for example, the parties had agreed to the supply of a lorry on 'hire purchase terms'. The House of Lords held that in the absence of any other evidence of the details of the hire purchase agreement this was too vague to be enforceable, and there was therefore no contract.

Acceptance of an offer must be unconditional, accepting the precise terms of the offer. Where the process of negotiation is long and difficult, it might be difficult to pinpoint exactly when an offer has been made and accepted. In such cases a court will examine the precise course of negotiations to ascertain whether the parties have reached agreement, if at all, and when. This process can be complicated when the so-called 'battle of forms' occurs. Rather than negotiating terms each time a contract is made many companies try to use standard conditions, which will be printed on headed stationery, such as order forms and delivery notes. The 'battle of forms' occurs when one party sends a form stating that the contract is on their terms, and the other party responds by sending back the forms and stating that the contract is on their terms. The general rule in these cases is that the 'last shot' wins the battle. Each new form issued is treated as a counteroffer, so that when one party performs its obligation under the contract the action will be seen as acceptance by the other side. One simple case that illustrates this is *British Road Services v Crutchley (Arthur V)* Ltd (1968). The plaintiffs delivered some whisky to the defendants for storage. The BRS driver handed the defendants a delivery note, which listed the company's terms of carriage. The note was accepted and stamped with Crutchley's terms and conditions and the court held that by accepting this, the BRS driver had accepted a counteroffer. Although many cases are simple, other more recent case law has held that the last shot will not always succeed.

It is a basic assumption that there is no acceptance until the act has been thoroughly performed. However, in some cases, part performance may amount to acceptance. In *Errington v Errington and Woods (1952)* a father bought a house in his own name for £750, borrowing £500 of the price from a building society. He bought the house for his son and daughter in law to live in and told them that they must meet the mortgage repayments. If they met the payments the house would be signed over to them on completion of the term. The couple moved in and began to pay the mortgage, but they never in fact made the promise to continue with the payments until the mortgage was paid off, which meant that the contract was unilateral. When the father later died, the people in charge of his affairs sought to withdraw the offer. The Court of Appeal held that it was too late to do this. The part performance of the son and daughter in law constituted an acceptance of the contract and the father and his representatives after death were bound by the resulting contract unless the son and daughter in law ceased the payments, in which case the offer was no longer binding. A request for information about an offer does not constitute a counteroffer, so the original offer remains open. If an offeree has to accept an offer in a specified manner, then only acceptance by that method or an equally effective one will be binding. Other important cases here are *Luxor (Eastbourne) Ltd v Cooper (1941) And Daulia Limited v Four Millbank Nominees Limited (1978).*

Communicating acceptance of an offer

An acceptance will not usually take effect until it is clearly communicated to the offeror. However, there are some circumstances where acceptance may take effect without it being communicated to the offeror. An offer may clearly state, or indeed imply, that acceptance need not be communicated to the offeror. An offeror who fails to receive an acceptance through their own fault may be prevented from claiming that the non-communication means they should not be bound by the contract. One important case here is *Holwell Securities Ltd V Hughes (1974).* Another important case is *Yates v Pulleyn (1975).*

The general rule for acceptances by post is that they take effect when they are posted, rather than when they are communicated. The postal rule was laid down in the case of *Adams v Lindsell (1818)*, when on the 2nd of September 1817, the defendants wrote to the plaintiffs, who were in the wool processing business, offering to sell them a quantity of sheep fleeces, and stating that they required an answer 'in course of post'. However, the defendants did not address the letter correctly and it did not reach the plaintiffs until the evening of September the 5th. The plaintiffs posted their acceptance the same evening, and it reached the defendants on the 9th of September. If the original letter had been correctly addressed, it would have reached the plaintiffs by the 7th of September. Because it was incorrectly addressed it did not and no reply was received and the wool was sold to a third party. The issue was whether a sale had been made before the sale of the wool to the third party. The court heard that the contract was concluded as soon as the acceptance was posted and that the defendants were bound from the evening of 5th September so should not have sold the wool to a third party. There are certain exceptions to the postal rule. The offeror may avoid the postal rule by making it a specific term of their offer that acceptance will only take effect when it is communicated to them.

The postal rule has limited application to modern communications technology. In *Entores Ltd v Miles Far East Corp,* (1955) offer and acceptance communicated by telex were valid because the method was so instantaneous that the parties were deemed to be dealing as if face-to-face, even though they were in different countries. The time when these forms of communication are used may cause problems in determining if a contract is made, as when a fax is sent out of office hours.

Now offer and acceptance in the case of electronic communication is governed by the Consumer Contracts (Information, Cancellation and Additional Charges) Regulations 2013 which replaced the Consumer Protection (Distance Selling) Regulations 2000. This gives the buyer the right to be informed of the right to cancel within seven days, description, price, arrangements for payment and identity of seller, and to be given written confirmation, without which a contract is not formed.

Ignorance of the offer

It is generally accepted that a person cannot accept an offer of which they are unaware, because in order to create a binding contract, the parties must reach agreement. This is a very important principle.

Tenders, auctions and the sale of land

The rules outlined above also apply to the sale of land and to sales by tender and auction. If a large organization, such as a company or government department needs to contract a supplier of goods or services, it will, more often than not, advertise for tenders, i.e., bids. Organizations wishing to supply goods or services will reply, detailing the price for these services. The advertiser will choose from the replies and contact the successful tender. As a general rule, the request for tenders is regarded as an invitation to treat, (see previous) so there is no specific obligation to accept any of the tenders sent. The tenders themselves are offers and a contract does not come into existence until one is accepted. However, where a party has issued an invitation to tender, it is bound to consider all correctly submitted tenders. One such case highlighting this is *Blackpool and Fylde Aero Club v Blackpool Borough Council (1990)*. Blackpool BC invited tenders from people who were interested in operating leisure flights from the local airfield. Tenders had to be submitted to the town hall by a stated deadline. The Aero Club submitted its application on time, but the council refused to consider it, as due to an error on their part, they mistakenly believed that the tender had been submitted after the deadline.

It was held that the council's invitation to tender was a unilateral offer to consider all tenders which fell within its rules. The tender constituted an offer which had been accepted by the Aero Club. The offer was accepted by any party who put in a tender. Thus the council were obliged to consider all tenders (acceptances) to their offer, including the Aero Club tender. They were not, of course, obliged to accept the tender. In some cases, however, an invitation for tenders may in itself be an offer. The main example of this is where the invitation to tender makes it clear that the lowest tender (or highest) will be accepted.

The implications of choosing to accept a tender depend on what sort of tender is involved.

Specific tenders

Where an invitation to tender specifies that a particular quantity of goods is required on a particular date, or between certain dates, agreeing to one of the tenders submitted will constitute acceptance of an offer, creating a contract between the parties.

Non-specific tenders

Some invitations to tender are not specific and may for example simply state that certain goods may be required, up to a particular maximum quantity, with deliveries to be made if and when requested. For example, an invitation to tender made by a hospital may ask for tenders to supply goods, if and when required. In this case, taking up one of the tenders submitted does not amount to acceptance of an offer in the contractual sense and there is no contract. The hospital may take the goods all at once, some at a time or none at all. It is not bound.

Auction sales

The parties to an auction sale are the bidder and the owner of the goods. The auctioneer supplies a service and is not party to the contract between buyer and seller.

Sale of land

The standard rules of contract apply to the sale of land, including buildings. However, the court applies the rules strictly in the case of land, tending to require very clear evidence of an intention to be bound before they state that an offer has been made.

In Harvey v Facey (1893) the plaintiffs sent the defendants a telegram asking 'will you sell us Bumper Hall Pen? Telegraph lowest cash price'. The reply arrived back stating 'Lowest price for Bumper Hall pen £900'. The plaintiffs then sent a telegram saying 'we agree to buy Bumper Hall Pen for £900. Please send us your title deeds'. On these facts, the Privy Council held that there was no contract. They regarded the telegram from the defendants as a statement of price only. It was therefore not an offer which could be accepted by the third telegram.

In practice there are rigid procedures involved in the sale of land. The first is the 'sale subject to contract', where the parties agree to the sale and the implication is that there is a good deal of proving and other work before a contract is in existence. The next stage is the exchange of contract, where the buyer and seller agree to the terms of the formal contract. Once the contracts are exchanged then the contract is binding and any backing out can result in a claim for damages and lost deposit.

Certainty of contract

In order to be viewed as a binding contract, an agreement must be absolutely certain. That is, it should not be vague or incomplete. One such case that amplifies this is that of *Scammell v Ouston (1941)* where the parties agreed that Ouston could buy a van from Scammell, giving his lorry in part exchange paying the balance over two-years on hire purchase terms. Scammell decided to back out and claimed that there was no contract between the parties. The House of Lords agreed, pointing out that the courts would uphold an agreement if there really was one, in this case the terms were too vague, particularly the agreement to pay on Hire Purchase Terms. In certain cases, parties may leave details vague, particularly when dealing with fluctuating prices and other factors. Provisions should be in the contract stating how they should be clarified.

Terms implied into contract by statute

In some cases, statute will override contract and will provide that certain provisions should be read into contracts even though they have not been specifically agreed between the parties. For example, under the Consumer Rights Act 2015, an agreement for the sale of goods can become binding as soon as the parties have agreed to buy and sell, with the details of the contract being laid down by law or determined by the standard of reasonableness.

In such a case, the parties do not even have to agree on a price. The buyer is entitled to pay a reasonable price. Terms implied by statute will be examined further on in this book.

Intention to create legal relations

One major principle of contract law is that of intention to create legal relations. If two or more parties make an agreement without the intention of being legally bound by it, the agreement will not be regarded as a contract. As far as intent to be legally bound is concerned, contracts can be divided into domestic and social agreements on one hand, and commercial agreements on the other. Where the agreement falls into the former category there is an assumption that the parties do not intend to create legal relations. The reverse is true when it comes to commercial agreements.

Domestic and social agreements

Where a husband and wife who are living together as one household make an agreement, the courts will assume that they do not intend to be legally bound, unless the agreement states otherwise. In *Balfour v Balfour (1919)* the defendant was a civil servant stationed in Sri Lanka. Whilst the couple were on leave in England, Mrs. Balfour was taken ill, and it became clear that her husband would have to return by himself. He promised to pay her maintenance of £30 per month. They eventually separated and the husband refused to make any more payments. The Court of Appeal decided he was not bound to make further payments, as when the agreement was made there was no intention to create legal relations. Likewise, agreements between parents and children are assumed not to be legally binding.

Social agreements and commercial agreements

The presumption that an agreement is not intended to be legally binding is also applied to social relationships between people who are not related. With both the above though, there can be exceptions. With commercial agreements There is a strong presumption in commercial agreements that the parties intend to be legally bound, and unless clear words are used this presumption stands. Where the words of a business agreement are ambiguous, the courts will favor the interpretation that suggests that the parties did intend to create legal relations.

The capacity to enter into a contract

The law states that individuals who enter into a contract must have the capacity to enter into a contract, otherwise it is voidable. Adults who have full capacity are able to enter into contracts and enforce them at law (unless they are illegal contracts).

The law sets out those who do not have legal capacity to contract, particularly providing special legal protection to those who are minors, or under a mental disability.

Minors and capacity in contract law

Individuals who are under the age of 18 are known as 'minors' under the Family Reform Act 1969. A minor can enter into a contract at law, however, such a contract is 'voidable' by the minor before they reach 18 (and for a time thereafter). This means that the minor can enforce the contract, but they can also terminate it if they wish. Once the minor reaches the age of 18, the contract becomes legally binding on both parties. However, there are exceptions to the general rule: a minor may need to enter into a contract to buy necessities, such as food, clothing, medicine and other things necessary for them and their lifestyle. Minors may also need to enter into legally binding contracts for their education, such as apprenticeships. These types of contract are enforceable against the minor, however, such contracts must be fair to be enforceable against the minor. So if a minor pays a reasonable price for items required in the circumstances, the minor is legally required to fulfil the contract (i.e. pay for the goods or service).

A case where such a contract has been enforced is that of *Doyle v White City Stadium* (1935), where there was an agreement to train a boxer. There was no money paid, but the contract was enforceable as it was considered that the contract was beneficial because of the training provided. Another case where the contract was held enforceable is *Clements v London & NW Rail Co* (1894) where certain benefits were removed following a contract of employment, but the contract was considered to be beneficial and was upheld.

When can a contract with minors be voided?

The courts may not uphold a contract if it is considered not to be to the benefit of the minor. For example, in the case of *De Francesco v Barnum* (1889), a minor aged 14 years old, entered into an agreement to train as a dancer on stage. However, the contract had conditions which were considered not beneficial to the minor and, therefore, the minor was not bound by the contact. In the 2006 case of *Proform Sports Management Ltd v Proactive Sports Management Ltd* the court had to consider a contract entered into by footballer Wayne Rooney (who was 17 at the time) with his agent. The High Court ruled that the contract was voidable because it was not an agreement equivalent to contracts of apprenticeship, education and service.

A 'voidable contract' is a contract that can be ended. The contract is still valid, but it can be avoided by the minor who can legally terminate the agreement – before reaching the age of 18 years, or within a reasonable time of coming of age. What is a reasonable time period will depend on the facts of the case. In the case of *Steinberg v Scala (Leeds) Ltd* (1923), the contract was voided because the minor was unable to keep up with payments. However, in the case of *Edwards v Carter* (1892) the court decided that the contract could not be rejected and the agreement was enforceable.

What happens if money has already been paid by a minor?

If money is paid by a minor under a contract, then usually this cannot be recovered unless it can be proved that the contract has not been beneficial to the minor. So, if a minor enjoys goods or services, then seeks to terminate the contract and recover money already paid – he cannot be reimbursed. In the case of *Pearce v Brain* (1929), a minor exchanged a motorcycle for a car, but found that the car had defects. The court decided that the contract must stand as he had used the car and, therefore, had enjoyed the benefit of it.

The Minors' Contracts Act 1987

This Act was introduced to protect minors alongside the common law (i.e., rulings of the courts). This Act also provides guarantees for minors contracting with adults. A contract is binding on the adult but not on the minor; however, if the minor ratifies the contract after having reached the age of 18 by, for instance, an act confirming a promise made when a minor – he is legally bound. Furthermore, the contact is not void while still a minor – and any money paid under the contract terms cannot be repaid unless there has been no benefit received. However, there are exceptions, the most likely of which to arise is that of a contract for 'necessities' as discussed above.

Corporations

A corporation is a legal entity that is treated by law as having a separate identity from the persons who constitute it. There are three main types of corporations: registered companies, corporations established by statute and chartered corporations. Each has a different level of contracting ability.

Registered companies

These are companies registered under the Companies Act 2006, which superseded the 1985 Companies Act and which covers most commercial companies. When registering, companies must supply a document that regulates their activities called a memorandum of association, which contains information including an objects clause, laying down the range of activities that their company can engage in. Under the 1989 Companies Act, which has been replaced by the 2006 Act, a company can be liable for a contract made outside its stated activities if the other party has acted in good faith.

Statutory companies

These corporations are created by an Act of Parliament, for specific purposes, the Independent Broadcasting Authority is an example, as are local authorities. The statute creating the particular corporation will specify the purposes for which that corporation may make contracts. Any contracted outside of these purposes is null and void.

Chartered corporations

These are corporation's set up by Royal Charter, which means that their rights are officially granted by the Crown. Examples are charities and some universities and other educational institutions. They have the same contractual capacity as an adult human being.

Formalities

We have discussed the fact that an agreement, with some exceptions, does not have to take a specific written form in order to be deemed a binding contract. A contract can be oral.

One famous recent case involving an oral contract *was Hadley v Kemp (1990)* where Gary Kemp was the songwriter in the group Spandau Ballet. He was sued by other members of the group for royalties received for the group's music. The basis of the claim was that there was an oral agreement to share royalties. They were unable to prove the existence of any oral agreement and their claim failed.

Contracts which must be made by deed

The Law of Property Act 1925 states that a contract for a lease of more than three years must be made by deed, which basically means that it must be put into a formal document, signed in front of witnesses.

Contracts which must be in writing

Some statutes lay down that certain types of contracts must be in writing. Most contracts involving sales of land must be in writing, under the Law of Property Act 1989. Other contracts that need to be in writing are those involving the transfers of shares in a limited company (Companies Act

2006 bills of exchange; cheques and promissory notes (Bills of Exchange Act (1882); and regulated consumer credit agreements, such as hire purchase agreements (Consumer Credit Act 1974, as amended by the 2006 Consumer Credit Act).

Contracts which must be evidenced in writing

Contracts of guarantee (where one party guarantees the obligations of another, such as parents guaranteeing a sons or daughters overdraft) are required to be 'evidenced in writing'. Contracts for the sale or disposition of land before 27th September 1989 are still covered by the old law prior to the Law of Property Act 1989. Evidenced in writing means that although the contract itself may not be a written one, there must be written evidence of the transaction. The evidence must have existed before one party tried to enforce the contract against the other, and it must be signed by the party against whom the contract is to be enforced.

Electronic contracts

Many transactions and other forms of trade are now conducted electronically. For example, most people will at least be familiar with, if not frequent users of, ATMs situated outside or inside banks. When a bank's customer withdraws money or uses an ATM for other purposes, an electronic transaction takes place. More and more business is now done electronically, often with the parties never physically meeting each other. Online shops, for example, allow potential customers to browse, select and purchase goods without ever asking a salesperson for advice or assistance. Negotiations, giving quotes or submitting tenders for work may all be done electronically and indeed are. A great deal of information is now passed electronically within organisations and from one organisation to another. This all raises a number of legal questions, specifically regarding electronic contracts. Some of the most important issues include whether an electronic contract is valid, that is, whether it must comply with certain formalities, whether electronic signatures are admissible as evidence of intent and agreement, and what law applies to an electronic contract (if it is between international parties). These issues are addressed overleaf.

Formalities of an electronic contract

Generally, as we have seen, contracts can take any number of forms. They can be by deed, in writing, evidenced in writing, oral, or implied from the conduct of the parties. Certain contracts, however, require a specific form, and will not be legal (though they may be equitable) if they fail to comply with the formalities. For example, as we have seen, a conveyance of land or any interest in land must, under s52 of the Law of Property Act 1925, be by deed, save for the exceptions listed in that section. Other contracts are required to be in writing.

So what form, if any, must an electronic contract take? The answer depends on the nature of the contract.

If writing is a requirement, do documents which are stored digitally on a computer hard drive comply? Schedule 1 to the Interpretation Act 1978 states: "'Writing' includes typing, printing, lithography, photography and other modes of representing or reproducing words in a visible form, and expressions referring to writing are construed accordingly." Since words stored digitally on a computer may be reproduced on a monitor or printed onto paper, it would appear that computer storage is covered by this definition. Nevertheless, individual cases may still have to be decided by the courts.

*

Electronic signatures

A signature is generally understood as evidence that the signatory approves of a document's contents. But does this ring true also for a person's name printed on a telex or fax, or reproduced in electronic mail? In *Good Challenger Navegante SA v Metalexportimport SA (2004)* the Court of Appeal held that for the purposes of s30 of the Limitation Act 1980 a typed name on a telex was a signature. The Court held that "...the typed name of the sender at the end of the telex not only identified the maker but led to the inference that he had approved the contents." This does not apply to all instances of typed names, however, and a formal contract with typed names at the end with spaces underneath where the parties are expected to write their names would be unlikely to fall within the reasoning given in the Good Challenger case.

Above all, the signature must be able to objectively show that the signatory, by signing or printing their name, approved of a document's contents and intended to be bound by them. It is irrelevant whether the contents have been read (unless there has been some misrepresentation). The courts confirmed in *Mehta v J Pereira Fernandes SA (2006)* that a person's name which is shown as part of an email address in the header of an email does not mean that the person intended to be legally bound by the contents of the email. The automatic insertion of an email address could not be considered as a signature. Under s7 of the Electronic Communications Act 2000 an electronic signature is anything in electronic form which:

- is incorporated into or otherwise logically associated with any electronic communication or electronic data, and
- is certified as such by the signatory.

Such a signature is admissible in evidence for the purpose of establishing the authenticity, the integrity, or both, of the electronic communication or data.

Certification of the signature requires the signatory to make a statement that the signature, its production, communication or verification, or a procedure applied to it, is a valid means of establishing the authenticity, integrity or both of the electronic communication or data.

Contracts concluded electronically

Article 9 of Directive 2000/31/EC, on electronic commerce, requires EU member states (not Britain following BREXIT-see below) to ensure both that contracts can be concluded by electronic means and that the law does not create any barriers against using such contracts or which deprive such contracts of their validity. In the UK, the Electronic Communications Act 2000 supports approved cryptography service providers and provides that electronic signatures are admissible in evidence. Some contracts, though, such as those which transfer rights in real estate, are exempt from these general principles. Article 10 of Directive 2000/31/EC requires certain information to be provided regarding electronic contracts, such as describing the technical steps to be followed to conclude the contract, and the technical means for identifying and correct input errors before placing orders.

However, following BEXIT the government states:

The eCommerce Directive no longer applies to the UK now that the transition period is over. If you are a provider of online services, you should take steps in response to these changes.

What has changed?

Rules relating to online activities in European Economic Area (EEA) countries may apply to UK online service providers who operate in the EEA now that the transition period is over.

The eCommerce Directive allows EEA online service providers to operate in any EEA country, while only following relevant rules in the country in which they are established. This framework no longer applies to UK providers as the UK has left the EEA and the transition period is over.

You should consider whether your services were previously in scope of the Directive, and if so, ensure that you are compliant with relevant requirements in each EEA country you operate in.

Depending on the nature of your online services you may already comply with these requirements. This could mean that there are little or no immediate changes you need to make to be compliant.

The government intends to fully remove the eCommerce Directive's Country of Origin principle from UK legislation, to bring EEA online service providers in scope of UK laws, which they were previously exempt from. As this principle is found in a number of pieces of legislation it will be removed at different points, when Parliamentary time allows.

****

1.2

Consideration and Contracts

In this chapter we look at the notion of consideration which is central to contract law.

English law states that a contract is not usually binding unless it is supported by consideration. Consideration is usually said to mean that each party to a contract must give something in return for what is gained from the other party. Very basically, if there is a dispute and you wish to enforce someone's promise to you, then you must prove that you gave something in return for that promise. The key case that defined 'consideration' is *Currie v Misa* (1875), which states that consideration can consist of a right, interest, profit, benefit, detriment, or forbearance.

Courts do not normally inquire into the adequacy of consideration provided by either party as long as there is clear evidence that both have contributed something of value in the eyes of the law. *See Stilk v Myrick (1809).*

There are two types of consideration: executed and executory, as described below. Consideration may be goods or services, a thing or a service. Many problems concerning consideration arise not when a contract is made but when one or other of the parties to the contract seeks to modify it, such as paying a lower price than agreed or supplying a different good or service.

Promisor and Promisee

In most contracts, it is the case that two promises will be exchanged, so each party to the contract is promisor and promisee. In a contract case, the claimant will often be arguing that the defendant has broken the promise made to the claimant and therefore the claimant will usually be the promisee. One example is if A contracts to build a conservatory and B promises to pay £5000 for the conservatory, there are two promises in this contract. A's promise to build a conservatory and B's promise to pay. If A fails to build the conservatory B can sue him. If the issue of consideration arises, B will seek to prove that his promise to pay £5000 was consideration for A's promise for building the conservatory. In that action, A will be the promisor and B the promisee. However, reverse the situation and B fails to pay, then A will sue and, if consideration is at issue, A will have to prove that his promise to build the conservatory was consideration for B's promise to pay. In that action, A will be the promisee and B the promisor.

'Executory' and 'executed' consideration

As mentioned above, consideration can fall into two categories: executory and executed. Executed consideration is the performance of an act in return for a promise. Executory consideration is when the person makes a promise, and the other person offers a counter promise – you promise to deliver goods to me and I promise to pay for them when they arrive, the promise is executory because it is something to be done in the future.

Consideration must be given in return for the promise or act of the other party. Something done, given, or promised beforehand will not be counted as consideration. A classic case concerning this arose in *Roscorla v Thomas (1842)*. The defendant sold the plaintiff a horse. After the sale was completed, the defendant told the plaintiff that the animal was 'sound and free from any vice'. This was not the actual truth and the plaintiff sued. The court held that the defendant's promise was unenforceable because it was made after the sale. If the promise about the horse's condition had been made before, the plaintiff would have provided consideration for it by buying the horse. As it was made after the sale, the consideration was past, for it had not been given in return for the promise.

There are two exceptions to the rule that past consideration is no consideration. The first is where the past consideration was provided at the promisor's request, and it was understood that payment would be made. The second is the bill of exchange. Under s27 of the Bills of Exchange Act 1882, an antecedent debt or 'liability' may be consideration for receipt of a bill of exchange.

The rules of consideration

Consideration need not be adequate

The law of contract regulates the making of bargains. As freedom of contract is vital, the law is not concerned with whether a party has made a good bargain or a bad one. Adequacy is given its normal meaning-the contract is enforceable even if the price does not match the value of what is being gained under the agreement. One such case that reflects this is *Thomas v Thomas (1842)*. Before he died Thomas expressed a wish that his wife should be allowed to remain in his house although there was no mention of this in his will. The executors carried out his wish but charged the widow a nominal ground rent of £1 a year. When they later tried to dispossess her, they failed.

Consideration must be sufficient

Consideration offered is sufficient provided that:

- It is real (White v Bluett (1853)

- It is tangible (Ward v Byham (1956)
- It has some discernible value (Chappel v Nestle (1960); and
- Economic value is measured against benefit gained.

Consideration must not be past

Consideration must follow rather than precede agreement. This prevents coercion by suppliers of goods and services.

Consideration must be of economic value

What this principle basically means is that there must be some physical value, rather than just an emotional or sentimental value.

Consideration can be a promise not to sue

If one party has a possible civil claim against the other, a promise not to enforce that claim is good consideration for a promise given in return. One clear example is if A crashes into B's car, then A can promise not to sue if B pays for the damage.

Performance of an existing duty

Where a promisee already owes the promisor a legal duty, then in theory performing that duty should not in itself be consideration. If the promisee does nothing more than they are already obliged to do, they are suffering no detriment and the promisor is only getting a benefit to which he or she is entitled.

Existing duties can be divided into three categories: public duties; contractual duties to the promisor; and contractual duties to a third party.

Existing public duty

Where a person is merely carrying out duties they are legally bound to perform – such as police officer or juror, doing that alone will not be consideration. However, where a promisee is under a public duty, but does something beyond the call of that duty, that extra act amounts to consideration. In *Glasbrook Brothers v Glamorgan County Council (1925)* the owners of a South Wales Mine asked the police to place a guard at their colliery during a strike. The police suggested that regular checks by mobile patrol would be adequate, but the owners replied that they wanted something more intensive and the police agreed at an extra cost of £2,200. After the strike the owners refused to pay saying that the police had a duty to protect their property. The courts held in favor of the police saying that the police did not have a duty to supply the cover they did, only the cover they deemed sufficient. Anything over and above was deemed consideration.

Existing contractual duty to the promisor

The position on contractual duties and consideration has changed from the traditional position whereby the performance of an existing contractual duty owed to a promisor was not consideration. In *Stilk v Myrick (1809*) two sailors deserted a ship during a voyage and the captain was unable to find replacements. The remaining crewmembers were promised extra wages for sailing the ship back to London, but the captain refused to pay on arrival and the sailors sued with the court holding that there was no consideration as the sailors had already contracted to sail the boat back to its destination.

In *Hartley v Ponsonby (1857*) half the crew deserted, and the remaining crew were offered extra wages to carry on the journey. At the end the captain refused to pay and the crew sued and won, as the courts held that there was consideration as the crew were to small to sail the boat adequately and extra money was justified.

An exception to the rule that performance of an existing contractual obligation owed to the promisor will not amount to consideration will occur where a party can be seen to receive an extra benefit from the other party's agreement to carry out his existing obligations. One such case that highlights this is that of *Williams v Roffey Brothers (1991)*. In this case the defendants (the main contractors) were refurbishing a block of flats. They sub-contracted the carpentry works to the plaintiff. The plaintiff ran into financial difficulties, whereupon the defendants agreed to pay the plaintiff an additional sum if they completed the work on time. It was held that where a party to an existing contract later agrees to pay an 'extra bonus' in order that the other party performs his obligations under the original contract, then the new agreement is binding if the party agreeing to pay the bonus has thereby obtained some new practical advantage or avoided a disadvantage. In this particular case, the advantage was the avoidance of a penalty clause and the expense of finding new carpenters, among other factors.

Existing contractual duty to a third party

In some cases two parties make a contract to provide a benefit to a third party. If one of the parties (A) makes a further promise to that third party to provide the benefit they have already contracted to provide, that further promise can be good consideration for a promise made by the third party in return-even though nothing more than the contractual duty is being promised by A.

One case that illustrates this *is Scotson v Pegg (1861)*. Scotson contracted to supply a cargo of coal to a third party, X, or to anyone X nominated. Scotson was instructed by X to deliver the coal to Pegg, and Pegg promised to unload the coal at a stated rate of pay. He subsequently failed to do the agreed unloading. Scotson sued Pegg, claiming that their promise to deliver coal to him was consideration for his promise to unload it. Pegg claimed that this could not be consideration, since Scotson was already bound to supply the coal under the contract with X. The court upheld Scotson's claim delivery of the coal was consideration because it was a benefit to Pegg, and a detriment to Scotson in that it prevented them from having the option of breaking their contract with X.

Waiver and Promissory estoppel

These are ways of making some kind of promise binding even where there is no consideration. Waiver has traditionally applied where one party agrees not to enforce their strict rights under the contract by, for example, accepting delivery later than agreed. One case that illustrates the doctrine of waiver is that of *Hickman v Haynes (1875*). A buyer asked the seller to deliver goods later than originally agreed and then when the delivery was made refused to accept it. The seller sued for breach of contract, the buyer responded by arguing that the seller was in breach, for delivering later than specified. The courts rejected the buyer's argument on the grounds that the delivery was made at the buyer's request.

Promissory estoppel (stopping the contract on the basis of a promise) is a newer doctrine than waiver, developing the concept. It was introduced by Lord Denning in the *Central London Property Trust Ltd v High Trees (1947)* where owners of a block of flats had promised to accept reduced rents in 1939. There was no consideration for their promise but Lord Denning nevertheless stated that he would estop them from recovering any arrears. He based his case on the decision in *Hughes v Metropolitan Railways (1875)*. In this case, under the lease the tenants were obliged to keep the premises in good repair, and in October 1874, the landlord gave them six months notice to do some repairs stating that if they were not done in time, the lease would be forfeited. In November the two parties began to negotiate the possibility of the tenants buying the lease, the tenants stating in the meantime that they would not carry out the repairs. By December the negotiations had broken down and at the end of the six-month notice period, the landlord claimed that the lease was forfeited because the tenants had not done the repairs. The House of Lords (now Supreme Court) held however, that the landlord's conduct was an implied promise to the tenants that he would not enforce the forfeiture at the end of the notice period, and in not doing the repairs, the tenants had been relying on this premise. It was seen that the six-month notice period began again when negotiations broke down.

The exact scope of the doctrine is a matter of debate, but certain requirements must be met:

- Estoppel only applies to the modification of discharge of an existing contractual obligation. It cannot create a new contract.
- It can only be used as a 'shield' and not a 'sword'.
- The promise not to enforce rights must be clear and unequivocal.
- It must be inequitable for the promisor to go back on his promise.
- The promisee must have acted in reliance on the promise, although not necessarily to his detriment.

Agreement by deed

When is a deed required?

Land law, The Law of Property Miscellaneous Provisions Act1989, requires all transfers of land or the creation of interests in land, such as gifts or mortgages, to be made by way of legal deed, otherwise it is void as far as the legal estate is concerned. A document will be a deed if:

- It makes clear on the face of it that it is intended to be a deed.
- It is validly executed as a deed by all those required to sign it.

- It is validly executed as a deed by an individual if it is signed by the individual in the presence of a witness who attests to the signature, or at their direction and in their presence and the presence of two witnesses who each attest the signature, and it is delivered as a deed by them or a person authorised to do so on their behalf.

When is the transfer deed fully effective?

In registered land, the transfer deed is legally effected only when it is lodged at the Land Registry for registration on the official Registered Title of the property. If the transfer is of unregistered land, the transfer deed is effective immediately to vest the legal estate in the purchaser, but the transfer must be lodged for first registration of title with the Land Registry within 2 months (otherwise the seller will hold the legal estate on bare trust for the purchaser). However, the 2-month period can be extended with good reason.

Rights that are overreaching

A purchaser will take the property subject to the beneficial interests of anyone they knew or ought to have known about (under the doctrine of 'notice'). A typical example is where the purchaser buys land subject to a trust, knowing that an individual has a life interest in the property and can remain in occupation until their death.

Overreaching is a process whereby the beneficiaries' equitable interests are effectively dissolved and lifted from the land, and then attached to the purchase price. The purchaser then takes the land free from the beneficiaries' equitable interests, whether or not he knew or ought to have known of them, and the beneficiary claims his entitlement from the money made through the selling of the property.

When does overreaching apply?

Overreaching is capable of applying only to the equitable interests listed in section 2 Law of Property Act 1925. These are generally those existing behind a trust and having a monetary value. Section 2(1) LPA 1925 provides that: "A conveyance to a purchaser of a legal estate in land shall overreach any equitable interest or power affecting that estate [and listed in the section] whether or not he has notice thereof."

Generally speaking, for overreaching to be effective the purchaser (which includes a mortgagee) must pay the purchase money/mortgage loan to all of the trustees (at least two, or a trust corporation). Provided this is done, the purchaser/mortgagee takes free of any beneficial interests existing behind a trust. The beneficiaries' equitable interests are then lifted from the land and automatically attached to the money paid by the purchaser (i.e., to the proceeds of sale).

****

1. 3

Terms of Contracts

In this chapter we look at the main terms of contracts and what must be inherent in a contract before it can be legally binding. Express terms of contract and implied terms are examined along with collateral agreements and unfair contract terms. Finally, we look at misrepresentation, duress and undue influence. Illegality of contract is dealt with in chapter 6.

Once a contract has been formed, it is necessary to define the scope of the obligations which each party incurs. Terms of contracts describe the respective duties and obligations of each party to the contract. As well as the contractual terms laid out and agreed by parties to a contract, called express terms, there may also be implied terms – terms that are 'read into' a contract because of the facts of the agreement and the apparent intention of the parties or the law on specific types of contracts.

Express terms of contract

In the Supreme Court judgement in *Marks and Spencer plc v BNP Paribas Services Trust Ltd, (2015),* Lord Neuberger stated that while the various terms of a contract have to be interpreted before implication of terms may be considered, the processes of interpretation and implication are different. See also *Wigan BC v Scullindale Global Limited (2021).*

Oral statements

In all transactions, except for the simplest, there will be some negotiations before a contract is made. These are usually oral statements or based on oral statements. Problems can arise following oral statements when parties cannot agree whether the statement was intended to be binding. In considering questions such as these a court will classify statements made during negotiations as either representations or terms. A representation is a statement that may have encouraged one of the parties to make the contract, but is not itself part of the contract, while a term is an undertaking that is part of the contract. Representation can also be construed as misrepresentation, which is a common cause of dispute. Whether a statement is either a representation or a term is mainly a question of the party's intentions. If the parties have indicated that a particular statement is a term of their contract, then the court will carry out that intention.

Written terms of a contract

Written terms can be incorporated into a contract in three different ways: by signature, by reasonable notice and by a previous course of dealing.

The parol evidence rule

Under this rule, where there is a written contract, extrinsic (parol) evidence cannot change the express terms laid down in that document. Extrinsic evidence includes oral statements and written material such as draft contracts or letter, whether relating to pre-contract negotiations or the parties' post contractual behavior. One case that illustrates the parol evidence rule is *Henderson v Arthur (1907)*. The plaintiffs and the defendant were parties to a lease that contained a covenant for the payment of rent quarterly in advance, although before the lease was drawn up the parties agreed that the rent could be paid in arrears. When the tenant was sued for not paying quarterly in advance, he pointed out this prior agreement. The court held that the terms of prior oral agreement could not be substituted for the terms of a later formal contract covering the same transaction. There are a few exceptions to the parol evidence rule, the following being the main ones:

Rectification

Where a document is intended to record a previous oral agreement but fails to do that accurately, evidence of the oral agreement will be admitted.

Partially written agreements

Where there is a written agreement, but the parties clearly intended it to be qualified by other written or oral statements, the parol evidence rule is displaced.

Implied terms

The parol evidence rule only applies where a party seeks to use existing evidence to alter the express terms of a contract. Where a contract is of a type that is unusually subject to terms implied by law and statute, parol evidence may be given to support, or to deny, the usual implication.

Collateral agreements

There is a way in which an oral statement can be deemed binding, even though it conflicts with a written contract and does not fall within any of the exceptions to the parol rule. If one party says something like 'I will sign this document if you will assure me that it means....' The courts may find that two contracts have been created, the written agreement and a collateral contract based on the oral statement.

Construction of express terms in contracts

The courts will sometimes have to determine the construction of an express term within a contract. The courts will have to 'seek the meaning which the document would convey to a reasonable person having all the background knowledge which would have reasonably been available to parties at the time of entering into the agreement'. The courts start by presuming that the parties meant what they said. The courts would also look at the outcome of the words and meaning to see if they create an absurdity or are inconsistent with the rest of the contract.

Implied terms

As well as the express terms laid down in the contract, further terms may sometimes be read into the contract by the courts. These implied terms are divided into four groups: terms implied by fact, terms implied by law, terms implied by custom and terms implied by trade usage. Terms implied by fact are terms not laid out in the contract, but which it is assumed both parties would have intended to include if they had thought about it, they may have left them out by mistake. In order to decide what the intention of the parties was, the courts have developed two tests, the 'officious bystander test, and the 'business efficacy' test.

The officious bystander test was laid down in *Shirlaw v Southern Foundries (1926)*. The Judge said, ...'that which in any contract is left to be implied and need not be expressed is something so obvious that it goes without saying: so that, if while the parties were making their bargain, an officious bystander were to suggest some express provision for it in the agreement, they would testily suppress him with a common 'oh, of course'. The business efficacy test covers terms which one side alleges must be implied to make the contract work, to give it business efficacy.

Terms implied by law are terms which the law dictates must be present in certain types of contract-in some cases whether the parties intended them or not.

In *Liverpool Council v Irwin (1977)* the defendants lived in a council maisonette that was part of a high-rise block in Liverpool. The block was in a bad condition and tenants withheld rent and the case went to court with the tenants arguing that the council was in breach of contract (tenancy). The council argued that there was no agreement to keep the block in good condition and the courts argued that good repair and safety were implied terms of contract. The council lost the case.

Other implied terms may arise from contracts governing the supply of goods and services, such as the Consumer Rights Act 2015. Terms implied by custom can be implied into a contract if there is evidence that under local custom they would normally be there. Terms implied by trade usage would normally be part of a contract made by parties in a particular trade or business.

The classification of contractual terms

There are three types of contractual terms, conditions, warranties and innominate terms. A condition is a term that the courts would regard as important in that it would clearly have negative consequences if breached. Where a condition is breached the injured party can regard the contract as repudiated, and need not render any further performance, and can also sue for damages.

Warranties denote contractual terms that can be broken without highly important consequences. This would be a minor term and would not entitle the party to terminate the contract it merely entitles him to sue. The Consumer Rights Act 2015 designates certain terms as warranties breach of which does not allow the buyer to treat the contract as discharged, but merely to sue for damages, for example, the right to quiet enjoyment.

One such case that illustrates the above is that of *Bettini v Gye (1876)* where a singer was engaged to sing for a whole season and to arrive six days in advance to take part in rehearsals. He arrived only three days in advance. It was held that the rehearsal clause was a warranty, as it was subsidiary to the main clause. The management were therefore not entitled to treat the contract as discharged. They should have kept to the original contract and sought damages for the three days' delay.

Innominate terms are terms that can be broken with either important or trivial consequences, depending on the nature of the breach.

Innominate terms were illustrated in *Hong Kong Fir Shipping Co Ltd v Kawasaki Kisen Kaisha (1962)* in which the defendants had chartered a ship for two years from the claimants. Twenty weeks of the charter were lost due to the condition of ship and incompetent staff. The agreement contained a clause stating that the ship was 'in every way fitted for ordinary cargo service'. There was no doubt that the defendants were entitled to bring an action for damages but instead decided to terminate the contract. The claimants counter sued, claiming that the breach did not entitle the defendants to terminate, only to claim damages. The Court of Appeal agreed, stating that the question to be asked was that whether as a result of the breach the defendants had been deprived of the whole of the benefit of the contract. As this was not the case, the termination was unjustified.

Unfair contract terms

Contract terms can be considered to be so unfair to one of the contracting parties that the courts have had to intervene to prevent an injustice. This has usually arisen within the context of exemption clauses and is controlled both by common law and the exemption clauses in contracts. Parts 1 and 2 of the Consumer Rights Act 2015 consolidate and replace the Unfair Terms in Consumer Contracts Regulations 1999 (UTCCRs) and relevant provisions of the Unfair Contract Terms Act 1977 (UCTA). The Unfair Contract Terms Act 1977 applies only to exemption clauses covering business liability and, since the CRA 2015, does not cover any exemption clauses that would be covered by the Act, i.e., in contracts between a trader and a consumer.

The Act defines a 'trader' as a person acting for purposes relating to that person's trade, business craft or profession. A 'consumer' is defined as an individual acting for purposes that are wholly or mainly outside the indiviual's trade, business, craft or profession *(see Overy v Paypal (Europe) Ltd 2012.*

For an exemption clause to be effective as a matter of contract law it must be incorporated into the contract. There are various ways in which an exemption clause can be incorporated into a contract. In the absence of a signature, the exemption may be incorporated by notice. It was emphasised in *Parker v South Eastern Ry (1877)* that it is notice of the terms that is important, not their actual reading or understanding.. It follows that if the notice is illegible or obscured by a date stamp, as in *Richardson, Spence and Co v Rowntree (1894)* it will be ineffective.

In certain cases, one party to a contract may seek to avoid incurring liabilities for breach of contract or may specify that their liability for such a breach will be limited, usually to a specific amount of damages. However, a clause that seeks to exclude all liability for uncertain breaches is called an exclusion clause. There are many examples such as holiday companies seeking to exclude all liability for holidays gone wrong or cancelled. Over the past 40 years the law has sought to control the use of these clauses, first by the efforts of judges and also by legislation such as the Unfair

Contract Terms Act 1977 and the Unfair Terms in Consumer Contracts Regulations 1999, now consolidated as described above by the CRA 2015.

Misrepresentation in contracts

Even in cases where a contract clearly meets the requirements of offer and acceptance, consideration and intent to create legal relations, it will still not be binding if, at the time the contract was made, certain factors were present which meant that there was no genuine concern. These are known as vitiating factors (because they vitiate, or invalidate, consent). The vitiating factors that the law recognizes as preventing a contract are misrepresentation, mistake, duress, undue influence and illegality. In these cases, the innocent party may set the contract aside if he wishes. If one party has been induced to enter into a contract by a statement made by the other party, and that statement is untrue, the contract is voidable and the innocent party may also be able to claim damages. For a misrepresentation to be actionable it must be untrue, a statement of fact not an opinion, and it must have induced the innocent party to enter into the contract.

It is worth noting that, following the amendments to the Consumer Protection from Unfair Trading Regulations 2008 (CPRs 2008) made by the Consumer Protection Amendment Regulations 2014, after October 1st 2014 consumers who entered into a contract for the sale or supply of a product by a trader or who entered into a contract to sell a product to a trader (for example selling a car to a dealer) or made a payment to a trader for the supply of a product, and that trader engaged in a prohibited practice in relation to that product, for example by giving misleading information, have an extended range of specific consumer 'rights to redress' under the CPRs (right to unwind, right to a discount, and specific rights to damages). This regime is separate to the consumers general remedies, but the consumer cannot make a claim twice for the same product. In addition, there is an amendment to s.2 of the Misrepresentation Act 1967 which removes the ability of consumers to recover damages under that legislation where they have a right to redress under the CPRs in respect of the misrepresentation,

There are four different types of misrepresentation, fraudulent misrepresentation, where there is clear deceit, negligent, where misrepresentation arises through acts of negligence but not deceit and innocent misrepresentation which is not fraudulent but is still clear misrepresentation. The effect of a misrepresentation is generally to make a contract voidable, rather than void, so the contract will continue to exist unless or until the injured party chooses to have it set aside by the courts by means of rescission. Rescission is an equitable remedy that sets the contract aside and puts the parties back in the position where they were before the misrepresentation. An injured party who decides to rescind the contract may do so by notifying the other party or, if this is not possible owing to the conduct of the party, by taking some reasonable action to indicate the intention to default.

A case that illustrates this is *Car and Universal Finance Co Ltd v Caldwell (1965)* where the defendant sold and delivered a car and was paid by cheque. The cheque bounced, by which time the car and buyer had disappeared. The defendant notified the police and the Automobile Association. While the police were investigating the buyer sold the car to a dealer who knew that the car was not the buyers to sell. Finally, the car dealer sold the car to the claimants who bought it in good faith. The Court of Appeal held that by contacting the police and the AA the claimant had made his intention to rescind the contract clear. As soon as this happened the ownership of the car reverted to him. This meant that at the time the car was sold back to the claimant the car was not anyone's to sell.

Another case illustrating this is *Whittington v Seale-Hayne (1900)* where the plaintiff's, breeders of prize poultry, were induced to take a lease of the defendant's premises by his innocent representation that the premises were in a sanitary condition. Under the lease, the plaintiff's covenanted to execute any works required by any local or public authority. Owing to the insanitary conditions of the premises, the water supply was poisoned, the plaintiff's manager and his family became very ill, and the poultry became valueless for breeding purposes or died. The court rescinded the lease and held that the plaintiffs could recover an indemnity for what they had spent on rates, rent and repairs under the covenants in the lease, because these expenses arose necessarily out of the contract. It refused to award compensation for other leases, since to do so would be to award damages, not an indemnity, there being no obligation created by the contract to carry on a poultry farm on the premises or to employ a manager, etc.

Representation and terms of a contract

Section 1 of the Misrepresentation Act 1967, s.2 as amended by The Consumer Protection Amendment Regulations 2014, described above, provides that where a misrepresentation becomes a term of the contract, the innocent party may bring an action for both misrepresentation and breach of contract. Under section 3 of this Act, as amended by the Unfair Contract Terms Act 1977, as amended by the CRA 2015, exemption clauses that attempt to exclude or limit liability for misrepresentations are operative only if reasonable. This provision is illustrated in *Walker v Boyle (1982)* where the seller of a house told the buyer that there were no disputes regarding the boundaries of the property. This misrepresentation appeared to entitle the buyer to rescind the contract and notwithstanding a clause seeking to deny this, the court granted a rescission.

Mistake

The general rule is that a mistake has no effect on a contract, but certain mistakes of a fundamental nature, sometimes called operative mistakes, may render a contract void at common law. If the contract is rendered void, then the parties will be returned to their original positions, and this may defeat the rights of innocent third parties who may have acquired an interest in the contract.

The reluctance of the courts to develop the common law doctrine of mistake is probably due to the unfortunate consequences for third parties that can result from holding a contract void. Equity at one stage intervened to create a more flexible doctrine, but this has been overruled. We discuss mistakes in more depth in the next chapter.

Rectification

Where there has been a mistake, not in the actual agreement but in reducing it in writing, equity will order rectification of the document so that it coincides with the true agreement of the parties.
The main conditions for this are that:

- The document does not represent the intention of both parties; or
- One party mistakenly believes that a term was included in the document and the other party knew of this error.
- There must have been a concluded agreement but not necessarily an enforceable contract. Rectification is an equitable remedy and is available at the discretion of the court.

Refusal of specific performance

Specific performance will be refused when the contract is void at common law. Equity may also refuse specific performance where a contract is valid at law, but only 'where a hardship amounting to injustice would have been inflicted upon him by holding him to his bargain' *(Tamplin v James (1879).*

Duress

This requires actual or threatened violence to the person. Originally, it was the only form of duress recognized by the law. This is highlighted by the case of *Barton v Armstrong (1975*) where a managing director was threatened with death if he did not purchase a former chairman's shares. The managing director was happy to purchase the shares notwithstanding the threats that had been made. It was held that the threats constituted duress and the contract was set aside. We will look at duress in more depth in chapter 7.

****

1. 4

Contracts And Illegality

In this chapter we look at the concept of legally unenforceable contracts and the effect of this on parties to a contract. We also look at modes of performance and breaches of common law and legislation generally, plus contracts prejudicial to public safety.

Although a contract, on the face of it, may contain all the elements of a valid agreement, such as offer and consideration, that contract may still be legally unenforceable. Contracts may be illegal at the time of their formation or because of the way they have been performed. A contract may be illegal when entered into because the contract cannot be performed in accordance with its terms without committing an illegal act. For example, a contract may involve a breach of the criminal law, or it may be a statutory requirement for the parties to the contract to have a license that they in fact do not have. A case that illustrates this is *Levy v Yates (1838).* In this case, there existed a statutory rule that a royal license was required to perform a play within 20 miles of London. In that case the contract was between a theatre owner and an impresario for the performance of a theatrical production where no royal license had been obtained. The contract was thus illegal at the time of its formation.

Illegal mode of performance

In some cases, a contract may be perfectly legal when it was made, but may be carried out in an illegal manner. A case that illustrates this is

Anderson Ltd v Daniel (1924). In this case, a statute provided that a seller of artificial fertilizer had to supply buyers with an invoice detailing certain chemicals used in its manufacture. The sellers failed to provide the invoice needed. Although not against the law to sell fertilizer it was against statutory rules not to supply an invoice. As a result, the sellers were unable to claim the price when the defendants refused to pay. A contract is obviously illegal if it involves a contravention of the law. However, a contract is also regarded as being illegal where it involves conduct that the law disapproves of as contrary to the interests of the public, even though the conduct is not actually unlawful. In both cases the transaction is treated as an illegal contract and the courts will not enforce it.

Contracts violating legal rules

Breach of common law

There are a number of factors that may make a contract illegal at common law, the most important where there is a contract to commit a crime or tort (negligent act). These are obvious breaches of the law. However, another very important area is contracts in restraint of trade. The issue of restraint of trade commonly arises and concerns those contracts that limit an individuals right to use their skills for payment, or to trade freely. These contracts fall into four groups:

- Contracts for the sale of a business where the vendor promises not to compete with the purchaser.
- Contracts between businesses by which prices or output are regulated.
- Contracts in which an employee agrees that on leaving employment they will not set up in business or be employed in such as way as to compete with their employer or ex employer. This is most common in business where personal skills and

reputation attract custom, such as advertising and the ex-employee may take with them valuable customers.

- Contracts where a person agrees to restrict their mode of trade by, for example, only accepting orders from one particular company. This is sometimes called a 'solus' agreement and is frequently used for petrol stations, in return for the land or lease the trader promises to use the product of the seller (*Esso Petroleum v Harper's Garage (Stourport) 1968).*

Any of the above can be held to create a restraint of trade, a general restraint if the contract completely prohibits trading, or a partial restraint if it limits trading to a certain time or area.

Breach of legislation

Some types of contracts are expressly declared void by statute. The two most important examples of contracts that are expressly declared void by statute are contracts in constraint of trade and wagering contracts.

Contracts in restraint of trade

As stated above, these are arrangements by which one party agrees to limit his or her legal right to carry out a trade, business or profession. A contract that does this is always viewed as *prima facie* void for two reasons:

- To prevent people signing away their livelihoods at the request of a party with stronger bargaining power
- To avoid depriving the public of the person's expertise.

These contracts are of several possible types as mentioned above-employee restraints, vendor restraints-preventing the seller of a business from unfairly competing with the purchaser and agreements of mutual regulation between businesses. However, these agreements might be upheld as reasonable:

- as between the parties-so the restraint must be no wider than to protect a legitimate interest.
- in the public interest-so the restraint must not unduly limit public choice.

The reasonableness of the restraint is also measured against factors such as duration and geographical extent.

Employee restraints

An employer can legitimately protect trade secrets and client connection, but not merely prevent the employee from exercising his or her trade or skill. Reasonableness is measured against certain criteria:

A restraint in a highly specialised business is more likely to be reasonable. In *Forster and Sons Ltd v Suggett (1918)* – the court held that a restraint of 5 years on an employee from engaging in glass or glass bottle manufacturing was reasonable given the time and money invested into their training. *Nordenfelt v Maxim Nordenfelt Guns and Ammunition Co Ltd (1894)* - the court held that a term prohibiting Nordenfelt from starting a competing business anywhere in the world for 25 years was reasonable.

Pursuant to the Nordenfelt principle, restraint of trade clauses are void and unenforceable unless they are reasonable by reference to the interests of the parties and the public. The restraint must also be reasonable in terms of time and space. Restraint of an employee in a key position is more likely to be reasonable.

An employer is not entitled to protect itself against the use of the skill and knowledge which the employee acquired during his or her employment. Those belong to the employee, who must be free to exploit them in the marketplace. Neither can an employer seek protection from competition per se since it is against the public interest that employees should be deprived of the opportunity to earn their living or to use their personal skills to the ultimate benefit of the community as a whole:

Herbert Morris Limited v Saxelby
[1916] AC 688.

Instead, the employer must demonstrate that the covenant protects a legitimate business interest. In the Herbert Morris case, Lord Parker defined this as "some proprietary right, whether in the nature of a trade connection or in the nature of trade secrets, for the protection of which such a restraint is reasonably necessary". The concept was further developed by Lord Wilberforce in *Stenhouse Australia Limited v Phillips [1974] 1 All ER 117,* who said:
"The employer's claim for protection must be based on the identification of some advantage or asset inherent in the business which can properly be regarded as, in a general sense, his property, and which it would be unjust to allow the employee to appropriate for his own purposes, even though he (the employee) may have contributed to its creation".

In other words, the employer is entitled to prevent the employee taking unfair advantage of confidential information and business connections to which he had access in the course of his/her employment.

An employee may be significant to the business without even being a member of staff as demonstrated in *Leeds Rugby Ltd v Harris (2005).* The duration of the extent must not be too long *(Home Counties Dairies v*

Skilton (1970) and the geographical extent too wide *(Fitch v Dewes (1921*). Similarly, the range of activities that the restraint covers must be no wider than is necessary to protect legitimate interests *(J A Mont (UK) Ltd v Mills (1993*).

Soliciting of clients can be prevented by such clauses, if not too wide *(M&S Drapers v Reynolds (1957*). Also, including clients not within the original scope of the restraint is not unreasonable *(Hanover Insurance Brokers Ltd and Christchurch Insurance Brokers Ltd v Shapiro (1994*). Attempting a restraint by other means is also void, including making contractual benefits subject to a restraint *(Bull v Pitney Bowes Ltd (1966)* and restraints in rules of associations *(Eastham v Newcastle United FC Ltd (1963).*

Vendor restraints

These are void for public policy to prevent an individual from negotiating away his or her livelihood and also because the public may lose a valuable service. Restraints are more likely to be upheld as reasonable since businesses deal on more equal bargaining strength, even if restraint is very wide *(Nordenfelt v Maxim Nordenfelt Co (1894).* The restraint must still protect a legitimate interest to be valid *(British Concrete Ltd v Schelff (1921*).

Agreements between merchants, manufacturers or other trades

If the object is regulation of trade, then they are void unless both sides benefit *(English Hop Growers v Dering (1928*). So they are void when the parties have unequal bargaining strength *(Schroder Publishing Co Ltd v Macaulay (1974)*-unless public policy dictates otherwise: *Panayiotou v Sony Music International (UK) Ltd (1994*).

Wagering contracts

Wagering agreements are bets and were rendered void by The Gaming Act 1845 which remained in force until the Gambling Act 2005, which came into force in stages to 2007.

The Act provides:

"All contracts or agreements, whether by parole or in writing, by way of gaming or wagering, shall be null and void, and no suit shall be brought or maintained in a court of law or equity for recovering any sum of money or valuable thing alleged to be won upon any wager..."

The Act does not make wagering agreements illegal it simply provides that neither party to such an agreement can legally enforce it. For the provisions of the legislation to apply, a wagering contract must be one in which there are two parties and the terms of the agreement are such that one party wins and the other loses. This means that football pools, for example, are not covered as its promoters take a percentage of the stake money and so gain by the transaction regardless of whether players win as well. The Act also covers gaming, which is defined by the Betting, Gaming and lotteries act 1963 as 'the playing of a game of chance for winnings in money or money's worth'. Games of chance include games that depend partly on skill and partly on chance. Athletic games and sports are excluded.

Competition law

Common law lays down certain controls on contracts in constraint of trade. These controls give only limited protection and actual legislation provides more adequate protection. One of the main goals of the

European Union, through Article 85, is to promote free trade between member states and clearly restrictive trade can affect this policy. Where a restrictive trade agreement could affect trade between member states it will only be valid if allowed under both EU and English law.

In terms of contracts in English law, the relevant legislation is now contained in the Competition Act 1998 Along with the Enterprise Act 2002. This Act prohibits a number of anti-competitive practices. The 1998 Act applies to agreements between undertakings, decisions by associations of undertakings or concerted practices that (a) may affect trade and (b) have as their object or effect the prevention, restriction or distortion of trade. For the Act to prohibit an agreement the effect of the agreement must be significant and not minor.

Contracts against public policy

There exists a wide range of contracts that are considered to be illegal because they are against public policy. As we discussed, public policy really means the interest of society at large and the contract must contravene it. Contracts promoting sexual immorality, for example, are seen as contravening public policy.

One case that illustrates this is *Armhouse Lee Ltd v Chappell (1996)* concerning a contract under which the defendants paid the plaintiffs to place adverts for telephone sex lines in magazines. When regulation concerning such publicity was tightened the defendants terminated the contract, as they no longer wished to advertise their services in this way. The plaintiffs brought an action for the money due under the contract and the defendants argued that the contract was illegal and unenforceable as it promoted sexual immorality. This defense was rejected by the Court of Appeal. The court held that though the adverts were distasteful the sex lines were generally accepted by society and were regulated by the telephone industry. There was no evidence, in the eyes of the Court of Appeal that any 'generally accepted moral code' condemned these telephone sex lines. It considered that contracts should only be found illegal under this heading if an element of public harm clearly existed.

Contracts prejudicial to public safety

The main types of contracts found illegal on these grounds are contracts with those living in an enemy country, contracts to perform acts which are illegal in a friendly foreign country and contracts which are damaging to foreign relations.

The effect of an illegal contract

The effect of an illegal contract will depend on whether it is illegal due to a statute or due to the common law. Where the contract is illegal due to a statute, in some cases the statute provides for the consequences of any illegality. Under common law an illegal contract is void and courts will not order it to be performed. The precise effects of an illegal contract depend on whether the contract is illegal at the time of formation or is illegal due to the way in which it was performed. Contracts illegal at the time of formation are treated as if they were never made, so the illegal contract is unenforceable by either party. Contracts illegal as performed are slightly different as to their effect. It will be possible to enforce the illegal contract if the illegal act was merely incidental to the performance of the contract. For example, a contract for the delivery of goods may not be tainted by illegality when the lorry driver is caught speeding or under the influence of drink. Where the contract is merely illegal because of the way it was performed, it is possible for either both or only one of the parties to intend illegal performance. If both parties are aware that a contract's performance is illegal, the consequences for this type of contract are the same as for a contract that was illegal at the time of its formation. When one party did not know of the illegal performance of the contract by the other party, the innocent party can enforce it. In some cases, it is possible to divide the illegal part of a contract from the rest and enforce the provisions which are not affected by the illegality-this is called severance. The illegal parts of the contract can be severed if they are relatively unimportant to the contract and if the severance leaves the nature of the contract unaltered.

****

1.5

Discharge of a Contract

In this chapter we look at the ways that a contract is effectively discharged and frustration of contract. We will also look at force majeur and the importance of force majeure clauses.

We look at the effects on the contract when it becomes impossible to fulfill because of the death of either party to a contract. Other areas are also explored.

A contract is said to be discharged when the rights and obligations in it come to an end. There are four ways in which a contract can come to an end: performance under the contract, i.e., natural end, end by mutual agreement, breach of contract and frustration. We should look at these areas in turn.

Performance under contract

This is the most obvious way of parties discharging their obligations and bringing the contract to a satisfactory end. In many cases, it is uncomplicated but there are some cases where one party may claim to have discharged their obligations and the other party disagrees. The law then must look at the question of what constitutes performance. The obvious and general rule is that performance must exactly match the requirements laid down in the contract. This is known as entire performance. If the first party fails to perform then the other party need pay nothing at all, even if the shortfall causes no hardship. This is the simple rule and obviously contracts can be more complicated, with claim and counter claim. The case of *Cutter v Powell (1795)* demonstrates the difficulty. A sailor had contracted to serve on a ship traveling from Jamaica to Liverpool. He was to be paid 30 Guineas for the voyage, payable when the ship arrived in Liverpool. However, he died during the journey. His widow sued for wages up until he died, but her claim was unsuccessful, as the court held that the contract required entire performance.

Similarly, in *Bolton v Mahadeva (1972)* a central heating system gave out less heat than it should, and there were fumes in one room. It was held that the contractor could not claim payment; although the boiler and pipes had been installed, they did not fulfill the primary purpose of heating the house.

The rule can also allow parties to escape from what has become an unprofitable contract to do so by taking advantage of the most minor departures from its terms.

In *Re Moore and Co Ltd and Landaur and Co (1921)* the contract concerned the sale of canned fruit that were to be packed into cases of 30 tins. On delivery it was discovered that although the correct number of tins had been sent, almost half the cases contained only 24 tins in each. This made no difference to the market value of the goods, but the buyers pointed out that the sale was covered by the Sale of Goods Act, which stated that goods sold by description must correspond with that description. The delivery did not, and the buyers were within their rights to reject the whole consignment.

Mitigation of the entire performance rule-Substantial performance

This doctrine allows a party who has performed with only minor defects to claim the price of the work done, less any money the other party will have to spend to put the defects right.

Severable contracts

A contract is said to be severable where payment becomes due at various stages of performance, rather than in one lump sum when performance is complete. Most contracts of employment are examples of this. Also, major building contracts also operate in this way, allowing for stage payments. In a severable contract the money due at the end of each stage may be claimed and the person carrying out the work under the contract can refuse to continue if the payments are not made.

Prevention of performance by one party

Where one party performs one part of the agreed obligation and is then prevented from completing the rest of the contract because of a fault of the other party, a quantum meruit can be claimed from the other party. Quantum meruit is an assessment of the amount performed to date and a reasonable price arrived at.

Breach of terms concerning time

The judgment here will be that of an assessment of whether 'time is of the essence' and the effect that completing the contract out of time has on the other party.

Force majeure clause

Force Majeure simply means circumstances beyond control. A person or business will only be able to rely on a force majeure clause if one is included in the relevant contract and it applies to them. English law does not imply force majeure relief into contracts that are silent on the matter. It is very unusual to find force majeure clauses in English leases.

Simply because a force majeure clause exists (that operates in a persons or business favour), doesn't necessarily mean they have the right to invoke the relief in all situations. Force majeure clauses are typically drafted to include specified events (often called force majeure events). Whether the current situation constitutes a force majeure event is a matter for interpretation that requires specialist legal advice. It is unlikely that a clause envisages coronavirus COVID-19 specifically, however it may specify events such as pandemics, epidemics and work stoppages and also include events such as:

- compliance with a law or governmental order, rule, regulation, or direction.
- any action taken by a government or public authority, including imposing embargo, export restriction or other restriction or prohibition.
- delays by suppliers or materials shortages.
- difficulty or increased costs in obtaining workers, goods or transport; or
- other circumstances affecting the supply of goods or services.
- It is also wise to consider how the outbreak is being classified by bodies such as the World Health Organisation at the time you're seeking to invoke the force majeure clause, as this may or may not support an argument or claim.

Force majeure clauses typically include a requirement, for the party seeking relief, to show that the event could not have been mitigated by preventative action. This demonstrates the point force majeure may only be invoked when the relevant event has prevented performance of the contract, not simply that the event exists, has caused economic hardship or that performance has become difficult or commercially undesirable.

Force majeure clauses typically include a requirement, for the party seeking relief, to show that the event could not have been mitigated by preventative action. This demonstrates the point force majeure may only be invoked when the relevant event has prevented performance of the contract, not simply that the event exists, has caused economic hardship or that performance has become difficult or commercially undesirable. Certain government agencies around the world have begun to issue "force majeure certificates" to some businesses in an attempt to prevent or stall breach of contract claims and limit liability.

Invoking a force majeure clause

The following non-exhaustive list contains some of the matters you should consider:

- force majeure clauses typically include a right for the unaffected party to terminate when the event has continued for a specified period of time. Although claiming force majeure relief may seem immediately beneficial to a business, it may have unintended consequences, such as triggering termination rights for customers.
- what do the contracts say? No force majeure clause is the same, therefore a one-size-fits-all approach will not work. Each relevant contract must be reviewed.
- have you communicated with your customers and suppliers? The outbreak continues to affect global trade and the number of cases and countries involved is increasing, so it may be that simple communication will suffice without the need to resort to legal action.

Force majeure clauses typically set out a procedure which must be followed to effectively claim relief under the clause. A person/business should obtain advice before invoking the clause to ensure that they have properly complied with that procedure. Recent case law suggests that failure to comply can jeopardise subsequent legal claims.

Further considerations

When faced with such circumstances, it is advisable to have each affected contract reviewed in its entirety, as there are likely to be several terms that are impacted, including but not limited to exclusivity, liability and liquidated damages, delivery and termination rights, change control regimes, governing law and jurisdiction.

With Covid-19, there are countless ways in which one can imagine the impact of the pandemic on business and commerce. Judges themselves will have felt the impact on a personal level and are likely to be sympathetic to anyone who seeks to rely on a force majeure clause. But parties should not assume that the clause will apply – the clause must be read carefully, and care must be taken to demonstrate that performance of the contract truly was rendered impossible or substantially more difficult as a result of the virus and its impact.

Frustration of contract

That an event has the effect of frustrating the contract is notoriously difficult to establish. In *Canary Wharf (BP4) T1 Ltd v European Medicines Agency* [2019] EWHC 335 (Ch), the Court held that the supervening effect of Brexit did not render impossible the EMA's continued occupation of its London headquarters.

The basic principle underlying frustration of contract is that, after a contract is made, something happens, through no fault of the parties own, to make fulfilment of the contract impossible. Although there are many situations that can make it impossible to fulfil a contract only certain cases can be seen as genuine frustration. When a contract is discharged by frustration both parties are excused performance of their future obligations and the application of the Law Reform (Frustrated Contracts) Act 1943 determines what happens to advance payments (such as deposits and any other payments due) made before the frustrating event and claims for reimbursement for contractual expenses and performance conferred prior to frustration.

The modern doctrine of frustration arose from *Taylor v Caldwell (1863)*. The parties in the case had entered into an agreement concerning the use of Surrey Gardens and music hall for a series of concerts and day and night fetes. Six days before the planned date for the first concert, the building was burnt down, making it impossible for the concerts to go ahead. The party planning to put on the concerts was sued for breach of contract but the action failed, as fulfillment of the contract was impossible.

The concept and practice of frustration of contract can be placed in three categories: events that make performance or further performance impossible; events that make performance illegal; and those that make it pointless.

Impossible to fulfill contract

A contract may become impossible to perform because of destruction or unavailability of something essential for the contract to be performed.

Death of either party to the contract

Unavailability of party. Contracts which require personal performance will be frustrated if one party, for example, is ill or is imprisoned, providing that the non-availability of the party substantially affects performance.

Method of performance impossible

Where a contract lays down a particular method of performance and this becomes impossible, the contract may be frustrated. A contract is unlikely to be frustrated simply because performance has become more expensive or more onerous than expected. The leading modern case on frustration is *Davis Contractors Co Ltd v Fareham UDC (1956)*. Davis, a construction company contracted to build 78 houses for a local authority. The job was to take eight months, at a price of £94,000. In fact, labor shortages delayed the work, which ended up taking 22 months and cost the builders £22,000 more than they had planned for. The defendant was willing to pay the contract price despite the delay, but Davis sought to have the contract discharged on the grounds of frustration arguing that labor shortages made performance fundamentally different from that envisaged in the contract (it intended to seek payment on a quantum meruit basis to cover costs). However, the House of Lords decided that the events that caused the delays were within the range of changes that could reasonably be expected to happen during the performance of a contract for building houses and the change of circumstances did not make performance radically different from what was expected. Therefore, the contract was not frustrated. Lord Radcliffe explained:

'it is not hardship or inconvenience or material loss which itself calls the principle of frustration into play. There must be as well such a change in the significance of the obligation that the thing undertaken would, if performed, be different from that contracted for'.

Illegality

If, after a contract is formed, a change in the law makes its performance illegal, the contract will be frustrated.

Performance made pointless

A contract can be frustrated where a supervening event makes performance of a contract completely pointless, though still technically possible. A contract can be rendered pointless if there has been such a drastic change of circumstances as to dramatically alter the nature of the contract.

Time of frustrating event

In order to frustrate a contract, the event in question must occur after the contract is made.

Limits to the doctrine of frustration

The doctrine of frustration will not be applied on the grounds of inconvenience, increase in expense or loss of profit. The case above that highlights this is *Davis Contractors Limited v Fareham UDC (1956).* It will also not apply where there is express provision in the contract covering the intervening event or where the frustration is self-induced.

A contract will not be frustrated if the event making performance impossible was the voluntary action of one party. If the party concerned had a choice open to him, and chose to act as to make performance impossible, then frustration will be self-induced, and the court will refuse to treat the contract as discharged. One such case that highlights this is *The Superservant Two (1990).* In this case one of the two barges owned by the defendants and used to transport oil rigs was sunk. They were therefore unable to fulfill their contract to transport an oil rig belonging to the plaintiff as their other barge (superservant one) was already allocated to other contracts. It was held that the contract was not frustrated. The defendants had another barge available but chose not to allocate it to the contract with the plaintiffs.

Where the event was foreseeable

If, by reason of special knowledge, the event was foreseeable by one party, then he cannot claim frustration. This was highlighted in *Amalgamated Investment and Property Co v John Walker and Sons Ltd (1976)* where the possibility that a building could be listed was foreseen by the plaintiff who had enquired about the matter beforehand. A failure to obtain planning permission was also foreseeable and was a normal risk for property developers. The contract was therefore not frustrated.

Breach of contract

A contract is breached when one party performs defectively, or differently from the agreement or not at all (actual breach) or indicates in advance that they will not be performing as agreed (anticipatory breach). Where an anticipatory breach occurs, the other party can sue for breach straight away, it is not necessary to wait until performance falls due.

One case illustrating this is *Frost v Knight (1872)* where the defendant had promised to marry the plaintiff once his father had died. He later broke off the engagement before his father died, and when his ex fiancé sued him for breach of promise, he argued that she had no claim as the time for performance had not yet arrived. This argument was rejected and the plaintiff's case succeeded. Any effect of a breach of contract will entitle the innocent party to sue for damages but not every breach will entitle the wronged party to discharge the contract. If the contract is not discharged it will still need to be performed.

There are three main circumstances where the innocent party may wish to seek to discharge the contract:

Repudiation – this is where one party makes it clear that they no longer wish to be bound by the contract, either during its performance or before performance is due.

Breach of a condition – Breach of a condition allows the innocent party to terminate the contract.

Serious breach of an innominate term- where the relevant term is classified as innominate, it will be the one that can be breached in both serious and trivial ways, and whether the innocent party is entitled to terminate or not will depend on how serious the results of the breach are. If the results are so serious as to undermine the foundations of the contract, the innocent party will have the right to terminate. Even when one of these three types of breach occurs, the contract is not automatically discharged. The innocent party can usually choose whether or not to terminate. If the innocent party chooses to terminate this must be clearly communicated to the other party.

Agreement

In some cases, the parties to a contract will simply agree to terminate the contract, so that one or both parties are released from their obligations. A distinction is usually made between bilateral discharge where both parties will benefit from the ending by agreement and a unilateral discharge where one party benefits. In general, an agreed discharge will be binding if it contains the same elements that make a contract binding when it is formed. Those that present the most problems are formality and consideration.

Consideration

Consideration is not usually a problem where both parties agree to alter their obligations since each is giving something in return for the change. Problems are most likely to occur when one party's obligations change. If the other party agrees to the change, their agreement will only be binding if put into the form of a deed or supported by consideration. Where consideration is provided in return for one party's agreement to change this is called 'accord'. The provision of consideration is called 'satisfaction'. The arrangement is often termed accord and satisfaction.

Formalities

This issue arises in connection with certain types of contracts (mainly concerning the sale of land) that must be evidenced in writing to be binding under the Law of Property Act (1925).

Remedies for breach of contract

There are a number of remedies available to the innocent party in the event of a breached contract. There are two main remedies, those under common law and equitable remedies. There is a third category that involves remedies arising from the party's own agreement.

****

Chapter 2

Business Law-Negligence and Duty of Care-General

In everyday parlance, negligence means a failure to pay attention to what ought to be done or to take the required level of care. Whereas its everyday usage implies a state of mind, the tort of negligence is concerned with the link between the defendant's behaviour and the risk that should have been foreseen.

Key definition of negligence

Negligence, as a tort, is generally defined as a breach of a duty of care. This duty of care is owed by one person to another. When damage is caused to a person, who then becomes a claimant, the type of damage has to be specified and also defined as actionable.

The loss or damage can arise in a number of ways, arising through misfeasance or nonfeasance and can consist of personal injury, damage to property or can be pure economic loss. It can also consist of psychiatric damage.

The duty of care-establishment of a duty

Certain relationships between people, recognised by the law and developed by the law, give rise to a legal duty of care. The following

Employer-employee

- Manufacturer to consumer
- Doctor-patient
- Solicitor-client

Essentially, carelessness by one party which affects another gives rise, or can give rise, to legal action by the injured party. It is up to the claimant to prove that damage has been caused and that the case falls into a specific situation that gives rise to a duty of care.

The neighbour principle

Donoghue v Stevenson 1932

Outside of the categories of established duty, a duty of care will be determined based on individual circumstances.

One of the most prominent cases relating to Tort and negligence is that of *Donoghue v Stevenson* (HL 1932) In this case, Mrs Donoghue and friend visited a café and Mrs Donoghue's friend bought her a bottle of ginger beer. The bottle was made of opaque glass. When filling Mrs Donoghue's glass, the remains of a decomposed a snail floated out of the bottle. Mrs Donoghue developed gastroenteritis as a result.

Mrs Donoghue brought an action against the manufacturers of the ginger beer. Lord Atkin formulated a general principle in this case, the **neighbour principle**, for determining whether a duty of care should exist. He stated:

"You must take reasonable care to avoid acts or omissions which you can reasonably foresee would be likely to injure your neighbour. Who then, in law, is my neighbour? The answer seems to be persons who are so closely and directly affected by my act that I ought reasonably to have them in contemplation as being so affected when I am directing my mind to the acts or omissions which are called in question".

The manufacturers were found liable as they owed her a duty of care that the bottle did not contain foreign bodies which would damage her health.

This principle was a landmark and established negligence as an independent tort.

Out of this judgement, which was further developed in the case of *Caparo Industries plc v Dickman* (1990), (which is further outlined below) also comes the concept of foresight, i.e., was the damage itself reasonably foreseeable. There must be a legal relationship of 'sufficient proximity' between the parties. There is also a requirement that it is 'just and reasonable' to impose a duty on the defendant.

Even where the courts are prepared to find that the circumstances are such as to be capable of giving rise to a duty of care, it is still likely that the claimant in a case could fail if he or she was an 'unforeseeable victim' of the defendant's negligence.

One such case which amplifies this is *Bourhill v Young* (1943) where the plaintiff in the case heard but did not actually see a crash caused by the motorcyclists (the defendants) negligence. The plaintiff later saw part of the aftermath of the accident and sued the defendant after suffering nervous shock, and lost the case, as harm to her of that type was not foreseeable.

Essentially, the legal proximity of claimant to defendant must be clearly established. In *Davis v Radcliffe* (1990), for example, Lord Goff stated that proximity referred to such a relation between the parties as rendered it just and reasonable that a duty should be imposed. Lack of proximity can, in some cases, be attributed to the failure of just and reasonable requirement in a case. A variety of factors are considered, such as the status of the parties and their relationship with one another, nature of injury or harm suffered and the particular way that the harm arises. One seminal case which further defined the boundaries of tort and negligence was that of *Hedley Byrne and Co v Heller and Partners Ltd* (1964). Lord Pearce observed:

"How wide the sphere of duty of care in negligence is to be laid depends primarily on the courts assessment of the demands of society for protection from the carelessness of others".

The case of Hedley Byrne concerned Economic loss through negligent information (see below).

Pure economic loss

Although financial loss incurred as a result of a negligent action against a person and property is normally recoverable, problems can arise with so called 'pure' economic loss, which is financial loss which has not been accompanied by any other damage. Cases of financial loss may arise as a result of either negligent information or advice, or of negligent conduct. In general, courts will assess these cases on a case-by-case basis, rather than rely purely on precedent.

Before the Hedley Byrne case, liability for negligent statements, or misstatements, which resulted in financial or other loss, existed in contract, in the tort of deceit or for breach of a fiduciary duty. In Hedley Byrne and Co v Heller and Partners Ltd the plaintiffs wanted to know if they could safely advance credit to their client, (A). The plaintiff's bankers sought references from the defendants (B) bankers, who gave favourable reports 'without responsibility'. The plaintiffs relied on the information and then suffered financial loss when A went into liquidation. In this case, it was held that no duty arose because of the disclaimer. However, importantly, in appropriate circumstances, a duty could arise.

It was accepted that reasonable foresight of the harm was not enough in itself, but that a 'special relationship' must exist where, to the defendant's knowledge the plaintiff relied upon the defendant's skill and judgement or his ability to make careful enquiry, and it was reasonable in the circumstances for the plaintiff to do so. The essence of Hedley and Byrne can therefore be equated with the concept of 'reasonable reliance'.

Another case highlighting the above is that of *Caparo Industries* where Lord Bridge said that in order for a duty to arise, it was necessary to show that the defendant knew that his statement would be communicated to the plaintiff, either as an individual or as a member of an identifiable class, specifically in connection with a transaction or transactions of a particular kind, and that the plaintiff would be very likely to rely on it in deciding whether or not to enter into a transaction.

Provided that the defendant is aware of the existence of the claimant either as an individual or as a member of an ascertainable class, there is no need that the defendant knows the identity of the claimant. A vital ingredient of the duty is the defendant's knowledge (actual or constructive) of the purpose for which the information is required. In Caparo Industries it was held that, in preparing the audit of the accounts of a public company, the defendants owed no duty either to the plaintiffs either as potential investors or as existing shareholders. The purpose of the audit was to report to the shareholders to enable them to exercise their rights in the management of the company, not to provide information which might assist them in making investment decisions.

In contrast to the position of auditors, surveyors appointed to value a house for mortgage purposes may owe a duty to the purchaser even though the primary purpose of the valuation is to enable the lender to decide whether to advance a loan.

This was illustrated in *Harris v Wyre Forest District Council* (1989). This has been justified on the basis that valuers are paid for their services at the mortgagor's expense and understand that a lot of purchasers rely on these reports.

Contributory negligence (disclaimers)

On the assumption that an appropriately worded disclaimer is brought to the claimant's notice, either before or at the time the statement is made, it can be argued that no duty arises because the claimant's reliance would not be reasonable.

However, according to the House of Lords in the case *Smith v Eric S Bush* (1989), the effect of ss.11 (3) and 13 (1) of the Unfair Contract Terms Act 1977 is to subject all exclusion notices which would at common law provide a reasonable defence to an action for negligence, to a test of reasonableness, as provided for in s2 (2) of the act (this only relates to business liability).

Contributory negligence, which is discussed further in the book, is in principle a defence and is available equally to a claim under the Misrepresentation Act 1967.

Third party reliance

There are certain situations in which a duty of care will be imposed on a person (A), who makes a statement to B, as a result that B acts upon it to another's detriment. It is well established, generally, that a solicitor owes no duty of care to third parties. However, this is not always the case. For example, in *White v Jones* (1995), a majority of the House of Lords held the defendant solicitors liable for failing to carry out their clients' instructions regarding his will, with the result that the plaintiffs (the intended beneficiaries) lost their legacy.

The duty under White v Jones is not confined to cases relating to wills. In *Gorham v British Telecommunications plc* (CA 2000) an insurance company was held to owe a duty of care to the customer's dependant wife and family where he had intended to create a benefit for them on his death. It was also held in *Spring v Guardian Assurance plc* (HL 1994) that an employer supplying a reference about an employee to a prospective employer owes a duty to the employee to avoid making untrue statements negligently or expressing unfounded opinions, even if held honestly and believed to be true. In this case, it was the opinion of the majority of the Lords that economic loss in the form of failure to obtain employment was clearly foreseeable if a careless reference was given and there was clear proximity of relationship as between employer and employee, so that it was fair, just and reasonable that the law should impose a duty on the employer.

Negligent acts

Although there was originally no liability for pure economic loss caused by acts of negligence, the Hedley Byrne case made major inroads into this area and, although this case was originally confined to misstatements, a trend has developed towards the formulation of a wider principle, applying to both statements and acts.

Damage to third party property

In some cases, damages to property belonging to a third party may prevent the claimant from carrying on their business. In other cases, their contract with the third party may be adversely affected. In neither case can the claimant recover any damages because of a long-established rule that no claim will lie in respect of foreseeable economic loss, unaccompanied by physical damage to the property in which the claimant has an interest, either proprietary or possessory.

Defective property

If a claimant has acquired property and discovers it is defective, and money has to be spent on repairing or replacing it, such economic loss can be recovered against a party who has a relevant contractual obligation with the defendant. The claimant cannot bring a claim within the ordinary principles of tort, i.e., those contained within Donoghue v Stevenson, because the claim is concerned with defective goods which can cause personal injury or damage to property rather than the defective product in question.

However, although this was traditionally the case, this fundamental principle was brought into question in the case of *Anns v Merton London Borough Council* (HL 1978). In this case, damages were held to be recoverable by a building owner against a local authority which had negligently inspected and approved defective foundations. In Anns, the decision was justified on the basis that the cause of action arose when the building became an imminent danger to the health and safety of the occupier, who could then recover the cost of averting the potential danger.

Another case which developed this principle was *Junior Books Ltd v Veitchi Co Ltd* (HL 1983). The defendants were held liable for the cost of replacing a defective good supplied by them, even though there was no danger to health and safety. This decision went a considerable way to recognising a general right of recovery for pure economic loss. However, cases following this one have made it very clear that no new principle has been established and each case is viewed on its own merit.

Following a number of cases, the whole issue was considered by the Court of Appeal in *Murphy v Brentwood District Council* (HL 1990). The Lords unanimously overruled the findings in Anns so far as it imposed a duty on local authorities, on the ground that where a defect in a building was discovered before any personal injury or damage to property other than the defective house itself had been done, the expense incurred by the building owner in rectifying the defect (including associated costs such as vacating the premises) was pure economic loss and therefore irrecoverable in tort.

There are problems with the decision in Murphy, however. It would seem clear enough that the builder may be liable in accordance with Donoghue v Stevenson principles where a latent defect causes personal injury or damage to another property. In addition, it was thought, by one of the Lords reviewing the case, Lord Bridge, that where a building remained a potential source of injury to persons or property on neighbouring land or on the highway, the owner ought in principle be able to recover in tort from the negligent builder any costs incurred in order to protect himself from potential liabilities to third parties.

Most significantly, the Lords attached weight to the fact that it is the claimant's knowledge of the defect which makes the defect one of quality only, and therefore the loss purely economic. However, such knowledge has not necessarily barred the right of recovery.

One such case which highlighted this was *Rimmer v Liverpool City Council* (CA 1984). In this case, the designers and builders of a council flat, the local authority, was liable to a tenant injured by a pane of dangerously thin glass. The tenant knew of the danger and had complained, to no avail. It was considered that it was not practical for the tenant to either leave the flat or to change the pane of glass himself, although damages were reduced for contributory negligence.

Psychiatric illness

In *Alcock v Chief Constable of South Yorkshire* (HL 1991) Lord Ackner stated that shock "involves the sudden appreciation by sight or sound of a horrifying event, which violently agitates the mind".

Shock must manifest itself in some recognisable psychiatric or physical illness. Mere grief or emotional upset is not actionable, although mental distress suffered as a result of negligently inflicted injuries may be taken into account in the assessment of damages for pain and suffering.

Shock victims fall into two (very) broad groups, those who are unwilling participants in the events causing shock (known as primary victims) and those who are merely passive and unwilling victims (secondary victims). In relation to the first group, Lord Ackner said that if the defendants negligent conduct foreseeably puts the plaintiff in that position it follows that there will be a sufficiently proximate relationship between them, though if personal injury of some kind to the plaintiff is reasonably foreseeable as the result of an accident the defendant is liable for psychiatric injury (even though no physical injury occurs) and the plaintiff need not prove that injury by shock was foreseeable because the defendant must take his victim as he finds him.

Subsequent cases have established three types of primary victim, namely those who are put in reasonable fear for their own safety, rescuers and those who reasonably believe that they are about to be, or have been, the involuntary cause of another's death or injury. Such persons will recover if shock to them was reasonably foreseeable or if personal injury of some kind was foreseeable.

Where shock victims fall within the second category of groups a more complex analysis is required. It was held in Alcock that in order to recover damages, the plaintiff had to prove the following:

- that his relationship to the primary victim was sufficiently close that it was reasonably foreseeable that he might suffer shock if he apprehended that the victim had been, or might be, injured;
- that he was temporally and spatially close to the scene of the accident or its immediate aftermath;
- that he suffered shock through sight or hearing of the accident or its immediate aftermath.

One matter not covered in Alcock was whether a plaintiff could recover for shock caused as a result of witnessing the destruction of property. In *Attia v British Gas plc* (CA 1988) it was held that there was no principle of law that shock in such circumstances could never be regarded as foreseeable. However, since the defendants in that case admitted to owing a duty in respect of the damage to the plaintiff's home, the shock issue was treated as one of remoteness rather than duty.

Omissions

In tort, as a rule, the defendant does not owe a duty to take positive action to prevent harm to others. For example, the failure of a public authority to exercise a statutory power, or a statutory duty, will not normally give rise to a common law duty (see *Stovin v Wise* HL 1996). The mere existence of statutory powers and duties did not create a parallel common law duty.

This was highlighted in the case of *Gorringe v Calderdale* (2004) where the highway authorities' failure to paint a marking or to erect a road sign warning of a dangerous stretch of road did not give rise to a duty of care to the claimant.

Negligence-breach of duty

Once it has been established that a duty of care is owed to a claimant, it must then be proven that the defendant was in breach of that duty.

The key definition of negligence and duty of care was defined in *Blythe v Birmingham Waterworks* Co (1856). In this case, a wooden plug in a water main became loose in a severe frost. The plug led to a pipe which in turn went up the street. However, this pipe was blocked with ice, and the water instead flooded the claimant's house. The claimant sued in negligence. In this case, Alderson B defined negligence as:

"the omission to do something which a reasonable man, guided upon those considerations which ordinarily regulate the conduct of human affairs, would do, or doing something which a prudent and reasonable man would not do".

The key word here is *"reasonable man"*. The standard of care required of the defendant is that of the hypothetical reasonable man. This standard is objective as it does not take into account particular traits of an individual. In *Hall v Brooklands Auto Racing Club* (1933) Greer LJ described such a person as:

- the 'man in the street'; or
- 'the man on the Clapham Omnibus; or
- 'the man who takes the magazines at home, and in the evening pushes the lawnmower in his shirt sleeves'

The reasonable person is therefore an 'average' person and not perfect.

The standard of reasonable care is invariable in the sense that the law does not recognise differing degrees of negligence but it is an infinitely flexible concept enabling the court in any given situation to impose standards ranging from high to low.

What is reasonable conduct varies with the particular circumstance, and liability depends ultimately what the reasonable man would have foreseen, which in turn may depend upon what particular knowledge and experience, if any, is to be attributed to him. However, although a defendant is not negligent if the consequences of his conduct were unforeseeable, it does not necessarily follow that the defendant will be responsible for all foreseeable consequences. In practice the courts evaluate a defendant's behaviour in terms of risk, so that he will be seen to be negligent if the claimant is exposed to an unreasonable risk of harm.

Special standards of care

There are certain situations in which the courts will apply a different standard of care from that of the 'reasonable' person:

- Where the defendant has a particular skill
- Where the defendant has a particular lack of skill
- Where the defendant is a child
- Where the defendant is competing in or watching a sporting event.

Skilled or professional defendants

The standard of care applied to professional with a particular skill or expertise is that of the reasonable person with the same skill or expertise. For example, a doctor would be expected to show a greater degree of skill and care to a patient than 'the man on the Clapham omnibus'. See below.

Magnitude of the risk

The degree of care which the law expects must be commensurate with the risk created. Two factors are involved, namely the likelihood that harm will be caused and the potential gravity of that harm. In the case *Bolton v Stone* (HL 1951) the plaintiff was standing in the road when she was struck by a cricket ball which had been hit out of the defendants ground. There was some evidence that this had happened before on an infrequent basis, i.e., six times in thirty years, so that the risk was one of which the defendants were aware and which was reasonably foreseeable. However, the defendants were not held liable because the risk was so small that they were perfectly justified in not taking any further measures to eliminate that risk.

Another case illustrating magnitude and gravity of the risk is that of *Paris v Stepney B.C* (HL 1951) where a person with one eye, a garage worker, became totally blind after being struck in the eye by a metal chip which flew from a bolt which he was trying to hammer loose. The defendants, his employers, were held liable for failing to provide him with safety goggles, even though they were justified in not providing such equipment to a person with normal sight. Although the risk was small, the injury to this particular person was very serious.

Another case which illustrates the magnitude of risk is that of *Watson v British Boxing Board of Control* (2001) where the board breached its duty in failing to inform itself adequately about the risks inherent to a blow to the head and by failing to provide resuscitation equipment to be provided at the ringside together with persons able to operate it. The degree of risk to which a claimant is exposed will also depend upon any physical abnormality from which he may suffer so that, if such abnormality is or ought to be known to the defendant, that is a factor which should be taken into account.

Characteristics of the defendant

The general legal standard does not take into account the personal characteristics of a particular defendant. Inexperience, lack of intelligence or other provide no defence to negligence. For example, a partially sighted driver owes the same level of duty as a normally sighted driver. However, two types of defendant require mention.

Evidence of negligence

It is for the claimant to prove, on a balance of probabilities, that the defendant was negligent. This is subject to the proviso contained within the Civil Evidence Act 1968 s.11, that proof that a person stands convicted of an offence is conclusive evidence in civil proceedings that he did commit it unless the contrary is proved. The effect of this provision is to shift the burden of proof where the claimant proves that the defendant has been convicted of an offence involving conduct complained of as negligent, such as careless driving.

In order to discharge the burden of proof the claimant must usually prove particular conduct on the part of the defendant which can be regarded as negligent. The claimant will not be able to do so, however, if he does not know how the accident was caused and, in such a case, the maxim *res ipsa loquitur* (the thing speaks for itself) may be relied on. This is a rule of evidence that the claimant, who is unable to explain how the accident happened, asks the court to make a *prima facie* finding of negligence, which it is then for the defendant to rebut if he or she can. There are three conditions necessary for the application of the doctrine which arose out of *Scott v London and St Katherines Docks Co (EC 1865):* there must be an absence of an explanation as to how the accident happened, the 'thing' which causes the damage must be under control of the defendant (or someone for whose negligence he is responsible) and the accident must be such as would not ordinarily occur without negligence.

****

2.2

Negligence-Causation and Remoteness of Damage

Causation

It must first be established that the breach was the cause of the damage, or materially contributed to the damage. In determining this issue, it is usual to employ the 'but for' test, the function of which is to eliminate those factors which could not have had any causal effect. One case which illustrates this is *Cork v Kirby Maclean 1952* Where a workman, an epileptic, was set to work painting the roof inside a factory, which necessitated his doing the work from a platform some 23 feet above the floor of the factory. The platform was some 27 inches wide and was used for the deposit of the workman's brush and bucket. There were no guard-rails or toe boards. The workman fell from the platform and was killed. In this case, Lord Denning stated:

...if the damage would not have happened but for a particular fault, then that fault is the cause of the damage; if it would have happened just the same, fault or no fault, the fault is not the cause of the damage.

Another case is *Barnett v Chelsea and Kensington Hospital Management Committee* (HC 1969) where the failure of a casualty officer to examine a patient, who subsequently died of arsenic poisoning, was held not to have been a cause of death because evidence showed that the patient would have probably died in any event. Difficulties may arise where the precise cause of the damage is unknown. In *McGhee v National Coal Board* (HL

1972) the patient contracted dermatitis as a result of exposure to abrasive dust at work. His employers were not at fault for the exposure during the normal course of his work but were found to be negligent for failing to provide washing facilities with the result that he was caked in dust for longer than necessary as he cycled home. The plaintiff succeeded on the ground that it was sufficient to show that the defendant's breach materially increased the risk of injury, even though medical knowledge at the time was unable to establish the breach as the probable cause. This decision had far reaching effects, particularly in cases of medical negligence.

An attempt was made in *Hotson v East Berkshire Area Health Authority* (HL 1987) to extend the principle so as to impose a liability in respect of the loss of a chance of recovery. In this case, the plaintiff injured his hip in a fall and, as a result of negligent medical diagnosis, suffered a permanent deformity the risk of which would have been reduced by 25 per cent had the proper treatment been given at the time. The Court of Appeal upheld the finding but this was overturned by the House of Lords on the grounds that there was no principle in law which would have justified a discount from the full measure of damages.

In cases where successive acts cause damage, the position is more complex. In *Baker v Willoughby* (HL 1970) the plaintiff's leg was injured through the defendant's negligence, and some time later, before the trial, he was shot in the same leg during a robbery. The leg was then amputated. It was held in this case that the plaintiff's right of recovery was not limited to the loss suffered only before the date of the robbery, but that he was entitled to damages that he would have received had there been no subsequent injury.

In another case, *Jobling v Associated Dairies Limited* (HL 1980) the defendant's negligence caused a reduction in the plaintiffs earning capacity. Three years later, but before the trial, the defendant was found to be suffering from another complaint, wholly unrelated to the original accident, which totally incapacitated him. The defendants were held liable only for the loss up to the time of the plaintiff's disablement.

Remoteness of damage

The plaintiff is not entitled to compensation for every consequence of the defendant's wrong. In order to contain the defendant's liability within reasonable bounds, a line is drawn, and the consequences that fall on the far side of the line are said to be too remote and not having been caused in law by the defendant's breach of duty.

There are a number of cases which have provided tests of remoteness of damage. In *Re Polemis and Furness, Withy and Co* (CA 1921) a ship's cargo of benzene had leaked filling the hold with inflammable vapour. Stevedores unloading the vessel negligently dropped a plank in the hold, and the defendant employers were held liable for the destruction of the ship in the blaze that followed because that loss was a direct, although unforeseeable consequence of the negligence.

Whilst not denying the relevance of foreseeability to the existence of a duty, the case did decide that it was not relevant in determining for what consequences the defendant should pay.

However, in another case, *Overseas Tankship (UK) Ltd v Morts Dock Engineering Co Ltd* (*The Wagon Mound)*, 1961 this approach was disproved. A test of reasonable foresight of consequence was substituted for that of directness. The defendants, in this case, negligently discharged into Sydney Harbour a large quantity of fuel oil which drifted to the plaintiff's wharf whilst welding was in progress. The plaintiff's discontinued their operations, but later resumed following an assurance that there was no danger of the oil igniting. A fire did eventually break out, causing damage to the wharf and to two ships upon which work was being carried out. It was found as a fact that some damage to the wharf was reasonably foreseeable by way of fouling the slipway, but that, in view of expert evidence, it was unforeseeable that the oil would ignite.

The defendants were, accordingly, held not liable.

Manner of occurrence

In *Hughes v Lord Advocate* (HL 1963) post office employees negligently left a manhole uncovered with a canvas shelter over it, surrounded by paraffin lamps. The plaintiff, aged eight, took none of the lamps into the shelter and knocked it into the manhole. There was an explosion, following an unusual combination of circumstances, in which the boy was badly burned. Although the explosion was unforeseeable, the defendants were held liable because burns from the lamp were foreseeable, and it was immaterial that the precise chain of events leading to the injury was not.

A contrasting case is that of *Doughty v Turner Manufacturing Co Ltd* (CA 1964) in which the defendant's employee dropped an asbestos cover into a vat of molten liquid which, due to an unforeseeable chemical reaction, erupted and burned a fellow worker standing nearby. It was held that, even if injury by splashing were foreseeable the eruption was not, and the plaintiff failed. This case is at odds with Hughes (above) because if it accepted that some injury by burning was foreseeable, then it ought not to matter that the way in which it occurred was not.

Type of damage

The exact nature of the damage need not be foreseeable, provided it is of a type that could have been foreseen. The difficulty here, of defining damage 'of a type' is illustrated by two contrasting cases. The first case,

*Bradford v Robinson Rentals Ltd (*HC 1967) a van driver sent on a long journey in an unheated vehicle in severe weather was able to recover damages for frostbite because, although not in itself foreseeable, it was in the broad class of foreseeable risk arising from exposure to severe cold.

The second case, *Tremain v Pike* (HC 1969) the defendant's alleged negligence caused his farm to become rat-infested with the result that the plaintiff contracted a rare disease by contact with rats urine. It was held that, even if negligence had been proved, the plaintiff could not succeed because although injury from rat bites or food contamination was foreseeable, this particularly rare disease was entirely different in kind.

Extent of damage

When considering the extent of damage, it doesn't matter that the actual damage is far greater in extent than could have been foreseen. In *Vacwell Engineering Co Ltd v B.D.H. Chemicals Ltd* (CA 1971) the plaintiffs purchased a chemical manufactured and supplied by the defendants, who failed to give warning that it was liable to cause a minor explosion on contact with water. The plaintiff's employee placed a large amount of the chemical in a sink and an explosion of unforeseeable violence badly damaged the premises. Since the explosion and subsequent damage were foreseeable, even though the extent was not, the defendants were held liable.

A similar rule operates where the claimant suffers foreseeable personal injury which is exacerbated by some pre-existing physical or psychic abnormality. This so called "egg-shell skull" principle imposes liability on the defendant for harm, which is not only greater in extent than, but which is of an entirely different kind to, that which is foreseeable. In *Smith v Leech Brain and Co Ltd* (HC 1962) a workman who had a predisposition to cancer received a burn on the lip from molten metal due to a colleague's negligence. The defendants were held liable for his subsequent death from cancer triggered by the burn.

The principle applies equally to a claimant who suffers from nervous shock. In *Meah v McCreamer* (HC 1985) the plaintiff underwent a marked personality change brought about by injuries received in a collision for which the defendant was responsible. This led him to commit a series of assaults for which he received a life sentence. He recovered damages for loss of liberty.

Intervening causes

In some cases, the claimant's damage is alleged to be attributable not to the defendant's breach of duty, but to some intervening event which breaks the chain of causation. Such an event is called a *novus actus interveniens* and is usually dealt with as part of the issue of remoteness because even though the damage would not have occurred "but for" the defendants breach, it may still be regarded in law as falling outside the scope of the risk created by the original fault. One such case that illustrates this is *McKew v Hollan*d and *Hannen and Cubitts* (Scotland) Ltd (HL 1969) where the plaintiff's leg occasionally gave way without warning as a result of the defendant's negligence. On one such occasion he fractured his ankle as a result of descending a flight of stairs where his leg gave way.

The defendants were held not liable for this further injury because, although foreseeable, the plaintiff's conduct was *so* unreasonable as to amount to a *novus actus.* However, each case on its own merit. Whether the issue is seen as *novus actus* or of contributory negligence (which is the more common approach) will depend upon the nature of the plaintiff's conduct and it may be that a positive act is more likely to break the causal chain than a mere omission.

Intervention of a third party

According to Lord Reid in *Dorset Yacht Co Ltd v Home Office* (HL 1970) the intervention of a third party must have been something very likely to happen if it is not regarded as breaking the chain of causation. The question is what is the potential liability of a defendant for the criminal act of another? In the case *Knightly v Johns* (CA 1982) the defendant negligently caused a crash on a dangerous bend in a one-way tunnel. The police inspector at the scene of the accident forgot to close the tunnel to oncoming traffic as he ought to have done in accordance with standing orders, so he ordered the plaintiff officer to ride back on his motorcycle against the flow of traffic in order to do so, and the plaintiff was injured in a further collision. It was said that, in considering whether the intervening act of a third party breaks the chain of causation, the test is whether the damage is reasonably foreseeable in the sense of being a 'natural and probable' result of the defendant's breach. A deliberate decision to do a positive act is more likely to break the chain than a mere omission. In this case, the inspector's errors amounted to tortuous negligence which cannot be described as the natural and probable consequence of the original collision, and the defendant was held not liable.

Intervening natural force

The defendant will not normally be held liable for damage suffered as the immediate consequence of a natural event which occurs independently of the breach. In the case *Carslogie Steamship Co Ltd v Royal Norwegian Government* (HL 1952) the defendants were held not liable for storm damage suffered by a ship during a voyage to a place where repairs to collision damage caused by the defendant's negligence were to be done, even though that voyage would not have been undertaken had the collision not occurred.

Contributory Negligence

Since the passage of the Law Reform (Contributory Negligence) Act 1945 contributory negligence is no longer a complete bar to recovery but, in accordance with s.1(1) of the act, will result in a reduction of damages to such an extent as is seen as just and equitable.

The Act applies where the damage is attributable to the fault of both parties, and 'fault' is defined in section 4 to mean "negligence, breach of statutory duty, or other act or omission which gives rise to a liability in tort or would, apart from this act, give rise to the defence of contributory negligence". The defence, therefore, applies to actions other than negligence, though it does not apply to deceit or intentional interference with goods - Torts (Interference with Goods) Act 1977 s.11).

Causation

The damage suffered must be caused partly by the fault of the claimant and it is therefore irrelevant that the claimant's fault was nothing to do with the accident. Thus, reductions in damages have been made for failure to wear a seat belt or a crash helmet and for travelling in a vehicle with a drunk driver.

One case which highlights this is *Jones v Livox Quarries Ltd (CA 1952).* The plaintiff, contrary to instructions, stood on a rear towbar of a vehicle and was injured when another vehicle ran into the back of it. In this case, damages were reduced as the claimant had exposed himself to risk. The claimant is expected to show an objective standard of care in much the same way as the defendant must to avoid tortuous negligence.

There are particular cases in contributory negligence, children, old or infirm persons and rescuers merit special attention.

*

Children

As a matter of law thee is no age below which it can be said that a child is incapable of contributory negligence. However, the degree of care expected must be apportioned to the age of the child. For example, in *Gough v Thorne (CA 1966)* a 13-year-old girl who was knocked down by a negligent motorist when she stepped past a stationary lorry whose driver had beckoned her to cross, was held not guilty of contributory negligence. However, in *Morales v Eccleston* (CA 1991) an 11-year-old boy who was struck by the defendant driver while kicking a ball in the middle of the road with traffic passing in either direction had his damages reduced by 75 per cent.

Old or infirm persons

When assessing whether such a person is guilty of contributory negligence, the age and infirmity and its impact on the alleged negligence is taken into account.

Rescuers

It is not very often, for obvious reasons, that a rescuer will be found guilty of contributory negligence. In *Brandon v Osborne, Garret and Co Ltd* (HC 1924) the defendants negligently allowed a sheet of glass to fall from their shop roof and the plaintiff, believing her husband to be in danger, tried to pull him away and injured her leg. She was held to not be contributorily negligent. A similar principle applies where the claimant is injured in trying to extricate himself or herself from a perilous situation in which the defendant's negligence has placed them, even though, with hindsight the claimant is shown to have chosen the wrong course of action. As with all such cases, each case is viewed on its own merit.

Apportionment

Apportionment is on a just and equitable basis according to the 1945 Act and, in assessing the claimant's reduction, the court may take into account both the potency of his act and the degree of blameworthiness to be attached to it. The Court of Appeal has held, in *Johnson v Tennant Bros Ltd* (CA 1954) that no apportionment should be made unless one of the parties is at least 10 per cent to blame.

However, the decisions concerning apportionment is left, mainly, to judicial discretion.

Violenti Non Fit Injuria

This maxim embodies a principle that a person who expressly or impliedly agrees with another to run the risk of harm created by that other person cannot then sue in respect of damage suffered as a result of the materialisation of that risk. The defence is called consent or voluntary assumption of risk and, if successful, is a complete bar to recovery.

For the defence to apply the defendant must have committed what would, in the absence of any consent, amount to a tort. The defendant must prove not only that the claimant consented to the risk of actual damage, but also that he or she agreed to waive their right of action in respect of that damage.

Knowledge of the risk

Knowledge of the risk does not amount to consent. It must be found that the claimant, with full knowledge of the risk, agreed to incur it.

Agreement

In relation to agreement, in addition to the claimant being willing to take the risk, there must be evidence that the claimant has expressly or impliedly agreed to waive his or her course of action. An express antecedent agreement to relieve the defendant of liability for future negligence operates in effect as an exclusion notice and is therefore subject to the Unfair Contract terms Act 1977. Section 2(1) renders void any purported exclusion of liability for death or personal injury caused by negligence and, in the case of other loss or damage, s.2(2) subjects such an exclusion to a test of reasonableness. Section 2(3) further provides that a person's agreement to, or awareness of, such a notice is not of itself to be taken as indicating his voluntary acceptance of any risk. These provisions only apply to business liability.

In some circumstances the conduct of the parties may enable an inference to be drawn that the claimant has impliedly agreed to waive his legal rights in respect of future negligence. One such case was *Morris v Murray* (CA 1990). The defence applied when, in poor weather conditions, the defendant, who to the plaintiff's knowledge was extremely drunk, took the plaintiff for a spin and crashed the aircraft immediately after takeoff.

With negligence cases in the sporting arena, the potential liability of the participant depends upon the standard of care owed. In any sporting event, the spectator may be taken to have accepted the risks incidental to the game, for example, being hit by a cricket ball whilst watching a game of cricket. In the case *Wooldridge v Sumner* (CA 1963) it was stated that sportsmen and women have a duty not to behave with reckless disregard for the spectator. This applies to the duty of care required between one player and another. In *Watson v British Boxing Board of Control* (2001) it was pointed out that where the plaintiff consents to injury by an opponent in a boxing ring he does not consent to injury resulting from inadequate safety arrangements by the sports governing body after being hit.

Ex Turpi Causa

Where an alleged wrong occurs whilst the claimant is engaged in criminal activity, the claim may be barred because ex *turpi causa non oritur actio (no action can be founded on an illegal act).* This principle is based on public policy and may also apply where the claimant's conduct is immoral. The difficulty is deciding which types of conduct are considered sufficiently heinous for the purposes of defence. Some cases have found that it will apply where it would be impossible to determine an appropriate standard of care, whilst others have suggested that the claimant ought not to succeed if to permit him to do so would be an affront to the public conscience.

In *Clunis v Camden and Islington Health Authority* (CA 1998) the plaintiff, who had a long history of mental illness, was convicted of manslaughter and ordered to be detained in a secure hospital. He sued the defendant for negligence for failing to take reasonable care to provide him with after care services following his discharge from hospital where he had been detained under the Mental Health Act 1983.

It was held that, despite a successful plea of diminished responsibility at the criminal trial, his action was barred on the grounds of public policy since he was directly implicated in the illegality and must be taken to have known that what he was doing was wrong.

In *Vellino v Chief Constable of Greater Manchester Police* (CA 2001) the claimant suffered brain damage when he attempted to escape from police custody by jumping though a window on the second floor. Negligence was claimed on the part of the arresting officers, alleging that they had stood by and let him jump. The Court of Appeal held that the claim was untenable because the defendant had to rely on his own criminal conduct in escaping lawful custody to found his claim.

2.3

Negligence-Employers Liability

In addition to common law duty, there is a large body of statutory obligations which the employer must abide by when protecting its workforce. In relation to accidents and other forms of negligence it is common for employers to sue both in negligence and breach of statutory duty. Employers have a statutory duty to insure against liability, as laid down by the Employers Liability (Compulsory Insurance) Act 1969.

Nature of the duty

Although there once existed the doctrine of common employment, in which there was an implied term in a contract of employment that employees accepted risks incidental to their employment, the law has changed significantly.

The doctrine of common employment was abolished in 1948 and, as the law has evolved, employers have a personal duty and a vicarious liability towards their employees. Traditionally, the duty is said to be threefold, which was highlighted in the case of *Wilsons and Clyde Coal Co Ltd v English* (HL 1938), namely "the provision of a competent staff of men, adequate material and a proper system and effective supervision". The duty is not absolute but is discharged by the exercise of reasonable care and is thus similar to the duty of care in the tort of negligence generally. Although most of the cases concern work accidents, the duty extends to guarding against disease and gradual deterioration in health as a result of adverse working conditions. This was illustrated in the case of

Thompson v Smith's Ship repairers (North Shields) Ltd (HC 1984). However, it does not extend to the prevention of economic loss by, for example, advising the employee to take out insurance nor the prevention of injury to health caused by self-induced intoxication.

Safe plant and equipment

The employer has a duty to take reasonable care to provide proper plant and equipment and to maintain them so as to keep them in good order. This includes the provision of protective devices and clothing appropriate to the job, and also a warning or exhortation from the employer to make use of such equipment.

One case which highlights this is *Bux v Slough Metals Ltd* (CA 1973) where the plaintiff, a foundry worker, lost the sight of one eye when splashed with molten metal. Although the employer had, in compliance with statutory regulations, provided protective goggles, he was held liable for breach of his common law duty, which extended to persuading and even insisting on the use of protective equipment. Most employees will now be protected by the Personal Protective Equipment at Work Regulations 1992, which impose a statutory duty to take all reasonable steps to see that protective equipment is properly used, though it is the employee's duty to use it.

In relation to injury caused by defective equipment, in the case *Davie v New Merton Board Mills Ltd* (HL 1959) it was held that the duty to provide proper tools was satisfied by purchase from a reputable supplier. This decision has now been reversed however, by the Employer's Liability (Defective Equipment) Act 1969, which renders an employer personally liable in negligence if two conditions are met: first, that the employee is injured in the course of his employment by a defect in equipment issued by the employer for the purposes of the employer's business and,secondly, that the defect is attributable wholly or partly to the fault of a third party, (whether identifiable or not. Such a third party could be the manufacturer. Strict liability is thus imposed upon the employer if his employee can prove that some third party was at fault, though contributory negligence can be used as a defence by that third party.

The employee might also be able to rely on the Provision and Use of Work Equipment Regulations 1992 which provide that employers must ensure that work equipment is so constructed or adapted as to be suitable for the purpose for which it is to be used or provided, and that such equipment is maintained in an efficient state.

Safe system of work

A safe system of work means the organisation of work, the manner in which it is to be carried out, the organising and planning of numbers of men and women and their tasks and the instructions given to these workers. One case illustrating this is *Johnstone v Bloomsbury Health Authority* (CA 1991) where it was held that requiring the plaintiff to work such long hours as might foreseeably injure his health could constitute a breach of duty.

In *Walker v Nortumberland County Council* (HC 1995) the plaintiff suffered a nervous breakdown as a result of the employers broken promise to provide a safe system of work to reduce his workload. Very little was actually provided and he suffered a second breakdown which forced him to stop work permanently. His employers were held liable for failing to provide a safe place of work in that they continued to employ him without adequate assistance. In *Waters v Commissioner of Police of the Metropolis* (2000) the House of Lords held that an employer is under a duty to take reasonable care to protect its employees from harm, including workplace bullying and psychiatric harm, where the employer knows or can foresee that an employee might suffer this harm through the acts of fellow employees.

In *Hatton v Sutherland* (2002) the Court of Appeal ruled that claims for stress induced psychiatric illness follow the standard principles governing personal injury claims in that no special control mechanisms are applied to claims for psychiatric or physical injury arising from stress at work. The ordinary principles of employer's liability apply and the questions to be determined are:

- was there a breach of employer's duty of care which caused psychiatric harm to the employee?
- Was the psychiatric harm to that particular employee reasonably foreseeable?

The duty of care does not arise where the employer is unaware of the employee's vulnerability to stress induced illness or of an imminent psychiatric breakdown.

Safe premises

The employer's obligation includes making the premises as safe as possible. However, the employer is not required to eliminate every foreseeable risk if the burden in so doing is too onerous. In *Wilson v Tyneside Window Cleaning* (CA 1958) where it was held that the duty exists equally in relation to premises in the occupation or control of the third party. In appropriate circumstances an employer must be expected to go and inspect the premises to see that they are reasonably safe for the work to be carried out on them. However, the fact that the employer does not have control of the workplace is important in determining whether he has been negligent. Most workplaces are now governed by the Workplace (Health, Safety and Welfare) Regulations 1992.

Scope of the duty

The scope of the duty relates to the employer-employee and does not extend to an independent contractor. The duty is personal and non-delegable, so that the employer does not discharge his duty by entrusting its performance to another, whether that be an employer or independent contractor.

Vicarious liability

The employer-employee relationship is the most common example of vicarious liability. The negligence committed by an employee can thus ultimately be the liability of the employer.

Occupiers liability

The occupier of a property in respect of loss or injury suffered by those who enter a property or its grounds lawfully is governed by the Occupiers Liability Act 1957. prior to this Act, the extent of liability owed by an occupier depended upon the relationship with the person injured. The OLA 1957 abolished this in favour of two categories:

- Lawful visitors, who were protected by the Act
- All others who were not protected

This Act was supplemented by the Occupiers Liability Act 1984 which covers injuries to trespassers. Section 2(1) of the 1957 Act provides:

(overleaf)

"An occupier owes the same duty, the 'common duty of care' to all his visitors, except in so far as he is free to, and does extend, restrict, modify, or exclude his duty to any visitor or visitors by agreement or otherwise".

Who is an occupier?

The Act contains no clear definition of an "occupier". This is simply a term to denote a person who has a sufficient degree of control over premises to put him under a duty of care towards those who lawfully come on to the premises. Control is the decisive factor and it is not material that the occupier has no interest in the land, he could be tenant, lessee, licensee, or any other person having the right to possession. One case illustrating this is *AMF International Ltd v Magnet Bowling Ltd* (HC 1968) where building contractors were held to be joint occupiers along with the building owners. A landlord who has let his property to a tenant will not be the occupier of the demised parts but will still be held to be the occupier of those parts, i.e., common parts, not demised to the tenant.

The premises

The definition of premises is wide and covers not only land and buildings. By s.1 (3)(a) of the Act, the statutory provisions extend to any fixed or moveable structure, including any vessel, vehicle, or aircraft. This is apt to include not only structures of a permanent nature but also temporary structures such as ladders and scaffolding.

Visitors

The statutory duty is owed only to visitors who, by s.1 (2) are those who would, at common law, have been either invitees or licensees. For a licence to have been inferred there must be evidence that the occupier has permitted entry as opposed to merely tolerating it, as there is no positive obligation to keep the trespasser out. Repeated trespass of itself confers no licence. However, in some cases the courts have gone to great lengths to infer the existence of a licence. One case illustrating this is *Lowery v Walker* (HL 1911) where members of the public had for many years used the defendant's field as a short cut to the railway station. The defendant had often prevented them from so doing but did nothing further to stop them until, without warning, he turned a savage horse loose in the field. The animal attacked and injured the plaintiff who then sued and succeeded in his action on the basis that he was a licensee not a trespasser.

There are a number of other types of entrant that must be considered. Those who enter premises for any purpose in the exercise of a right conferred by law are treated, by s.2(6) of the Act as having the occupier's permission to be there for that purpose (whether they have it or not). Secondly, s.5(1) provides that where a person enters under the terms of a contract with the occupier there is, in the absence of express provision in the contract, an implied term that the entrant is owed the common duty of care and, according to *Sole v W.J Hallt Ltd* (HC 1973) he may frame his claim either in contract or under the 1957 Act. It is further provided by s.3(1) that where a person contracts with the occupier on the basis that a third party is to have access to the premises, the duty owed by the occupier to such third party as his visitor cannot be reduced by the terms of the contract to a level lower than the common duty of care. Conversely, if the contract imposes upon the occupier any obligation which exceeds the requirements of the statutory duty, then the third party is entitled to the benefit of that additional obligation. Thirdly, those who use public or private rights of way are not visitors for the purposes of the 1957 Act, though the user of a private right of way is now owed a duty under the Occupiers Liability Act 1984 (see later).

Exclusions

As has been outlined, the duty owed to a contractual entrant is governed by the terms of the contract and a person who enters under a contract to which he is not party is, at the very least, owed a duty of care. In the case of no-contractual entrants, it is clear that, at common law, an occupier may be able to exclude or limit his liability by notice, provided that reasonable steps are taken to bring it to the visitor's attention and that the notice is clear and not misleading in any way. One case that illustrates this is *Ashdown v Samuel Williams and Sons* (CA 1956) where it was held that the plaintiff, who was injured by the negligent shunting of a railway wagon upon the defendants premises, was defeated in her claim by exclusion notices erected by the defendant saying that person entered at their own risk and no liability would be accepted for loss or damage, whether caused by negligence or otherwise.

The basic principle is that if an occupier can prevent people from entering his premises, then he can equally impose conditions, subject to which entry is permitted. However, the power of the occupier to exclude or restrict his liability for death or injury has been severely reduced by s.2 of the Unfair Contract Terms Act 1977. This section provides that a person cannot, by reference to a contract term or to a notice, exclude or restrict his liability for death or personal injury caused by negligence unless the term or contents of the notice satisfies the requirement of reasonableness. The operations of s.2 of the Act is confined to those situations where there is business liability which is defined in s.1(3) as liability for breach of duty arising from things done in the course of a business or from the occupation of premises used for the business purposes of the occupier.

*

Common duty of care

The common duty of care is defined in s.2 (2) as:

"a duty to take such care as in all circumstances is reasonable to see that the visitor will be reasonably safe in using the premises for the purposes for which he is invited or permitted to be there"

This is similar to the common duty of care and may extend to taking steps to see that a visitor does not deliberately harm other visitors by foreseeably likely conduct. Whether the occupier has charged it depends on the facts, taking into account such matters as the nature of the danger, the purpose of the visit and the knowledge of the parties. In particular, there is provision in the act for Children, those with special skills, warning notices and independent contractors.

Children

The Act provides that the amount of care which an occupier can expect from a visitor will depend on certain factors. By s.2(3)(a) the occupier must be prepared for children to be less careful than an adult. However, case law has sought to balance responsibility between occupiers and parents.

The level of care expected will depend on the nature of the risk and the age and awareness of the child. For example, in the case *Titchener v BRB* 1983 no duty was owed to a 15-year-old boy who was struck by a train whilst walking on a railway line at night as he was aware of the dangers posed by his activity.

Special skills

Section 2(3)(b) provides that:

"An occupier may expect that a person, in the exercise of his calling, will appreciate and guard against any special risks ordinarily incident to it, so far as the occupier leaves him free to do so".

In the case *Roles v Nathan* (CA 1963) the defendant was held not liable for the death of two chimney sweeps killed by carbon monoxide fumes while sealing up a flue in the defendant's boiler. If the same people had fallen through the floor because of a rotten floorboard the position would have been different.

Warnings

The occupier may, in accordance with s.2(4)(a) of the Act, discharge his duty by warning his visitor of the particular danger, provided that the notice is effective and the warning is sufficient to ensure that the visitor is reasonably safe. Warning notices must be distinguished from exclusion notices. By sufficient warning the occupier discharges his duty, whereas exclusion purports to take away the right of recovery in respect of a breach. To be effective a warning must sufficiently identify the source of the danger.

Independent contractors

Where a visitor suffers damage due to faulty construction, maintenance or repair work by an independent contractor employed by the occupier, s 2 (4)(b) provides that the occupier will not be liable if it was reasonable to entrust the work to a contractor and he took such steps as he reasonably ought to see that the contractor was competent and had done the work properly. The occupier is not necessarily expected to check work of a technical nature although in the case of a complex project he may be under a duty to have the contractor's work supervised by a qualified specialist such as an architect or surveyor.

Defences

The provisions of the Law Reform (Contributory Negligence) Act 1945 apply and s.2(5) of the 1957 Act provides that an occupier is not liable in respect of risks which the visitor willingly accepts, thus allowing for the defence of *volenti non fit inujuria.* However, where there is business liability within the meaning of the Unfair Contract Terms Act 1977, s.2(3) of that Act provides that a person's agreement to or awareness of a notice purporting to exclude liability for negligence is not of itself to be taken as indicating his voluntary acceptance of the risk.

The Occupiers Liability Act 1984

The 1984 OLA extended the protection of the law to cover:

Trespassers

People lawfully exercising rights of way

Visitors to land covered by section 60 of the National Parks and Access to the Countryside Act 1949 and 'right to room' legislation.

The 1984 Occupiers Liability Act governs the liability of an occupier to "persons other than his visitors" in respect of injury suffered by them on the premises due to the state of the premises or to things done or needing to be done to them. The term "persons other than his visitors" includes trespassers and persons exercising private rights of way, but those using public rights of way.

The scope of the duty

Section 1(3) of the 1984 Act provides that the occupier owes a duty if:

- he is aware of the danger or has reasonable grounds to believe that it exists;
- he knows or has reasonable grounds to believe that the non visitor is in the vicinity of the danger concerned or that he may come into the vicinity of the danger; and
- the risk is one against which, in all the circumstances of the case, he may be reasonably expected to offer the non-visitor some protection.

Whilst paragraph (c) clearly adopts an objective test, paragraphs (a) and (b) import a subjective element in that the existence of a duty depends upon the occupier's actual knowledge of facts which should lead him to conclude that a danger exists. If the occupier is not aware of these facts, he may not owe a duty.

In the case *Rhind v Astbury* (2004) the claimant accepted that he was a trespasser when he dived into shallow water to retrieve a football, but he argued that his injury was caused by a fibreglass container on the bed of the lake which constituted a danger within the meaning of s.1 (3) of the 1984 Act. The Court of Appeal held that the claimant had failed to establish a duty of care under s.1(3) since the defendant was unaware of the existence of the container and had no reasonable grounds for suspecting that the danger existed.

It is to be noted that the statutory duty applies only to personal injury or death. Liability for loss of, or damage to, property is expressly excluded by s. 1(8).

Defences

Section 1(5) of the Act provides that the occupier may, in appropriate cases, discharge his duty by taking reasonable steps to warn of the danger or to discourage persons from incurring the risk. Whether a warning is effective will depend among other things upon the nature of the risk and the age of the entrant.

The defence of *volenti non fit injuria* is preserved by s.1(6) of the Act. It is normally limited to dangers arising from the state of the premises. The plaintiff was held to have willingly accepted the risk as his own, within the meaning of s.1(6) of the Act in the case of *Rathcliffe v McDonnell* (CA 1999). In this case, the plaintiff, having drunk four pints agreed to go open-air swimming with his friends. He climbed over the gate of a college swimming pool. Although conscious of a warning sign he dived in the pool and suffered horrific injuries as a result.

The Court of Appeal rejected his claim for damages on the grounds that he was aware of the risk and had willingly accepted it.

As far as the defence of *ex turpi* is concerned, it was held in *Revill v Newberry* (CA 1996) that the fact that the plaintiff was a burglar did not take him outside the protection of the law, so that he was entitled to succeed in negligence when the defendant unintentionally shot him. There was, unsurprisingly, a substantial reduction in damages for contributory negligence.

Exclusion notices

There is no mention in the Act of excluding liability to the non-visitor, and the provisions of the Unfair Contract Terms Act 1977 do not apply to the 1984 duty. Trespassers pose problems because depending upon the point at which they enter the premises, they may be less likely to see a notice than a lawful visitor.

One suggested solution is that the duty under the 1984 Act is a minimum which cannot be excluded so that even the lawful visitor would be protected by it, even though he was aware of an exclusion notice.

Independent contractors and trespassers

At common law, the liability of a contractor to the trespasser rests upon ordinary negligence principles. The fact that the claimant is a trespasser in relation to the occupier is not relevant except in so far as the trespasser's presence may be less foreseeable. One case which illustrates this is *Buckland v Guildford Gas Light and Coke Co* (HC 1949). The defendants, who had erected electricity cables on a farmer's land close to the top of a tree, were held liable for the death of a young girl who climbed the tree and was electrocuted.

Breach of statutory duty

Breach by the defendant of an obligation under statute (other than one which expressly seeks to impose liability in tort) may, apart from giving rise to any criminal sanction laid down in the Act, also enable a person injured by the breach to bring a civil action for damages for breach of statutory duty. This is a tort in its own right independent of any other form of tortuous liability. Whether a claimant can sue depends on whether the statute confers a right of civil action or can be interpreted as conferring this right.

The claimant must prove that the legislature intended to create a right to sue. In *Cullen v Chief Constable of the Royal Ulster Constabulary* (2003) the House of Lords upheld the previous decisions that the claimant could not rely on the tort of breach of statutory duty for the failure of the police to give him reasons for delaying his access to a solicitor, on the ground that the duty concerned could be enforced through judicial review. In a few instances, Parliament has expressly made known its intention, but in the majority of cases statute is silent on the issue. It is for the courts to decide what the intention of an Act is and, to this end, certain guidelines have been established. The basic proposition is that a breach of statutory duty does not, by itself, give rise to a private law action. Such an action will arise, however, if it can be shown that, on the proper construction of the statute, the duty was imposed for the protection of a limited class of the public and Parliament intended to confer upon members of that class a right to sue for breach. There is no general rule for determining whether the Act does create such a right, but if no other remedy is provided for its breach that is an indicator in the claimant's favour.

If the Act does contain other provision for enforcing the duty that is an indication of an intention that it was to be enforced by those means alone and not by private law action.

In determining whether, in any particular case, a civil action for breach of statutory duty will lie, the starting point is to look at precedent or for a clearly stated Parliamentary intention. In the absence of either it is in all cases a question of ascertaining the fundamental purpose the legislation intended to achieve, and that can only be done through a consideration of the Act as a whole.

The elements of the tort-Duty owed to the claimant

In establishing that breach of the particular duty will, in principle, ground a right of action, the claimant will, in most cases, have established that the obligation was imposed for the benefit of a limited class. The claimant must then prove that he is a member of that class.

In the case *Hartley v Mayoh and Co* (CA 1954) the widow of a fireman electrocuted while fighting a fire at the defendant's factory had no cause of action because the regulations existed for the benefit of "persons employed" and her husband was not so employed.

*

Defendant and breach of duty

The claimant must prove that the claimant was in breach. This can only be ascertained by having regard to the precise wording of the Act to determine the nature of the obligation. Some obligations are absolute, such as those contained within health and safety Acts.

Damage of the contemplated type

For the claimant to succeed the harm suffered must be of a type which the act was designed to prevent. In the case, *Gorris v Scott* (1874) the plaintiff's sheep were swept overboard the defendant's vessel during a storm. The sheep were not penned, contrary to statutory regulations, but the plaintiff failed in his action because the object of the regulations was to prevent the spread of disease, not to afford protection from the dangers of the sea. Another case illustrating this is *Donaghey v Boulton and Paul Limited* (HL 1968) where the plaintiff slipped and fell through an open space in an asbestos roof on which he was working. In breach of their duty the defendants had failed to provide him with adequate crawling boards but argued that the object of the regulations was to prevent workers from falling through fragile roofing materials, not through holes in the roof. This argument was rejected and the House of Lords held the defendants liable.

Causation

The burden rests upon the claimant to prove on a balance of probabilities that the breach of statutory duty caused or materially contributed to the damage. In this respect there is no distinction between this tort and a common law negligence action, so that the claimant must show that he would not have been injury were it not for the defendant's breach. The claimant must also show that the damage is not too remote and the usual test of reasonable foresight applies.

A problem arises where the claimant's own wrongful act puts the defendant in breach. In *Ginty v Belmont Building Supplies Ltd* (HC 1959) a regulation binding upon both parties required the use of crawling boards on a fragile roof. The defendant had provided the boards and given full instructions to the plaintiff how to use them. The plaintiff neglected to use them and fell through the roof. Both parties were clearly in breach of their statutory obligation but it was held that the plaintiff was the sole cause of his injury and his action failed.

Even if the claimant is in breach of his statutory duty he will fail in his action if it is his own deliberate folly which puts the defendant in breach. However, this will be mitigated by the actions of the defendant if he is also in breach.

****

2.4

Negligence-Liability for Defective or Dangerous Products

Part 1 of the Consumer Protection Act 1987, which came into force on 1st March 1988, creates a strict liability for dangerous goods.

Part 1 was enacted to give effect to an E.C. Directive of 1985, requiring the harmonisation of law on product liability throughout the E.C. If the Act doesn't apply in certain circumstances a claimant may still be able to sue for negligence. When claiming damages for harm suffered as a result of a defective product, the claimant must prove that he or she suffered damage caused wholly or partly by a defect arising from a specific product.

The Act (s.2.(2)) outlines who the potential defendants might be in such cases:

- the producer of the product;
- any person who holds himself out to be a producer by putting his name or trademark or any other distinguishing mark on the product;
- an importer of the product into a Member State from a place outside the E.C. in order to supply it to another in the course of his business.

The term 'producer' is defined in s.1(2) to mean either the manufacturer, or the person who won or extracted the product, or, where the product has not been manufactured, won, or abstracted but the essential characteristics of which are attributable to an industrial or other process having been carried out, the person who carried out that process.

Furthermore, by s.2(3) the mere supplier (e.g., Retailer) is liable if he fails within a reasonable time to comply with the plaintiff's request to identify one or more of the persons to whom s.2(2) applies, or to identify his own supplier.

'Product' is defined in s.1(2) as any goods or electricity. Component parts and raw materials also fall within the definition of product as distinct from the overall product in which they are comprised. For example, the brakes in a car would be the responsibility of both manufacturer of brakes and the supplier of the finished car.

The meaning of 'defect'

A product is defective, according to s.3(1) if its safety is not such as persons are generally entitled to expect. The safety of a product expressly includes safety "with respect to products comprised within that product" (i.e., components and raw materials) and a product may be unsafe not only if there is a risk of personal injury but also if it poses a risk of damage to property. When determining what people are entitled to expect, s.3(2) provides that account shall be taken of all the circumstances including the following specific matters:

- the way in which and the purposes for which the product has been marketed, its get-up, and warnings and instructions for use accompanying it:
- what might reasonably be expected to be done with or in relation to the product;
- the time when the product was supplied by its producer to another.

The reference in (a) to the purposes for which the product has been marketed may indicate that a balance must be struck between known risks associated with a product and the benefits which it seeks to confer. With regard to (b), a product which is clearly intended for a particular use may not be defective if it causes damage when put to an entirely different use. With (c) it is the time of supply by the producer to another which is relevant not the time of supply to the consumer.

Liability under the Act is considerably stricter that under common law. One case that illustrates this is *A and others v National Blood Authority* (2001). The claimants had been infected with Hepatitis C, through blood transfusions which had used blood products obtained from infected donors. The defendants argued that the product was as safe as might be expected, and also that the defect in the particular transfusion could not have been detected). Given the strict liability under the Act, it was held that factors which would have been relevant in a negligence action were completely irrelevant and the defendants were found to be liable under the Consumer Protection Act.

Definition of "damage"

Section 5(1) defines damage for the purposes of Part 1 as death or personal injury, or loss of or damage to property (including land), although claims for damage to property are limited in several respects. First, the defendant will not be liable for damage to the defective product itself, nor for damage to any product supplied with a defective component comprised in it. Secondly, there is no liability unless, at the time of the damage, the property was "of a description of property ordinarily intended for private use, occupation of consumption" and was intended by the claimant mainly for such purposes (s.5(3)). A person who suffers damage to his business property must therefore sue in negligence as opposed to under the Act.

Defences

Section 4(1) of the Act provides for defences as follows:

- The defect is attributable to compliance either with a domestic enactment or community law.
- The defendant did not at any time supply the product to another. A broad definition is given to "supply" in a later part of the act to include not only the usual types of supply contract but also gifts.
- The defendant supplied the product otherwise than in the course of his business and either he does not fall within s.2(2) (he is not a producer, "own brander" or importer) or he does so only by virtue of things done other wise than in a view to profit.
- The defect did not exist at the relevant time. By s.4(2) the "relevant time" means, in relation to electricity, the time at which it was generated. With all other products it means, in the case of a defendant to whom s.2(2) applies the time when he supplied the product to another and, in the case of a supplier, the time of the last supply by a person who is within the ambit of that section.
- The state of scientific and technical knowledge at the relevant time was not such that a producer of products of the same description as the product in question might be expected to have discovered the defect if it had existed in his products while they were under his control. This is called the "development risk" or "state of the art" defence.

The defect constituted a defect in a product containing the defendant's component part (or raw material) and was wholly attributable to the design of the overall product or to compliance by the defendant with instructions given by the producer of the overall product.

Common law negligence

Where the Consumer Protection Act does not apply, the claimant must rely on existing common law remedies. If the claimant acquires defective goods under a sale or similar supply contract the remedy is to sue the supplier for breach of implied undertakings relating to quality. Although these contractual obligations are generally imposed only upon those who supply in the course of business, they are strict and entitle the claimant to recover both in respect of goods which simply fail to work or which are less valuable than those contracted for, and where the defect causes personal injury or damage to property. If the claimant does not have a contract, an action in tort may be pursued.

The duty of the manufacturer

The duty owed by a manufacturer to the consumer was stated in Donoghue v Stevenson (Hl 1932) by Lord Atkins as follows:

"A manufacturer of products, which he sells in such a form as to show that he intends them to reach the ultimate consumer in the form in which they left him with no reasonable possibility of immediate examination, and with the knowledge that the absence of reasonable care in the preparation or putting up of the products will result in an injury to the consumer's life or property, owes a duty to the consumer to take that reasonable care".

The term "products" includes not only comestibles, but many other diverse products such as shoes, vehicles, toys and so on. The manufacturer's duty extends to the packaging of the product and to any labels, warnings or instructions for use which accompany it. If the manufacturer of a finished product incorporates a component made by another, he is under a duty to check on its suitability and may be liable for failure to do so should it turn out to be defective. Where products are already in circulation when the defect is discovered, the manufacturer must take reasonable steps to warn of the danger or to recall the products.

Manufacturer and ultimate consumer

The term "manufacturer" has been interpreted to include any person who actively does something to the goods to create the danger, such as assemblers, servicers, repairers, installers and erectors.

In *Malfroot v Noxal Limited* (HC 1935) an assembler was held liable when the side car which he had negligently fitted to a motorcycle came adrift and injured the plaintiff. Mere suppliers may come within the rule, even though they may be unaware of the danger and do nothing to create it. In the case *Andrews v Hopkinson* (HC 1957) a second-hand car dealer was liable for failing to check that an 18-year-old car was roadworthy, with the result that the plaintiff was injured in a collision caused by a failure of the steering. Apart from the end user of the product, the "ultimate consumer" is any person who may foreseeably be affected by it. In the case *Stennet v Hancock and Peters* (HC 1939) the defendant was held liable for negligently fitting a metal flange to a wheel of a lorry, so that it came off when the vehicle was in motion and struck the plaintiff.

Proof of negligence and damage

The burden rests upon the claimant as in any other negligence action. However, damage caused by a defect in manufacture as opposed to a defect in design, may easily give rise to an inference of negligence. On the other hand, if it is equally probable that the defect arose after the manufacturing process and is wholly unconnected with anything that the manufacturer may have done, claimant will fail.

The defendant will no longer escape liability however, merely by showing that he had a fool-proof system of manufacture and quality control, because the very fact of the defect may be evidence of negligence in the operation of that system by a person for whom the defendant is vicariously liable. Where the alleged defect is in relation to the design of the product, the claimant may face greater difficulty in that the issue of negligence is to be judged in the light of current knowledge which must be proved to have been such as to render the damage foreseeable.

As far as damage is concerned, liability only exists in respect of personal injury or damage to other property, although consequential financial loss is also recoverable. Pure economic loss is, however, irrecoverable.

****

Chapter 3

Business Law-Employment Law Generally

A Snapshot of The Main Areas of Employment Law
In this chapter, we will look, generally, at the main areas which cover employers and employees in the workplace. . In addition, it should be noticed that certain areas of employment law either have or will change from 2026 through 2027 owing to the introduction of the Employment Rights Act 2025, as outlined below:

The Employment Rights Act 2025
Significant changes to employment law in 2026 will include reforms to statutory sick pay, parental leave rights, and the establishment of the Fair Work Agency, among other key updates.

Key Changes in Employment Law for 2026

1. **Statutory Sick Pay (SSP) Reforms**:

    - From **April 2026**, the Lower Earnings Limit will be abolished, allowing more workers to qualify for SSP from the **first day of absence** instead of after three days. The weekly rate of SSP will increase from approximately £118.75 to £123.25 or 80% of the employee's normal weekly earnings, whichever is lower

2. **Parental Leave Rights**:
    - Employees will be entitled to **paternity leave** and **unpaid parental leave** from their first day of employment, eliminating previous minimum service requirements .
3. **Fair Work Agency**:
4. A new **Fair Work Agency** will be established to oversee compliance with national minimum wage, statutory sick pay, and holiday pay requirements. This agency aims to strengthen worker rights and ensure fair treatment in **Changes to Unfair Dismissal Claims**:
    - The time limit for bringing claims to an employment tribunal will extend from **three months to six months** for most claims, including unfair dismissal and discrimination C. Additionally, the 12-week limit for unfair dismissal claims related to industrial action will be removed, providing greater protection for striking workers .
5. **Anti-Harassment Duties**:
6. Employers will be held liable for harassment of employees by third parties (e.g., customers) during the course of their employment, requiring them to take reasonable steps to prevent such claims
7. **Fire and Rehire Practices**:
    - Stricter regulations will be implemented regarding "fire and rehire" practices, making dismissals automatically unfair in most circumstances unless the employer faces financial difficulty .
8. **Increased Collective Redundancy Protective Award**:
    - The protective award for collective redundancies will double from **90 days' pay to 180 days' pay**, increasing the

financial protection for employees during redundancy processes .

These changes represent a significant shift in employment law, aimed at enhancing worker protections and modernizing labor market regulations.

Employment law general

The framework of employment law applies as soon as a job is applied for. Employers have legal obligations when drawing up a job description, specification and shortlist for a particular job. Essentially, prospective employers must not discriminate against a candidate on the grounds of age, sex, race, religion or disability. There are laws to prevent this. Nor can any other factor such as trade union membership serve to work against an employee.

Right to work checks

Employers must check that a job applicant is allowed to work for them in the UK before employing them. They must see the applicant's original documents. They must also check that the documents are valid with the applicant present. Finally, they must make and keep copies of the documents and record the date they made the check. The employer could face a civil penalty if they employ an illegal worker and have not carried out a correct right to work check.

The full guidance on carrying out right to work checks can be found at gov.uk/government/publications/right-to-work-checks-employers-guide.

The Immigration Act 2016

The Immigration Act 2016 came into force in May 2016 to make it more difficult for illegal migrants to live and work in the UK.

As well as tightening existing provisions to target those abusing the system and willing to disobey UK immigration controls, the 2016 Act also includes measures aimed at preventing the exploitation of vulnerable migrants.

Right-to-work checks

Employers are expected to complete prescribed RTW checks against all recruits (regardless of nationality) to ensure they only employ individuals with the right to work in the UK. Failure to do so will leave an employer open to a civil penalty (of up to £20,000 per breach) if found to be employing an illegal worker. Compliant RTW checks secure a statutory excuse to civil liability for illegal working.

As of 1 October 2022, employers must carry out one of the following prescribed checks before employment begins:

1. a manual right to work check on a physical document or combination of documents as set out in the Home Office's Right to Work Checklist. This is where original documents are seen in person, checked to ensure validity and identity, and a copy – signed and dated original seen - retained on file. This is the only acceptable way to check a British or Irish national who provides an expired passport, or a birth certificate together with proof of National Insurance number (as well as a number of other documents).
2. a Home Office online right to work check (using a share code generated by an employee or prospective employee who holds a biometric residence permit or card, or a digital immigration status)
3. a right to work check using IDVT through the services of an approved provider This is where a third-party provider (from the Home Office's list of approved providers) conducts a check on the

employer's behalf. The employer will incur a fee for this service which is set by the individual provider and will vary by contract. Providers can only check current passports that belong to British and Irish nationals. Candidates with any other type of document, or an expired passport, cannot be checked via this route. Employers must still ensure they keep copies of the document as well as the check carried out for the statutory excuse to be established.

Employing EU, EEA and Swiss citizens

How you check EU, EEA or Swiss citizens' right to work in the UK has not changed, even though the UK has left the EU. They could still use their passport or National Identity Card until 30 June 2021.

After 30 June 2021, the new immigration rules for recruiting people from outside the UK will apply. You will not need to make retrospective checks for existing employees.

Employers will also need a sponsor license to employ EEA and Swiss citizens coming to the UK to work from 1 January 2021.

References prior to taking up a post.

Only certain industries such as those regulated by the Financial Services Authority are required to give a reference by law. Other employers do not have to give a reference but if they do it should be fair and accurate. Some employers may only give a factual reference stating dates of employment, job title and salary. Prospective employers must only approach a job applicant's current employer with the candidate's permission.

Prospective employers usually ask for references either prior to appointment or prior to interview. References vary but usually a previous employer should not provide a blatantly discriminatory reference which could jeopardize the chance of getting a job. However, they are under an obligation not to conceal certain facts, such as reasons for dismissal. The courts have taken the view that the duty is to provide a reference that is in substance true, accurate and fair. This was established in the key case of Spring v Guardian Assurance (1994) IRLR 460 where the complainant argued that a reference provided by a former employer was in breach of an implied term in the contract of employment that any reference would be compiled with all reasonable care. The House of Lords (now the Supreme Court) concluded that an employer has a duty to take reasonable care in compiling a reference by ensuring the accuracy of the information upon which it is based.

In a 2015 case, Mefful v Citizens Advice Merton and Lambeth Limited 2015, an employee of eight years' standing was made redundant. While employed, he had two significant periods of absence - one for stress and grief, and the other for shoulder pain and total hearing loss in one ear.

He brought and won an unfair dismissal claim. A claim for disability discrimination was ongoing.

He applied for (and was offered) a new job, and his new employer asked his former employer for a reference, including whether there had been any absences from work (and why), and whether the former employer would re-employ him. It also asked other questions about his performance.

If an employer gives a reference, it has a duty to take reasonable care to ensure it is true, accurate and fair and that it is not misleading. This duty is owed to both the employee and to the new employer.

The former employer in this case gave information about the periods off work but did not explain them. It said it would not re-employ him and did not answer the other questions about his performance. The prospective employer withdrew the job offer because of the reference.

The employee successfully claimed victimization and disability discrimination against his former employer. The Employment Tribunal (ET) found that:

- There had been a failure to explain the employees' periods of absence - to put them in context, given his disability. They were also overstated.
- The manager providing the reference had a negative view of the employee because of his legal claims against the employer. The gaps in the reference were, in the ET's view, deliberate, and intended to show the employee in a bad light.
- The reference misrepresented the employee's eight years of employment and was neither balanced nor fair.

In Summary

References can include:

- basic facts about the job applicant, like employment dates and job descriptions
- answers to questions that the potential employer has specifically asked about the job applicant that are not usually given as basic facts, like absence levels and confirming the reason for leaving.
- details about the job applicant's skills and abilities
- details about the job applicant's character, strengths and weaknesses relating to the suitability for the role they have applied for

Previous employers will usually be asked to provide the basic facts and possibly answer some additional questions. However, previous managers and colleagues might also be asked to provide character details. A reference must be a true, accurate and fair reflection of the job applicant. When opinions are provided, they should be based on facts. Personal references can sometimes be provided from individuals who know the job applicant such as a teacher. References should not include irrelevant personal information.

When are employment references needed?

References can be required at any stage of the recruitment process. Job applications should say if references will be required and at what stage of the recruitment process they will be needed. Employers must only seek a reference from a job applicant's current employer with their permission.

Job offers and references

If a job applicant is offered a job, there are two types of job offer that can be made: a **conditional** job offer. This can be withdrawn if the applicant doesn't meet the employer's condition, for example, satisfactory references; an **unconditional** job offer. Once an unconditional offer is made this cannot be withdrawn and if accepted a contract is formed. Once an employer has received satisfactory references and informed the job applicant an unconditional job offer can be made. Employees should consider waiting until they get an unconditional offer before handing in their notice. For guidance on job references go to: www.acas.org.uk/providing-a-job-reference.

Immigration skills charge

The Immigration Skills Charge Regulations 2017, as amended by The Immigration Skills Charge (Amendment) Regulations 2020, came into force 6 April 2017. Since then, employers must now pay an Immigration Skills Charge of up to £1,000 per year for each skilled migrant they employ.

These regulations mean that employers must pay a fee, called the Immigration Skills Charge, for every skilled migrant they sponsor under the Tier 2 (General) or Tier 2 (Intra Company Transfer) categories. The fee per migrant is £1,000 per year for larger sponsors and a reduced rate of £364 for smaller companies sponsors. For each additional six-moths the fee is £182 for smaller sponsors and £500 for larger sponsors

It is the employer's responsibility to pay this fee, and failure to do so will mean that a certificate of sponsorship is invalid. For more details go to: UK visa sponsorship for employers: Overview - GOV.UK (www.gov.uk)

Applying for a job and application forms

When filling in an application form, it is clear that you should stick to the truth. In all cases, if it is found that you have lied when filling in an application form then that is a reason for dismissal. Few employers check educational qualifications and professional qualifications. This meant that in the past people were being employed to carry out jobs that they were not necessarily qualified to do. Companies now exist to check out CVs and application forms so honesty is the best policy.

Under the Immigration, Asylum and Nationality Act 2006 (which came into force on 29/2/2008), and which replaced the 1996 Immigration and Asylum Act, your employer must ask you for a National Insurance number or some evidence that you have the right to work in the UK. Employers have an obligation to carry out this check on all new employees. For employees who started work between 27/1/1996 and 28/2/2008 the 1996 Act applies. For full details of the kind of checks that need to be carried out and the sanctions against employers who do not comply visit the Home Office website on www.ukba.homeoffice.gov.uk.

Employers must also ask for criminal convictions. You do not have to reveal these if they are `spent'. This means that they happened long enough ago for the Rehabilitation of Offenders Act 1974 to allow you to keep them secret. If you are required to work with children or vulnerable adults, you will need to provide a certificate of disclosure. This is an official document which can be obtained from the Disclosure and Barring Service which has replaced the Criminal Records Bureau under the Protection of Freedoms Act 2012. It lists any relevant previous convictions.

Checking up on prospective employees on social media

One Recruitment company suggests that 70% of employers use social networks to screen candidates. Its study also found that the same percentage are also using online search engines to research potential employees. The general rules are that employers should inform applicants if they are going to look at social media profiles and give them the opportunity to comment. The searches should also be proportionate to the job being applied for. Implementation of the General Data Protection Rules might tighten the enforcement of such guidelines.

See further on in this chapter for more about GDPR effective from May 2018.

Other rights in the workplace

There are many rights (and obligations) at work, which begin from the day your employment commences. These are covered in depth throughout this book. To summarise a few of the fundamental areas:

Time off for public and workforce duties

All employees are entitled to reasonable time off to perform public duties, including serving as a magistrate or a local authority councillor. Your contract of employment may give you a right to paid time off for such duties. In addition, trade union representatives, union learning representatives, company pension trustees and designated health and safety representatives are also entitled to paid time off work to carry out duties.

Losing or leaving a job

There are two types of notice period: statutory and contractual. Statutory notice is the minimum legal notice that can be given. Employers should give the employee:

- **one week's notice** if the employee has been employed by the employer continuously for one month or more, but for less than two years.
- **two weeks' notice** if the employee has been employed by the employer continuously for two years, and one additional week's notice for each further complete year of continuous employment, up to a maximum of 12 weeks. For example, if an employee has worked for 5 years, then they are entitled to 5 weeks' notice.

Employees must give their employer a minimum of one week's notice once they have worked for one month. This minimum is unaffected by longer service.

However, contractual notice is the amount of notice that the employer can set out in the terms and conditions of employment which can be longer than the statutory notice.

For example, the statutory notice an employee must give to an employer is one week, however, an employer can state within the terms of employment that an employee must give one month's notice.

Dismissal without notice

In a few cases employers may dismiss someone without notice on the grounds of gross misconduct. Gross misconduct occurs when an employee has committed a serious act such as theft, violence, physical abuse, serious breach in health and safety or gross negligence. Employers should give employees a clear indication of the type of issues that could constitute gross misconduct, and it is still important to follow a fair procedure as for any other disciplinary offence.

What is automatic unfair dismissal?

Some reasons for dismissal are classed as 'automatically unfair' when the reason for dismissal is proscribed by certain statutory provisions as inadmissible. Employees are protected from 'automatic' unfair dismissal. Inadmissible reasons include certain health and safety-related scenarios, such as:

- undertaking designated health and safety activities.
- dismissal of health and safety representatives or committee members for carrying out certain functions.
- raising health and safety concerns through other means.
- leaving or staying away from a dangerous workplace; or
- taking action to prevent danger.

Notably, dismissal for an inadmissible reason is always deemed to be unfair and employees do not need two years' service to bring such claims. Damages for ordinary unfair dismissal are capped at the lower of £86,444 or a year's salary, but employment tribunals can award uncapped damages for an automatic unfair dismissal.

Fixed term contracts

Generally, no notice of the expiry of a fixed-term contract will need to be given, however, if the contract is terminated by giving notice before its expiry date then the correct amount of statutory notice should be given.

Failure by the employer to give the correct notice period may amount to a breach of contract and employees may make a claim to an employment tribunal.

The *Unfair Dismissal and Statement of Reasons for Dismissal (Variation of Qualifying Period) Order 2012* increased the qualifying period for the right to claim unfair dismissal to **two years** for employees whose employment commenced on or after 6 April 2012. Before this, section 108 of the *Employment Rights Act 1996* provided that employees had to have been continuously employed by their employer for at least **one year** to claim protection against unfair dismissal. In a variety of unfair dismissal cases specified by legislation, particular reasons for dismissal will be "automatically unfair". In these cases, there is normally no requirement for a continuous period of employment.

You'll need to check quickly - you've got 3 months less a day from the date you were sacked to start acting for an unfair dismissal.

If you change your mind

If you resign in the 'heat of the moment' (e.g., during an argument) and you change your mind, you should tell your employer immediately. They can choose to accept your resignation or not.

Payment during notice period

You're entitled to your normal pay rate during your notice period, including when you're:

- off sick

- on holiday
- temporarily laid off
- on maternity, paternity or adoption leave.
- available to work, even if your employer has nothing for you to do.

'Payment in lieu' of notice period

Your employer can ask you to leave immediately after handing in your notice. If they do, they'll probably offer you a one-off payment instead of allowing you to work out your notice period - called 'payment in lieu'. You can only get payment in lieu if it's in your contract, or if you agree to it. If you don't agree to it, you can work out your notice period.

Gardening leave

Your employer may ask you not to come into work, or to work at home or another location during your notice period. This is called 'gardening leave'. You'll get the same pay and contractual benefits.

Relocation of work

If your employer moves the location of their business, your situation depends firstly on the terms of your contract of employment. Some contracts include a mobility clause which says you must move within certain limits. The notice period to move must be reasonable as do all the other aspects of moving. You may decide not to move because of increased travel time and costs, moving house, family situation or children's education. If you don't have a mobility clause in your contract, and the relocation is more than a short distance, you can decide not to move. In this case, your employer may make you redundant. See Chapter 6, Being Made Redundant. When you are facing redundancy there is a right to a trial period in any alternative job that you have been offered.

Redundancy is a dismissal so if you feel badly treated you may be able to claim for unfair dismissal.

If your employer decides to relocate:

- Check your contract of employment to see if there is a mobility clause.
- Find out whether your employer is offering a relocation package and, if so, whether you think it is reasonable.
- Discuss the matter of moving with your employer and state your intentions. If you decide to move talk to your employer about a trial period in the job.
- If you decide not to relocate and your employer considers that you are being unreasonable and refuses you a redundancy payment, you can take the matter to an Employment Tribunal (see Chapter 9) for them to decide whether you or your employer are being unreasonable. Note that fees apply.

Public and bank holidays

There is no statutory right to public and bank holidays as paid leave. This will generally be incorporated in your contract. Your employer may also count public and bank holidays as part of your annual leave. This is legal under the Working Time Regulations 1998 (see further in this book).

Transfer of a business

If your company is taken over, or if you work for the public sector and your job is transferred to the private sector, your terms and conditions of employment transfer automatically to the new employer, subject to conditions. Continuity of employment is guaranteed. You have the right to raise objections about your contract being transferred to another company. However, this can he fraught with problems.

The transfer of contracts is known generally as the transfer of undertakings, covered by the Transfer of Undertakings (Protection of Employment) Regulations 2006, as amended by the Collective Redundancies and Transfer of Undertakings (Protection of Employment) (Amendment) Regulations 2014 and is complex.

Sunday working

Certain groups of workers have protection in relation to working on a Sunday. They include shop workers and people who work in the betting industry. The aim was to allow those who do not wish to work on a Sunday to resist pressure to do so. However, if you have agreed a contract of employment that says you will work on Sunday then you do not have protection. Only employees who work in the above occupations have protection. For all other occupations, Sunday is just another day.

There is also no legal right to extra pay for work on a Sunday although most contracts of employment will incorporate agreed overtime rates.

Insolvency of employer

If your employer goes bankrupt and cannot pay wages, the state will make up at least part of the pay. You can claim for statutory redundancy pay, for up to eight weeks. As well as basic wages you can claim any holiday pay up to 6 weeks, unpaid pension contributions and the basic award for unfair dismissal. You must apply to the employer's representative, usually the liquidator or receiver. You will be given a form which you should fill in and send off to the address on the form. HMRC will pay you any statutory sick pay, statutory maternity pay, statutory paternity pay and statutory adoption pay.

*

Suspension on medical grounds

In certain situations, usually for health and safety reasons, employers may feel obliged to suspend an employee from work on medical grounds. There are certain regulations under which medical suspension can apply - these usually involve working with chemicals or radioactive material or lead. There are also certain regulations in the Food Preparation industry which might lead to a suspension. This is because your Employer feels that you are a danger to your fellow employees!

Finally, if a pregnant woman is not able to carry out her normal duties, and no suitable alternative work can be provided, she can also be medically suspended from work.

If you are suspended from work on medical grounds in line with one of the qualifying regulations or conditions, then you are entitled to full pay for up to 26 weeks (as long as you have at least 1 month's service). Any dismissal during this protected period is unfair. This does not apply if you are physically or mentally unfit for work. (If this is the case you will be entitled to some sick pay). It purely means that you are not capable of carrying out certain activities due to your condition. If you are offered suitable alternative work but refuse this, then no payment may be due to you. If your employer does not pay you, you can take a claim to an employment Tribunal, within three months.

Employment through agencies

Whereas once agency employment was tenuous, to say the least, all agency workers have some degree of protection under the 1973 Agencies Act. Legislation which came into effect from 1st October 2011 (Agency Workers Regulations 2010) has strengthened these rights. If you are working for an employment agency you may or may not be legally an employee. At the very least you will be a worker hired out to an employer to perform a service. Whether or not you are an employee, agency workers have basic rights:

-All agency workers are covered by health and safety law, where the agency has a responsibility not to place you in a job for which you are not appropriately qualified and the company hiring you has a responsibility for providing a healthy and safe working environment.

-All agencies, and therefore agency workers, are covered by discrimination law, which also covers the hiring company.

-All agency workers are entitled to be paid the National Minimum Wage.

-All agency workers are entitled not to work more than an average of 48 hours a week unless you sign an agreement with the agency to the contrary.

-All agency workers should receive five weeks and three days paid annual leave once you have worked for more than 12 weeks.

Some agencies have been circumventing this by saying that your pay includes holiday pay and that they therefore do not have to pay extra if you take a break. It is unclear as to whether this is legal or not. As an agency worker you may also be entitled to statutory maternity pay or paternity pay, depending on your earnings and how long you have worked for the agency. You are also allowed to join a union.

If you are an agency worker and you accept a permanent post then you are expected to work out a period of notice as an agency temp before becoming permanent. The company can also agree to pay the employer a lump sum to release you from your contract.

Agency worker rights from April 2020

The Swedish Derogation (referred to as 'pay between assignments' contracts) is abolished from 6 April 2020, so all agency workers are entitled to the same rate of pay as their permanent counterparts after 12 weeks. All agency workers are entitled to a key information document that clearly sets out the type of contract they will have and the pay they'll receive.

Other basic protections for agency workers are:

-You have the right to be paid by your agency, on the agreed day, even if the hiring company has not paid the agency.

-You must be consulted before any changes are made to the terms of employment or terms and conditions of employment.

For a full resume of rights, you should visit:
www.citizensadvice.org.uk/work/agency-workers/check-your-rights-as-an-agency-worker

Trade Union rights

The government has passed regulations aimed at curbing disruption caused by strikes. In July 2022, the Conduct of Employment Agencies and Employment Businesses (Amendment) Regulations 2022 came into force, allowing employers for the first time to use agency workers to carry out the work of striking employees.

In addition, in October 2022, The Transport Strikes (Minimum Service Levels) Bill was introduced into Parliament and is expected to come into force in 2023. If enacted it would:

- Require employers and trade unions to agree a minimum service level during transport strikes over a three-month period.

- Remove protection against automatic unfair dismissal from any staff specified in the agreement striking during the period.
- Potentially allow employers to obtain a court order preventing the strike if specified staff did go on strike.
- Potentially make a strike unlawful if a union does not take reasonable steps to prevent specified staff striking (allowing civil proceedings against the union with potential liability of up to £1m).

So, the government once again is seeking to curb union powers through legislation.

The law generally

A person has the right to decide whether they want to join a trade union or not. Employers are not entitled to know whether they are in a union. They should certainly not be asked questions at an interview about union membership, views, or activity. Since 2004, Employers have not been allowed to offer incentives to an employee to leave a union, for example a higher pay rise to non-union employees.

If a person thinks they have been turned down for a job, or overlooked for promotion, because of their union membership or activity they should take further advice as this is a form of discrimination which is unlawful. The same applies if they think that they have been dismissed due to union membership or union activity. A special level of compensation is available for this.

A person can join any union of their choice, but obviously it is sensible to join a union which represents workers in specific jobs.

Employers only must deal with a union if that union is formally "recognised" by the employer. This is a legal process which the union must go through to get certain rights and protection. Views are more likely to be considered by an employer when the union is "recognised" by an employer.

Where the union is "recognised", the employer is legally obliged to discuss certain matters with the union, such as pay and terms of employment. Redundancy is another area that employers must consult the union on. In certain circumstances a person is entitled to time off work for union meetings - but the employer does not have to pay when attending a union meeting. Some employers do give some paid time off to attend a union meeting, particularly when those meetings are important - pay offers or redundancy terms for example.

Representation

All workers now have the right to have a representative with them during formal disciplinary or grievance meetings. This can be a union rep but does not have to be. A person has the right to have a union rep with them even if the employer does not recognise any union. This is a right.

Trade Union Officials

As an elected representative of a trade union a person becomes entitled to certain rights and protection. A person can take paid time off to attend training courses and carry out union duties for example.

Strike action

Employees enjoy some protection if they go on official strike action called by a trade union. This protected period was increased to 12 weeks from October 2004, and it can be longer in certain situations - where an employer has made no attempt to negotiate, or employees have been "locked out" by an employer are examples. A person is not protected against dismissal if they take unofficial strike action. See the section in Chapter 10, Trade Unions, about the Trade Unions Act 2016, which became effective in March 2017 and which affects the rights to strike.

Whistleblowing

The general duty that confidential information must not be disclosed has always been subject to an important common law exception, that disclosure may be justified when it is in the public interest. The Public Interest Disclosure Act 1998 introduced new sections into the Employment Rights Act 1996 making it automatically unfair to dismiss workers or subject them to any detriment where they have made a protected disclosure. as reflected in changes to the regulations coming into effect on 25th June 2013, disclosure of information is only protected where the worker honestly believes on reasonable grounds that it tends to show that a criminal offence is being committed, there has been failure to comply with a legal obligation, a miscarriage of justice has taken place, there is a danger to health and safety at work, damage to the environment or the deliberate concealment of any of these.

An important case in this area is Chesterton Global Ltd and Nurmohamed (Court of Appeal) 2017. In this case, an estate agent raised concerns of accounting malpractice, which he alleged were designed to reduce the amount of commission paid to around 100 senior managers, including himself. The Court of Appeal had to decide if the estate agent's disclosure 'was in the public interest' a key requirement for statutory whistle blowing protection. The Court held that the estate agent's disclosure satisfied the 'public interest' requirement despite the concerns affecting the company's staff only and the whistleblower's personal interest in the issue.

The Data Protection Act

Privacy at work is an issue which is gaining more prominence. Employers are able to collect increasing amounts of data about employees. The Data Protection Act 2018, which is the UK's implementation of the General Data Protection Regulations (GDPR) (see below) provides some important rights which people should be aware of. This Act gives Employees some control over information that their employer holds over them.

The Act gives all workers the right to be told about the type of information their employer holds over them, how that information is to be used and about anyone else with access to it. The employer must ensure that all information kept is confidential. Certain types of data, such as information about sexuality and religion cannot be kept. Employers can hold or use such sensitive data only in certain situations, such as when required to do so by law.

You have the right to see a copy of any information held about you. The Regulations cover data kept on electronic or paper files. You can expect to see personnel files and other information held on file about you. The legislation also allows you to see reference information provided about you. An employer has an obligation to provide information promptly and can require a worker to pay a fee of up to £10 for producing the information. An employee can refuse to disclose information if it means putting at risk a third party or requires disproportionate effort.

If any problems are experienced in this area there is the right to make a complaint to the information commissioner's office.

The General Data Protection Regulation (GDPR) (Regulation (EU) 2016/679) and BREXIT

The UK is committed to maintain an equivalent regime post-Brexit to minimise the impact on UK data controllers and processors and to this end the Government passed the European Union (Withdrawal) Act 2018 and the Data Protection, Privacy and Electronic Communications (Amendments etc.) (EU Exit) Regulations 2019 (The **Exit Regulations**) which serve to ensure EU law as it exists on exit day, including GDPR, will be incorporated into UK law.

From that point, at the end of the transitional period, the UK legislative regime will comprise the Data Protection Act 2018, the Privacy and Electronic Communications Regulations 2003 and the 'UK GDPR'.

Monitoring at work

Most employers will carry out some form of monitoring in relation to their employees and this is accepted. However, where monitoring goes beyond the accepted boundaries of employee performance it needs to be done in a way that is lawful and fair. The Information Commissioner has set out guidance for employers in the Employment Practice Data Protection Code. Although the code is not a legal obligation itself, if your employer is not adhering to it he or she may be breaking the law on which it is based. For more information on the code of practice you can visit the website of the Information Commissioner at: www.informationcommissioner.gov.uk

In Summary, The Data Protection Act 2018 lays out that:

Everyone responsible for using personal data must follow strict rules called 'data protection principles'. They must make sure the information is:

- used fairly, lawfully and transparently.
- used for specified, explicit purposes.
- used in a way that is adequate, relevant and limited to only what is necessary.

- accurate and, where necessary, kept up to date.
- kept for no longer than is necessary.
- handled in a way that ensures appropriate security, including protection against unlawful or unauthorised processing, access, loss, destruction or damage.
- There is stronger legal protection for more sensitive information, such as:
- race
- ethnic background
- political opinions
- religious beliefs
- trade union membership
- genetics
- biometrics (where used for identification)
- health, sex life or orientation
- There are separate safeguards for personal data relating to criminal convictions and offences.

Your rights

- Under the Data Protection Act 2018, you have the right to find out what information the government and other organisations store about you. These include the right to:
- be informed about how your data is being used.
- access personal data
- have incorrect data updated.
- have data erased.
- stop or restrict the processing of your data.
- data portability (allowing you to get and reuse your data for different services)

- object to how your data is processed in certain circumstances.
- You also have rights when an organisation is using your personal data for:
- automated decision-making processes (without human involvement)
- profiling, for example to predict your behaviour or interests.

Modern Slavery and Human Trafficking Statements

The government has been ramping up its efforts to ensure that large organisations publish annual modern slavery and human trafficking statements. This is a legal requirement for commercial organisations with a total turnover of at least £36 million per year. In 2018, the Home Office wrote to 17,000 businesses reminding them of their companies' responsibility to publish an annual statement and warning them that "continued non-compliance will not be tolerated".

While there is no strict legal timetable for publication, the government's guidance recommends that statements be published within six months of the end of the organisation's financial year.

For example, if your organisation's financial year runs from 1 April to 31 March, publication for the financial year ending 31 March 2022 is expected by 30 September 2022.

Use of social media in the workplace

Overview

Social media is the term used for internet-based tools used on computers, tablets, and smart phones to help people keep in touch and enable them to interact. It allows people to share information, ideas and views. Social media can affect communications among managers, employees and job applicants; how organisations promote and control their reputation; and how colleagues treat one another. It can also distort what boundaries there are between home and work.

Some estimates report that misuse of the internet and social media by workers costs Britain's economy billions of pounds every year and add that many employers are already grappling with issues like time theft, defamation, cyber bullying, freedom of speech and the invasion of privacy.

Legal considerations

The Human Rights Act 1998 Article 8 gives a 'right to respect private and family life, home and correspondence'. Case law suggests that employees have a reasonable expectation of privacy in the workplace.

The General Data Protection Regulations 2018 cover how information about employees and job applicants can be collected, handled and used. The Information Commissioner's Office has published an employment practices code.

The Regulation of Investigatory Powers Act 2000 covers the extent to which organisations can use covert surveillance.

Developing a policy

Employers should develop a policy setting out what is and what is not acceptable behaviour at work when using the internet, emails, smart phones, and networking websites.

The policy should also give clear guidelines for employees on what they can and cannot say about the organisation. Any policy should be clear throughout about the distinction between business and private use of social media. If it allows limited private use in the workplace, it should be clear what this means in practice.

In working out a policy for use of social media, the employer, staff and unions or staff reps (if there are any) should agree the details. The policy should aim to ensure employees do not feel gagged; staff and managers feel protected against online bullying; and the organisation feels confident its reputation will be guarded.

Disciplinary procedures

An employer should try to apply the same standards of conduct in online matters as they would in offline issues. To help an organisation respond reasonably, the employer should consider the nature of the comments made and their likely impact on the organisation. It would help if the employer gave examples of what might be classed as 'defamation' and the penalties it would impose. The employer should also be clear in outlining what is regarded as confidential in the organisation.

Blogging, tweeting and emails

If an employee is representing the company online, the employer should set appropriate rules for what information they may disclose and the range of opinions they may express. Bring to their attention relevant legislation on copyright and public interest disclosure. Some rules should be included on the use of social media in recruitment, which managers and employees should follow. When recruiting, employers should be careful if assessing applicants by looking at their social networking pages - this can be discriminatory and unfair.

Email is an integral part of many people's working lives. An organisation should have clear rules on how staff use their work email, whether it may be monitored and if there are time limits for deleting emails no longer required for business purposes. Additionally, an organisation may want to provide guidance for staff on how to make the best use of email and ensure that it does not place unnecessary stress and pressure on them. Research commissioned by Acas suggested organisations may benefit from providing staff with email management strategies to help effectively manage inboxes. Other areas identified in the research included encouraging staff to use the 'delay send' function when sending an email out-of-hours. This means that colleagues receive email during normal working hours rather than at home, which can adversely affect their work-life balance.

Excessive use of the internet at work

In Hall v Weightmans, January 2020, an employment tribunal found that the employee's dismissal for excessive internet use discovered during a disciplinary investigation was fair and that the appeal procedure followed was "textbook". In this case, during an interview to investigate why H had allegedly brought her daughter and grandchildren to the firms' premises to share lunch and then leaving them on site unaccompanied, H alleged she had been working on her computer whilst her family had been present. The report showed that H had been online, but not for work purposes, along with a further period of 1.25 hours earlier in the day when she was on duty and browsing the internet for personal reasons. A further investigation of her internet history for the whole month demonstrated a consistently high usage for non-work related searches across most working days at a level which was unacceptable, as evidenced by 117 pages of data showing hundreds of entries recording access to shopping/airline web sites such as Evans, Shoeaholic, Ryan air, Easyjet and Debenhams.

An ET found H's dismissal to be fair. The employer had clear hard evidence of H's internet usage, which was at odds with her explanation. In addition, the tenor of H's explanations had appeared to be dishonest, and so there had been a loss of trust in her. It was therefore reasonable to believe that her conduct amounted to gross misconduct for which the employer was entitled to dismiss her summarily. The dismissal procedure followed was fair, complied with ACAS guidelines and was within the range of reasonable responses.

Language requirements in the workplace

Language requirements can be a legal minefield. Although customer-facing public sector staff must be fluent in English, the legal position for private companies wanting to introduce a similar policy is less clear. Regulations made under the Immigration Act 2016 that came into effect on 22 December 2016 brought into force the Code of Practice and introduced the requirement for public sector workers who speak to the public as a regular and intrinsic part of their role to be fluent in English (and English or Welsh in Wales). There is no equivalent fluency requirement for the private sector.

Imposing language requirements

While employers are generally free to draw up their own requirements for roles within their business, they should not breach their duties under the Equality Act 2010 by discriminating against those with a 'protected characteristic'.

Whereas businesses may see it as desirable to have all employees with perfect command of the English language, imposing such a requirement is potentially discriminatory. The most obvious risk is that of indirect race discrimination as the provision, criteria or practice (PCP) disadvantages those whose mother tongue is not English and will therefore only be defensible if the employer is able to show objective justification (and that it is proportionate means of achieving a legitimate aim).

In practice, this is likely to mean that, so long as an employee's command of the language is sufficient for them to carry out their duties, an obligation on such employees to have a greater or better command of the language (absent any other good reason) is potentially discriminatory. This means that different roles can have differing language requirements, and one would expect, for example, customer-facing roles such as working on reception to have a higher requirement than roles which require minimal interaction in English, for example, cleaning roles.

Disciplinary action or performance management will clearly not be appropriate in circumstances where the employee does not meet the more demanding language requirements of the employer but has sufficient grasp of the language to carry out the role. Any such action taken could amount to a detriment.

Potential problems

Employers considering exercising a degree of control over language in the workplace should bear in mind the following:

In 2010, an employment tribunal found that an instruction to a Polish worker not to speak Polish at work was direct race discrimination (*Dziedziak v Future Electronics Ltd*) In 2015, the Employment Appeal Tribunal agreed that an instruction to only speak a particular language in the workplace could be discriminatory (although on the facts of the case, *Kelly v Covance Laboratories Ltd*, it was held not to be because the employer's instruction was based on a genuine concern that the employee may have been an animal rights activist)

The Equality and Human Rights Commission Employment Code of Practice states: "Employers should make sure that any requirement involving the use of a particular language during or outside working hours, for example during work breaks, does not amount to unlawful discrimination"

The Default Retirement Age

The Default Retirement Age (DRA) was phased out between 6th April and 1st October 2011. The change gives people the freedom to continue working for longer. Employers, in the past, (and until 30th September 2011) could make staff retire at 65 even if they were fit and healthy enough to do the job. This could be achieved by giving six months' notice to the employee.

The last day employees could be retired using the DRA was 30th March 2011. Employers could still use the DRA between 30th March and 6th April but had to use the 'short notice provisions'. Under these an employee could claim compensation (subject to a maximum of eight weeks wages).

Between 6th April and 30th September, only people who were notified before 6th April 2011, and whose retirement date is before 1st October, could be compulsorily retired. From 1st October, employers could not be able use the DRA to compulsorily retire employees.

Changing an employment contract

If an employer cannot reach an agreement with an employee or worker, they may decide they need to change the written terms in their contract. If there are more than 20 people affected, employers will need to consult staff representatives ('collectively consult').

****

3.2

Employment Contracts-Implied Duties of the Employer/Employee

Into every contract of employment are implied a number of obligations insofar as these are not inconsistent with the express terms of the individual contract of employment. These duties are based on principles developed by the courts in the decided cases.

Implied duties may be classified as follows:

a) to be ready and willing to work.

b) to use reasonable care and skill.

c) to obey lawful orders.

d) to take care of the employer's property.

e) to act in good faith.

To be ready and willing to work

The fundamental duty owed to an employer by an employee is to turn up to work and to work at the direction of the employer in return for wages. Two interesting cases have arisen in relation to this. In Miles v Wakefield Metropolitan District Council (1987) M was a superintendent registrar of births deaths and marriages, working 37 hours per week, three of which were on Saturday morning. As part of industrial action, M refused to carry out marriages on Saturday mornings, although he was willing to do his other work. Wages were deducted, M sued for lost wages and the employer won, with the House of Lords (Supreme Court) saying that where an employee refuses to perform the full range of duties and had been told that he would not be paid if he did not, then the employers were entitled to withhold the whole of his remuneration, (3hrs) although he attended for work and carried out a substantial part of his duties.

To use reasonable care and skill

This has two aspects:

a) The duty not to be unduly negligent.

b) The duty to be reasonably competent.

If an employee is negligent during his work, he may be regarded as being in breach of contract. In Lister v Romford Ice and Cold Storage Ltd (1957) a lorry driver, employed by the company, carelessly reversed his lorry and injured a fellow employee, who was his father. The employers paid damages to the father but claimed indemnity from the son, because of negligence. This was held to be the case.

Duty to be reasonably competent

If an employee is incompetent this may be a breach of contract. In Hamer v Cornelius (1858) this was held to be the case.

To obey lawful orders

An employee is under a duty to obey all the lawful orders of his employer, i.e., those which are within the scope of the contract. In Price v Mouat (1862) a lace salesman was ordered to card (pack) lace, but he refused and was dismissed without notice. He claimed wrongful dismissal, and this was held because the order was not one which was within the scope of his contract.

An employee, therefore, is not obliged to do any act which is deemed to fall outside the ambit of his individual contract of employment. The question of the introduction of new technology has caused problems here and must be linked to the scope of managerial prerogative in introducing new work techniques. In Cresswell v Board of Inland Revenue (1984) the Revenue wished to introduce a computer system to assist with the PAYE system. Most of the work associated with the system had been done manually. Did the employers have the ability to change the nature of the working system? Did the employers have the ability to change the nature of the working system? Held: employees were expected to adopt the new methods and techniques in fulfilling their contracts if the employer provided the necessary training in new skills.

To take care of employer's property

An employer is under an obligation to take reasonable care of his employer's property. In Superflux v Plaisted (1958) the defendant had overseen a team of vacuum cleaner salesmen and had negligently allowed fourteen cleaners to be stolen from his van. Held: he was in breach of his contract of employment.

To act in good faith

His implied duty has several different aspects, which together form the basis of a relationship of trust. There is the duty not to make a secret profit, i.e., not to accept bribes.

This principal was clear from the case of Reading v AG (1951) which concerned a member of the armed forces, in which Lord Normand said:

---though the relation of a member of his majesty's forces is not accurately described as that of a servant under a contract of service--he owes to the Crown a duty as full fiduciary as the duty of a servant to his master--and in consequence--all profits and advantages gained by the use of his military status are to be for the benefit of the Crown'.

Duty to disclose certain information.

There appears to be no general duty on an employee to inform his employer of his misconduct and deficiencies: Bell v Lever Brothers (1932). However, there is one important exception, namely where the employment of that particular person is made more hazardous by virtue of an undisclosed defect on part of the employee.

Covenants in restraint of trade

A covenant in restraint of trade is a clause in a contract, which purports to limit an employee's rights to seek employment when and where he chooses upon leaving his employment. This is usually done as a protective measure by an employer when he might suffer because of disclosure of confidential information or for other such reasons.

There are difficulties, however, in enforcing such covenants and the employer has to demonstrate that the covenant is justified. A court will look at such factors as the time that the covenant runs, geographical area that it covers and public interest when considering the reasonableness of such covenants. If a covenant is found to be unreasonable, the contract as a whole is not necessarily regarded as void, unless it is impossible to distinguish the covenant from the rest of the contract. If the covenant can be severed from the rest of the contract, without altering the nature of the agreement, the unreasonable clause may be struck out: see Commercial Plastics LTD v Vincent (1965).

If an employer breaks the contract of employment by wrongfully dismissing an employee, the employee may disregard any covenant in the contract which purports to limit his right to seek employment elsewhere: see General Billposting v Atkinson (1909).

Patents

Under common law, unless the contract dealt with the matter, an employee would not normally be entitled to the benefit of any invention made by him if allowing him to do so would be a contravention of the implied duty of the employee to act in good faith. The Patents Act 1977 (as amended), ss-39-47, gives ownership of an invention to the employee inventor unless the invention was made in the course of the duties for which he was employed. Any disputes are dealt with by the patents court.

Duties of the employer

By virtue of common law, and a number of statutory provisions, employers have a considerable number of obligations towards employees. The main examples are:

To pay contractually agreed remuneration

An employer is under no obligation to provide work as long as remuneration is paid. This, however, has been questioned in recent times, particularly in relation to skilled employees. Lord Denning said, in Langston v AUEW (1973): 'In these days an employer, when employing a skilled man, is bound to provide him with work. By which I mean that the man should be given the opportunity of doing his work when it is available and when he is ready and willing to do it'. Therefore, a failure to provide work of a nature that the employee is used to could be regarded as constructive dismissal.

There are three exceptions to the rule, one is piecework, the second is where the nature of the employment is such that the actual performance of the work forms part of the consideration supplied by the employer, the employee may be entitled to compensation over and above the contractual wages. These situations are sometimes referred to as 'names in lights' clauses. The other exception is when an employee is taking part in limited industrial action.

To pay the National Minimum Wage and National Living Wage

The National Minimum Wage (NMW) is the minimum pay per hour most workers in the UK are entitled to by law. The rate varies depending on age and whether a person is an apprentice.

Apprentices and the National Minimum Wage

Apprentices are entitled to the apprentice rate of the National Minimum Wage if they are either:

- Under 19
- 19 or over and in the first year of their apprenticeship

Apprentices over 19 who have completed the first year of their apprenticeship are entitled to the National Minimum Wage for their age.

Entitlement to the National Minimum/Living Wage

A person must be at least school leaving age (the last Friday in June of the school year in which the person turns 16) to get the National Minimum Wage. A person must be over 23 to get the National Living Wage.

Almost all workers are entitled to the National Minimum Wage, including:

- Casual workers
- Part-time workers
- Temporary workers

There are some types of workers who don't qualify:

- self-employed people running their own business.
- company directors
- volunteers or voluntary workers
- workers on a government employment program, such as the Work Program
- members of the armed forces
- family members of the employer living in the employer's home
- non-family members living in the employer's home who share in the work and leisure activities, are treated as one of the family and are not charged for meals or accommodation, for example au pairs.
- workers younger than school leaving age (usually 16)
- higher and further education students on a work placement up to 1 year
- workers on government pre-apprenticeships schemes
- people on the following European Union programs: Leonardo da Vinci, Youth in Action, Erasmus, Comenius
- people working on a Jobcentre Plus Work trial for 6 weeks.
- share fishermen.
- prisoners
- people living and working in a religious community.

Work experience and internships

A person will not get the National Minimum Wage or National Living Wage if they are:

- a student doing work experience as part of a higher or further education course.
- of compulsory school age
- a volunteer or doing voluntary work.
- on a government program
- work shadowing

The National Minimum Wage is worked out as an hourly rate, but it applies even if the employee is not paid by the hour.

To treat employees with trust and confidence

In Courtaulds Northern Textiles Ltd v Andrew (1978) the EAT held'---there is an implied term in a contract of employment that employers will not, without reasonable and proper cause, conduct themselves in a manner calculated or likely to destroy or seriously damage the relationship of trust or confidence between the parties' A series of cases have firmly established this principle.

To observe provisions relating to holidays and other statutory entitlements such as maternity and paternity leave

The written statement provided to employees under the 1996 Act ought to state the holidays to which the employee is entitled and whether the employee is entitled to holiday pay and if so, how much. There are relatively few statutory provisions. Section 94 of the Factories Act 1961 provides that women and young persons who work in factories must have a holiday on bank holidays and the Wages Councils and Agricultural Wages Board have the power to fix holiday pay for workers in the industries over which they have jurisdiction.

In addition to holidays there are other statutory entitlements such as maternity and paternity leave plus adoption leave which must be adhered to.

To observe provisions relating to hours of work

The hours which an employee is required to work are determined by reference to his individual contract of employment and the written statement supplied to the employee ought to state these. There are certain statutory provisions, section 7 of the Sex Discrimination Act 1986 (now replaced by the Equality Act 2010) removed the majority of limitations imposed concerning the hours to be worked by women. Part V1 of the Factories Act 1961 limits the working day to no more than nine hours for young people. In addition, see below, the Working Time Regulations 1998. These have introduced specific regulations controlling the working week and cover a broad variety of workers, not only employees.

To permit employees time off work for public duties

The 1996 Act provides that an employer must permit an employee to have time off work for the purpose of carrying out work as:

a) Justice of the peace (work relating to this)
b) a member of a local authority
c) a member of a statutory tribunal
d) a member of a regional health authority or an Area or District educational establishment.
e) a member of a governing body of a local authority maintained educational establishment.

To indemnify employees

An employer is under an obligation to indemnify his employees in respect of any expenses incurred in performing their duties under the contract of employment, for example traveling expenses. In certain circumstances however, the employee may be under an obligation to indemnify the employer for any loss sustained: see Lister v Romford Ice and Cold Storage LTD (1957)

To provide references

As we have seen in chapter one, there is no obligation on an employer to supply character references for employees although, in practice, employers normally supply them since failure to provide one speaks for itself. The legal effect of references means that if an employer does provide one, it ought to be correct for several reasons:

If a reference is defamatory, the defamed employee may bring an action against the employer, although the defence of qualified privilege is available to the employer, i.e., the employer may show that the statements were made without malice.

Negligent misstatement. A person who acts in reliance on a reference, which has been issued negligently, may apparently bring an action to recover any loss sustained as a consequence.

Working Time Rights

Under Europe's Working Time Directive, most people now have seven basic rights to proper time off, rest breaks and paid holiday. As BREXIT will not have an immediate impact on employment law this is likely to remain unchanged until further notice.

Who has working time rights?

These working time rights apply to all employees and workers from the first day of employment. The rights apply to most agency workers, home-workers and freelancers. Only those who are self-employed and are genuinely running their own business do not have the right to paid annual leave.

Working time rights do not apply to:

1. individuals who are self-employed and who are genuinely running their own business.
2. individuals who can choose freely their hours and duration of work (such as a managing executive).
3. the armed forces, emergency services and police are excluded in some circumstances.
4. domestic servants in private houses.

Working time rules also apply differently to some groups of workers (e.g. those who have to travel a long distance from home to get to work) and in some sectors or workplaces (e.g. security, hospitals, or air, road or sea transport) or when there is an emergency or accident.

Rest breaks

You have the right to a rest break of at least 20 minutes where you work for a continuous period of six hours or more during a working day / shift. If you are under 18, however, you are entitled to a 30-minute break after working four and a half hours. Additional or longer breaks may be provided for in your contract. A lunch break or coffee break can count as a rest break.

The requirements are:

- the break must be in one block.
- it cannot be taken off one end of the working day - it must be somewhere in the middle.
- you are allowed to spend it away from the workplace.

Your employer can say when rest breaks can be taken provided they meet these requirements.

You do not have an automatic right to be paid for rest breaks. Whether you receive pay for rest breaks will depend on your contract.

Daily rest periods

You have the right to a rest period of 11 uninterrupted hours every working day. If you are under 18, you are entitled to a 12 hour uninterrupted rest period per working day. This rest period must be continuous and uninterrupted.

Weekly rest breaks

You have the right to a rest period of either:

- 24 hours in every 7 day period or
- 48 hours in every fortnight

This rest period must be continuous and uninterrupted. Employers have a duty to make sure that you take your breaks.

48 hour working time limit

You have the right not to work more than 48 hours a week on average. This limit is averaged over a 17-week period. This means that it is legal to work more than 48 hours in some weeks, so long as you work less in others.

You can opt out of this right unless you work at night but should not be pressured to opt out. The opt-out must be voluntary and must be in writing.

You have a right to opt back in again to working time protection at anytime, but you must give your employer at least 7 days notice. You may be required to give more notice - up to 3 months if you previously agreed to this with your employer in writing.

Young workers and working time limits

The weekly working time limits for young workers are 8 hours a day and 40 hours per week.

For most young workers these are absolute limits. A young worker's working time is not averaged over a reference period, so in one week they must not work more than 40 hours. The opt-out provisions do not apply to young workers.

Young workers will only be able to work more than 8 hours per day, or 40 hours per week if they are needed to:

- keep the continuity of service or production.
- respond to a surge in demand for a service or product.

And provided that:

- there is no adult available to do the work.
- their training needs are not negatively affected.

For further detailed information about your working time rights and how these can be enforced please see the TUC guide, 'Enforcing your Basic Workplace Rights'.

Holiday pay

If you work regular hours and get the same pay each week, then holiday pay is simply the same as your normal pay. If your normal pay includes regular bonuses, shift premiums or contractual overtime payments, then these should also be included in your holiday pay. If your weekly pay varies because your hours vary from week to week, then your weekly holiday pay should be the average weekly pay you earned over the last 12 weeks. An interesting case relating to holiday pay is The Sash Windows Workshop Ltd v and Another v King (ECJ) 2015 where a salesperson agreed with his company that he would be self-employed, rather than be engaged on an employment contract. Crucially, this meant that he was not given annual leave. After he retired, he claimed that he was owed 13 years backdated holiday pay because he was really a worker. The case went to the ECJ, which concluded that the onus is on the employer to provide paid annual leave to individuals who are really 'workers' regardless of how they are labelled and whether they ask for paid leave.

Holiday pay paid throughout the year

When paid holidays were first introduced in 1998, some people found a change to their pay slip. Their take home pay was still the same, but now made up of two elements. First was their basic pay, which had been reduced from what it had been in previous pay packets. The difference was made up with a new element called holiday pay. The employer then said that there was no need for paid holidays as you were getting your holiday pay throughout the year and should save up for it.

Paying holiday pay in this way is now illegal in Scotland but still legal in England and Wales. However, the amount specified must be a genuine addition. See the next chapter for more about holiday pay entitlement.

Special hazards

If your work involves special hazards or heavy physical or mental strain, and you are a night worker, then you cannot work more than eight hours in any 24. This is not an average but an absolute limit.

****

3.3

Terminating Employment

There are a number of ways in which a contract of employment may come to an end-termination by way of contract, termination in breach of contract and termination by methods external to the contract. Under common law, a contract of employment can be validly terminated by an employer giving notice to an employee in accordance with the terms of the contract or, in the absence of such a term, by giving reasonable notice. If sufficient notice was given, the employee had no further rights and this meant that dismissal could be entirely arbitrary. However, in recent times provisions have been introduced whereby an employee may be entitled to compensation for loss of job even though he was given notice. It should be noted that once notice has been given, it can only effectively be withdrawn with the consent of the other party.

Dismissal with notice

The length of notice, which must be given by an employer to an employee, is determined by reference to the following criteria to be applied in the following order:

a) Express terms of the contract. If the contract of employment expressly rovides for a period of notice, this must be observed unless that period is less than the statutory minimum to which that employee is entitled under d) below.

b) In the absence of an express term it may be impossible to imply a term into the contract, for example, by custom. Again, such a period may not be less than the statutory custom.
c) If there is no express or implied term of the contract, the courts may rely on a reasonable period. What is "reasonable" depends upon such factors as the status of the employee, salary, length of employment with that employer, age etc. The "reasonable" period cannot be less than the statutory minimum. In the absence of any of the above criteria, or where they produce a period less than the following, the statutory minimum in s 86 of the 1996 Act (ERA) must be applied in respect of those employees covered by that section. Section 86 provides that for an employee continuously employed for between one month and two years, the notice period is one week; for an employee employed for more than two years, he is entitled to one week for each year of continuous employment subject to a maximum of twelve weeks notice after twelve years of employment. These rights do not apply to a contract for the performance of a specific task, which is not expected to last for more than three months.

Constructive dismissal

Constructive dismissal is when you're forced to leave your job against your will because of your employer's conduct. The reasons you leave your job must be serious, for example, they:

don't pay you or suddenly demote you for no reason.
force you to accept unreasonable changes to how you work – e.g., tell you to work night shifts when your contract is only for day work.
let other employees harass or bully you.

Your employer's breach of contract may be one serious incident or a series of incidents that are serious when taken together. You should try and sort any issues out by speaking to your employer to solve the dispute. If you do have a case for constructive dismissal, you should leave your job immediately - your employer may argue that, by staying, you accepted the conduct or treatment.

Summary dismissal

Summary dismissal is where an employer dismisses an employee without giving the employee the amount of notice to which that individual is entitled. If there is no justification, such dismissal is wrongful, and an action can be brought. The remedy for wrongful dismissal is damages representing the loss of wages during the period of notice that ought to have been given. In addition, wrongful dismissal may also be unfair dismissal within the meaning of the 1996 Act.

Circumstances which justify summary dismissal

The question of what justifies summary dismissal is not one that can be answered with a simple rule since each case must be decided according to the circumstances. However, a general principle has emerged that summary dismissal is justified if the conduct of the employee is such that it prevents further satisfactory continuance of the relationship. This was the finding in Sinclair v Neighbour (1967).

The status of the employee in question is a relevant consideration as is the fact that the employee has a history of misconduct as opposed to an isolated incident.

*

Dismissals Procedure

If the contract states that dismissal is to be according to an established pattern (e.g., that there will be two warnings before dismissal occurs) it is a breach of contract if the procedure is not observed. (Tomlinson v L.M.S Rly (1944).

If the contract states that the dismissal may only occur for certain specified reasons, a dismissal is wrongful if the reason for the dismissal is other than specified in the contract.

However, it should be noted that the 2002 Employment Act introduced the obligation on an employer to include a statutory disciplinary and grievance procedure which must be in the contract or written terms and must be followed before any dismissal proceedings can take place.

Waiver of rights

If an employee's conduct justified a summary dismissal, the right must have been exercised within a reasonable time of the conduct, which allegedly justified the action since delay may amount to a waiver of the breach of contract.

Employee leaving

An employee is entitled to terminate employment at any time by giving the amount of notice required by the contract. If the employee is deemed to have been entitled to terminate employment by reason of the employer's conduct that may constitute a constructive dismissal and the fact that he gave notice makes no difference.

If an employer's attitude causes an employee to terminate his contract without notice, this may well constitute constructive dismissal and the employee may act accordingly.

Termination by agreement

The parties to a contract of employment as with any other contract may terminate their relationship by agreement at any time upon such terms as they may agree, e.g., payment of money as a golden handshake. It should be noted that a termination by agreement is not a dismissal for the purposes of the redundancy and unfair dismissals provisions of the 1996 Act. However, the tribunals are concerned to ensure that any alleged agreement to terminate a contract of employment is real and not merely a result of pressure imposed on an employee who is unaware of the significance of agreeing to terminate the contract and who faces dismissal as an alternative to so agreeing.

Termination by frustration

Frustration occurs whenever the law recognizes that without default of either party a contractual obligation has become incapable of being performed because the circumstance in which performance would be called for would render it a thing different from that which was undertaken by the contract (Lord Radcliffe in Davis Contractors v Fareham UDC (1956)).

In the context of a contract of employment, the term frustration means that circumstances have arisen, without the fault of either party, that make it impossible for the contract to be performed in the way that may be reasonably expected and the contract automatically terminates without the need for notice to be given. Frustration of the contract is not deemed to be dismissal for legislative purposes. Examples of frustration may be sickness. In Notcutt v Universal Equipment Co (1986), a worker with 27 years service, who was two years from retirement suffered a permanently incapacitating heart attack. The court decided that this rendered performance of the contract impossible and therefore the contract was frustrated as he was unable to fulfil his obligation to work. The employee was therefore not entitled to sick pay during his period of notice.

Imprisonment is another example; however, this has caused problems. In 1986, the Court of Appeal allowed a four year apprenticeship contract to be frustrated by a six months Borstal sentence: FC Shepherd LTD v Jerrom (1986). In this case the court held that such a period of imprisonment made the performance of the contract impossible. As with sickness, the courts will tend to look at each case on its own merits without applying hard and fast rules.

Action for wrongful dismissal

An employee who has been wrongfully dismissed may bring an action for damages against his former employer representing the amount of wages owed to him in respect of work already done and in respect of wages that the employee would have earned had he been given the amount of notice to which he was entitled. The amount of wages lost is determined by the ordinary principles of common law and includes all sums connected with the job, such as loss of tips etc. Damages for wrongful dismissal cannot normally include compensation for injured feelings or pride or the fact that future earnings may be affected.

The object of damages is to compensate the injured party for what he actually lost, not to punish the party in breach of contract, and therefore the courts have developed principles to ensure that the employee who has been wrongfully dismissed receives compensation only for his actual loss.

In the case of Brighton & Sussex University Hospitals NHS Trust v Akinwunmi, 2017, Mr Akinwunmi ('Mr A') was a consultant neurosurgeon for the NHS trust. Mr A had poor relationships with a number of fellow surgeons and had previously complained that he was being bullied - and brought a race discrimination claim to the Employment Tribunal, which was settled. It had been agreed that Mr A would take an unpaid three month sabbatical. During this sabbatical, Mr A raised some concerns about patient safety and alleged that his colleagues were turning away NHS patients whilst accepting private work. His colleagues claimed that he was incompetent, and his practices were unsafe. A complaint was made to the police that Mr A had also threatened to assault one of his colleagues. The police decided to take no further action - but the Trust failed to notify Mr A of this.

A decision was made to limit his sabbatical to three months, Mr A appealed against this decision, but his appeal was not upheld, and his absence from work became unauthorised. Mr A argued that it was impossible for him to return to work as there were various serious outstanding issues with his colleagues and this could be a risk to patient safety. Mr A was also concerned the police might arrest him if he returned to work and came into contact with the colleague he was alleged to have threatened. The Trust stated that the complaints could not be dealt with until he returned. A disciplinary hearing was held and Mr A was dismissed because of his unauthorised absence. Mr A brought claims for unfair dismissal, automatic unfair dismissal because of whistleblowing and victimisation. The ET dismissed Mr A's claims for whistleblowing and victimisation but did find that his dismissal was unfair. On appeal the Employment Appeal Tribunal agreed that dismissing Mr A for his unauthorised absence was unfair because the full context of the absence was not taken into consideration by the Trust. The EAT held it was unreasonable for the Trust to expect Mr A to return to work before trying to resolve the outstanding issues and improve working relationships. The EAT agreed that insisting Mr A return to a workplace where people's lives could depend on good working relationships was particularly unreasonable.

The EAT noted that the Trust's witnesses were found to be 'disingenuous' when giving evidence.

Damages against employee

Where an employee fails to give sufficient notice to his employer, the employer may sue the employee for damages representing the loss, which stems from the breach of contract. In practice, such actions are infrequent because the loss is often minimal.

Specific performance

Specific performance is an order from the court directing that the parties to a contract perform their contractual obligations. It is a fundamental principle of labor law that specific performance is granted to compel performance of a contract of employment and this principle is now embodied in s 235 of the Trade Union and Labour Relations (Consolidation) Act 1992.

Injunction

An injunction is an order from a court forbidding certain conduct, e.g., the breaking of a term of the contract of employment. Hence it may be used to prevent a breach of a covenant restraining an employee from taking employment with a rival of his former employer. The courts usually refuse to grant an injunction if it compels performance. By virtue of the Trade Union and Labour Relations Act 1992, no court may issue an injunction if the effect of such an order would be to compel an employee to do any work or to attend any place to work.

However, where the injunction compelling performance is to the benefit of the employee, the court may be prepared to grant such an order. In Hill v CA Parsons LTD (1972) the defendant employers wished to enter into an agreement with an organisation of workers whereby it was agreed that all employers in certain sections, including the plaintiff, would be obliged to join that organisation. This arrangement was legal at the time but under the Industrial Relations Act 1971 it would have been invalid. The plaintiff did not wish to join the organisation and he was dismissed with four weeks' notice. The Court of Appeal held that he was wrongfully dismissed since he was entitled to at least six months notice and furthermore an injunction was awarded which prevented the employee from being dismissed until that time elapsed by which time he would have a remedy under the 1971 Act.

Declaration

A declaration is an order from the court, which simply determines the rights of the parties in the case. It has no binding force in itself and is not available to all employees, being restricted to those persons whose employment is derived from statute.

Written statement of reasons for dismissal

An employee who has been continuously employed for 2 years who has been dismissed, subject to the statutory provisions of the 2002 Act and the following of a formal procedure, is entitled to receive, upon request, a written statement of the reasons for his dismissal. The employer must supply the reason in writing within 14 days of the request. A claim may be presented to an industrial tribunal by an employee that his employer has "unreasonably" refused to provide a written statement of the reasons for dismissal or that it is inadequate or untrue. The right to a written statement only arises where the employee has been dismissed by his employer.

Suspension

In accordance with the general principle that an employer fulfils his contractual obligations by paying wages in accordance with the contract of employment, he may suspend an employee on full wages without breach of contract. An employer may only suspend an employee without pay if the contract expressly or impliedly provided for this. If the contract does not so provide, it is a breach of contract. Therefore, an employee who is suspended without contractual authority may treat himself as dismissed and claim accordingly.

Unfair Dismissal

The present law relating to unfair dismissal is to be found in the Employment Rights Act 1996. The significance of the concept of unfair dismissal is that it represents a further, and most important, step towards recognizing the property right which an employee has in his job. Additionally, it is no longer possible for an employer to end a contract by simply giving notice and thereby totally discharging his responsibilities. The threat of dismissal is no longer quite so important since the employee has a remedy if the threat is implemented. The 1996 Act provides that, subject to certain specified exceptions, every employee has the right not to be unfairly dismissed. It should be noted that a complaint of unfair dismissal does not depend upon the employer having acted in breach of contract but simply that the employer has terminated the contract in circumstances which are unfair. Certain categories of employees are excluded: employees who, at the effective date of termination of the contract have been continuously employed for less than one year, two years if employed after 6th April 2012, persons over retiring age, persons employed in the police service, share fishermen, employees who ordinarily work outside Great Britain, employees employed on fixed term contracts and persons covered by a designated dismissals procedure agreement.

Dismissal

If an action for unfair dismissal is to succeed, the employee must first establish that he was dismissed within the meaning of the Act. The employee must establish constructive dismissal if alleged.

The Act provides that:

"an employee shall be treated as dismissed by his employer if the contract under which he is employed by the employer is terminated by the employer whether it is so terminated by notice or without notice or where under that contract he is employed for a fixed term, that term expires without being renewed under the same contract or the employee terminates that contract, with or without notice, in circumstances such that he is entitled to terminate it without notice by reason of the employers conduct".

The Act refers to the concept of so-called "constructive' dismissal. If an employee leaves employment entirely voluntarily, there is no dismissal but if he leaves because of the employers conduct then it may be deemed "constructive."

The courts and tribunals have been concerned to define the circumstances in which an employee is entitled to regard himself as having been constructively dismissed. In Western Excavating LTD v Sharp (1978) the tribunals found that sufficiently unreasonable behaviour on the part of the employer entitled an employee to leave his job and claim constructive dismissal. However, the Court of Appeal rejected the unreasonableness test and established that the correct test is one based on strict contractual principles. Accordingly, an employee is only able successfully to argue constructive dismissal where the employer has breached the contract in such a way as to justify the employee in treating himself as discharged from further performance. The action of an employer may involve breach of an express or implied term.

When is dismissal unfair?

The expression "unfair dismissal" is in no sense a commonsense expression capable of being understood by the person in the street. Whether a dismissal is unfair is affected, but not conclusively determined, by whether one or both parties has broken the terms of the contract of employment. The employer cannot, in seeking to show that a dismissal was not unfair, rely on alleged misconduct not known to him at the time of the dismissal. An otherwise fair dismissal is not automatically rendered unfair by a failure to give proper notice.

Reasonableness. It is for the employer to establish the reason for the dismissal. The tribunal must then satisfy itself as to whether the employer acted reasonably or unreasonably. The EAT laid down the following general principles in Iceland Frozen Foods v Jones (1982):

a) In applying the provisions of the 1996 Act a tribunal must consider the reasonableness of the employers' conduct and not simply whether they (the members of the tribunal) consider the dismissal unfair.

b) In judging the reasonableness of the employer's conduct, a tribunal must not substitute its own decision as to what was the right course to adopt for that of the employer.

c) In many cases there is a band of reasonable responses to the employees' conduct within which one employer might take one view and another quite reasonably another.

d) The function of the tribunal is to determine whether in the particular circumstances the decision to dismiss fell within the band of reasonable responses, which a reasonable employer might have adopted. If the dismissal falls within the band, it is fair. If it falls outside the band, it is unfair.

In deciding whether an employer acted reasonably, the industrial tribunal is required to have regard to the provisions of the ACAS Code of Practice-Disciplinary Code of Practice and Procedures in Employment. In broad terms, this provides that the disciplinary rules and procedures ought to have been made known to each employee and that a disciplinary procedure ought to contain certain essential procedures. It should be noted that the maximum compensatory awards for unfair dismissal increased to £86,444 from April 2019.

Reasons for dismissal

There are five categories of reasons, which, if one is established by the employer, may make the dismissal fair provided that the tribunal is satisfied that the employer acted reasonably. These are as follows:

a) Capability or qualification
b) Conduct
c) Redundancy
d) Illegality of continued employment
e) Some other substantial reason.

In addition, an employer in certain circumstances can dismiss an employee for reasons connected to pregnancy. Usually, it is automatically unfair to do so unless the employer can establish that at the effective date of termination, because of her pregnancy, she:

a) is or will have become incapable of adequately doing the work she is employed to do or: or
b) cannot or will not be able to do the work she is employed to do without a contravention (either by her or her employer) of a duty of restriction imposed by law.

In Brown v Stockton on Tees Borough Council (1988) the House of Lords (Supreme Court) held that if a woman was selected for redundancy because she is pregnant, such a dismissal is automatically unfair. Indeed, Lord Griffith stated that "it surely cannot have been intended that an employer should be entitled to take advantage of a redundancy situation to weed out his pregnant employer".

However, even where the circumstances of a and b above apply, the dismissal is still unfair if the employer has a suitable vacancy, i.e., appropriate for a pregnant woman to do and not substantially less favorable than her existing employment in relation to the nature, terms and place of employment, which he fails to offer her.

Another case highlighting unfair dismissal was that of Georgia O'Brian v Bolton St Catherine's Academy. Ms O'Brien's ordeal began in 2011 when she was assaulted by a pupil at Bolton St Catherine's Academy whilst assisting a colleague with a disruptive student. Her physical injuries were not long-lasting in comparison with her mental reaction, resulting in an absence from the school and subsequent termination of her employment in January 2013. In March 2017, the Court of Appeal confirmed that the decision of the Employment Tribunal in November 2014 was correct and should stand. In 2014, the Employment Tribunal found that Ms O'Brien's condition amounted to a disability and that her termination of employment was discriminatory and unfair. The school went on to appeal the decision and in September 2015 the Employment Appeal Tribunal

(EAT) allowed the school's appeal. However, in March 2017, the Court of Appeal overturned the EATs decision.

Another interesting case was that of Michael Hayward v Chadwick's Butchers. Michael Hayward had worked for Noel Chadwick, described to Manchester Employment Tribunal as a small and well-respected butchers in Wigan, for seven and a half years before he was dismissed for recommending a discount from online retailer Fresh Meat Packs North West to his then-girlfriend on Facebook.

Hayward was subsequently dismissed for gross misconduct and breach of contract by father and son directors John and Paul Chadwick for 'advertising' what they believed to be a competitor and breaching the company's social media policy. The tribunal heard the pair, whose business did not have a formal HR function, had already decided to dismiss Hayward before they brought him into a disciplinary meeting in April 2016.

The 37-year-old said he was not issued a written or verbal formal warning, despite requesting one, nor was he given the opportunity to have someone with him at the meeting or given an explanation regarding his actions. As no appeal was arranged within a few weeks of his sacking, Hayward eventually lost confidence in Noel Chadwick and did not follow up the matter.

The tribunal also heard that Hayward had been 'pulled up' on his use of social media before he posted the offer, but there was no warning given to him that suggested such behaviour could lead to his dismissal.

Allowing Hayward's unfair dismissal claim, Judge Keith Robinson called Noel Chadwick "fanciful" for suggesting it experienced any financial or reputational loss because of the Facebook post.

"Hayward's misdemeanour, if one can call it that, was minor," the judge continued. "This is not an advertisement; this [matter] was a wholly mishandled dismissal root and branch. The claimant was dismissed summarily in a process that was reprehensible."

The judge awarded Hayward a £6,091 payout – £4,891 in lost wages and compensation, and £1,200 to reimburse his tribunal fees.

Three other recent interesting cases based around unfair dismissal are:

Genus and Kelly v Fortem Solutions Ltd 2018. Two repair contractors who were fired for gross misconduct after they were discovered to have used company vehicles for personal purposes were unfairly dismissed, While the pair were at fault for misusing the vans, the tribunal found their employer failed to thoroughly investigate the issue before dismissing them.

Evans Nixon v Staffordshire Southwest Citizens Advice Bureau 2018 involved a long-standing CAB employee who had been dismissed for redundancy after a series of funding cuts. A selection exercise had been undertaken to determine who was made redundant, and the Claimant argued that she had been unfairly disadvantaged in the scoring process while less experienced colleagues had been retained. She also argued that her age and her disability (she suffers from a brain disorder called leukoencephalopathy) were factors in the CAB's decision to dismiss her.

The Employment Tribunal considered her case and found that the individual scores had not been discussed with her, and she also had not been given a chance to dispute the scores before the CAB had taken the decision to terminate her employment. On that basis, the Claimant's dismissal had been procedurally unfair. However, the Tribunal found that there was no disability or age discrimination.

Talon Engineering Ltd v Smith 2018. Mrs. Smith worked for a motorcycle manufacturer, Talon Engineering Ltd, and sent an email to a company that

Talon dealt with calling one of her colleagues an unpleasant name. Following an investigation into her conduct, Mrs. Smith was called to a disciplinary meeting, but her Union rep was unable to attend on the allotted day. Several alternative dates were suggested by Mrs. Smith and her rep, the first being 2 weeks ahead. Talon was not willing to delay the hearing to accommodate Mrs. Smith's companion and so it went ahead in her absence. Mrs. Smith was found to have committed gross misconduct and was summarily dismissed. She appealed and her appeal was rejected. Mrs. Smith then brought a claim in the Employment Tribunal for unfair dismissal.

The Tribunal found that Talon had a potentially fair reason for dismissing Mrs. Smith, i.e., conduct, but concluded that no reasonable employer would have refused a further short postponement of the disciplinary hearing and gone ahead in her absence. It was noted that the further delay to ensure Mrs. Smith's attendance and grant her the opportunity to be heard and accompanied would have been a short one.

Talon appealed to the Employment Appeal Tribunal (EAT), however, the EAT upheld the finding of unfair dismissal. The EAT also considered the right to be accompanied under section 10 of the ERA 1996, which says that the employer must postpone the hearing to allow the employee's chosen companion to attend if the proposed alternative is within 5 working days.

The EAT found that Talon appeared to believe that because Mrs. Smith's union rep suggested dates which did not fall within 5 working days, they were not obliged to reschedule the hearing.

Dismissal for trade union reasons

References in this section are to the Trade Union and Labour Relations (Consolidation) Act 1992. Trade Union membership or activities. Except in exceptional cases, a dismissal is automatically unfair if the employee can establish that the principal reason for it was that the employer was, or proposed to become, a member of an independent trade union, or that the employee had taken or proposed to take part in the activities of an independent trade union at any appropriate time or that the employee was not a member of any or a particular trade union, or had refused or proposed to refuse to become or remain a member.

Other reasons for dismissal

An industrial tribunal cannot determine whether a dismissal was fair or unfair if it is known that at the date of dismissal the employer was conducting or instituting a lock out or the complainant was taking part in a strike or other industrial action, unless it is shown:

a) that one or more relevant employees of the same employer have not been dismissed: or

b) that any such employee has, before the expiry of the period of three months beginning with the employee's date of dismissal, been offered re-engagement and that the complainant has not been offered re-engagement.

National security

If an employee has been shown to have been dismissed on grounds of national security, as evidenced by a certificate signed by or on behalf of a minister of the Crown, the tribunal must dismiss the complaint. In Council of Civil Service Unions v Minister for the Civil Service (1985) (the GCHQ case), the court held that the requirements of national security outweighed those of fairness when the minister decided to ban trade unions at GCHQ, without consultation with the trade unions. Workers who refused to give up their trade union membership were subsequently fairly dismissed.

Procedure

Using early conciliation before you make your claim

You can't make a tribunal claim without going through 'early conciliation' first. Early conciliation is when ACAS tries to help you reach an agreement with your employer. You must go through early conciliation by a deadline, which is usually 3 months less 1 day from the date of the thing you're complaining about. When you've finished early conciliation, you'll have at least a month to make your tribunal claim.

An employee who considers that he has been unfairly dismissed may present a complaint to an Industrial Tribunal within three months of the effective date of termination or within such further period as the tribunal considers reasonable in a case where it is satisfied that it was not reasonably practicable for the complaint to be presented within a period of three months. The claim can be online or by post. For more details on claiming go to: www.gov.uk/employment-tribunals/make-a-claim. This website also deals with Industrial Tribunals in Scotland and Northern Ireland which operate differently. More advice can be found at: https://www.citizensadvice.org.uk.

Where the dismissal is unfair (failure to offer re-engagement where the dismissal is connected with a lockout or strike) the time limit is six months from the date of dismissal. A copy of the application is sent to the employer as respondent. If the employer wishes to contest any aspect of the complaint, he must enter a "notice of appearance" within 14 days, although tribunals have a wide discretion to grant an extension of time. Once this has happened, a date is set down for the hearing of the case by an industrial tribunal.

Pre-hearing Assessments

Under the Industrial Tribunals Regulations (S1 1985/16) provision is made for a pre-hearing assessment of the case to be made at the request of either of the parties or on the notion of the tribunal itself. At the tribunal, it is for the complainant to establish that he was dismissed (unless dismissal is conceded). It is then for the tribunal to satisfy itself as to whether the dismissal was fair or unfair in accordance with the principles stated above. If the dismissal is found to be unfair, the tribunal will consider the remedies, which may be awarded.

An appeal, on a point of law only, lies from an industrial tribunal to the Employment Appeal Tribunal.

Remedies

Reinstatement and re-engagement orders. If the Tribunal finds the dismissal unfair, it must explain to the complainant the remedies available and ask if he wishes to be reinstated or re-engaged. If the employee indicates that this is his wish, then the Tribunal must consider whether it is practicable for the employer to comply with such an order. If the employer complies, but not fully, with a reinstatement or re-engagement order then, unless the tribunal is satisfied that it was not practicable to comply with the order, an additional award of compensation must be made.

If a reinstatement or re-engagement order is made but not complied with at all or if no such order is made, the tribunal must make an award of compensation based on the following:

a) basic award, the amount of which is calculated in line with redundancy payments.

b) compensatory award, being an amount that the tribunal considers just and equitable in all the circumstances having regard to the loss suffered by the complainant in consequence of the dismissal in so far as the loss is attributable to action taken by the employer subject to a maximum limit.

****

Chapter 4

Business Law-Company Law General

People who wish to enter into business activity will need to do so through some form of business structure, depending on their aims and objectives. In the UK, there are four principal business structures through which people can pursue their objectives:

1. **The sole proprietorship**-which is the simplest business structure, being that of an individual carrying on some form of business activity on his or her account (self-employed). The sole proprietorship is not incorporated, nor does the sole proprietor carry on business in partnership with someone else. Sole proprietorship does not have 'corporate personality' and the sole proprietor owns all the assets and all responsibilities for debts and liabilities. Sole proprietorships are not subject to the Companies Act 2006 and so do not need to file accounts at Companies House, although they need to complete their own tax returns.
2. **The ordinary partnership**-two or more persons who wish to engage in business together will usually form a partnership.
3. **The limited liability partnership** (LLP) discussed below.
4. **The company**-discussed in detail below.

Partnerships

There are three different forms of partnership:

a) the ordinary partnership
b) the limited partnership, which is a form of partnership that can be

formed under the Limited Partnership Act 1907. This is a rare form of partnership which won't be discussed further.

c) the limited liability partnership, referred to above and discussed further on.

The relationships between partners

The Partnerships Act 1890 establishes rules governing the rules between partners. Most partnerships will have a partnership agreement that spells out the rights and obligations of partners. Where a partnership agreement does not exist, ss 24 and 25 of the PA 1890 implies a number of default terms into the agreement. These default terms include the below:

- All partners are entitled to share equally in the profits and must also contribute equally to the firm's losses.
- Every partner may take part in the management of the firm.
- No new partners may be admitted to the firm without the consent of the other partners.
- The agreement between partners can only be altered with the express consent of the other partners.
- The majority of the partners cannot expel a partner unless express power to do so has been agreed by other partners.

Partners and third parties

Sections 5-18 of the PA 1890 regulate the relationships between partners and third parties. This includes the extent to which the partners can contractually bind the firm and other partners to a third party, and the extent to which the firm and other partners can be liable for acts or omissions of a single partner that cause a third party to sustain loss.

Limited Liability Partnerships

Under the Limited Liability Partnerships Act 2000, it is possible to create a different form of business association called a limited liability partnership. Under the LLPA 2000, a LLP becomes a corporate body with a legal personality separate from that of its members. It follows therefore that members of a LLP will not normally become liable for the debts of the LLP. The law relating to ordinary partnerships does not relate to a LLP.

Many of the detailed provisions relating to LLP's are to be found in secondary legislation, in particular the Limited Partnership Regulations 2001. These regulations apply some of the provisions of the CA 2006 and the Insolvency Act 1986 to LLP's with some modifications to reflect the different nature of an LLP.

Formation of an LLP

An LLP is created by registration with the registrar of companies. Once the registrar has registered an LLP and issued a certificate of incorporation, a new corporate body with a separate legal personality of its own is created. Section 2 (1) of the LPA 2000 provides that:

Two or more persons associated for carrying on a lawful business with a view to profit must have subscribed their names to an incorporation document which is to be delivered to the registrar of companies.

Companies

The main distinction between a company and a partnership, as we have seen above, is that the company is treated as a separate entity, or person, in law. The partnership, on the other hand is not seen as a separate entity and consists only of those who have chosen to join together for business purposes.

One other crucial distinction is that a company will pay corporation tax, whilst a partnership will pay only that tax due as an individual liability. A company has access to what is known as "limited liability". This is where the liability for debt of directors is limited. Not all companies are limited companies. If a company is not limited there is no requirement to file accounts at Companies House. Partnerships have no such access to limited liability.

A company can separate ownership from control. People who subscribe to a company and purchase its shares do not necessarily have any control over the company or a hand in running the business. This is especially the case in a large Public Limited Company, where shareholders receive a return on their investment in the company. A further distinction and advantage for a company is in the area of raising finance. The company as a separate entity can raise finance in its own right, mortgage any assets by way of a floating charge, and generally enjoy access to finance that is not available to a partnership.

Incorporation

Companies and LLP's, as opposed to sole proprietorships and ordinary partnerships, are created through the process of incorporation. Incorporation brings into being a 'body corporate', as defined by s 162(2) of the CA 2006.

A company can become incorporated through an Act of Parliament, by Royal Charter or through incorporation by registration. the most common method of incorporation is through registration. Indeed, the provisions of CA 2006 generally apply only to companies incorporated by registration.

Incorporation by Act of Parliament happens when, for example, through the passing of legislation, companies are set up to manage the process created by the legislation, such as the London Olympics and Paralympic Games. Incorporation by Royal Charter applies to companies that are created by the monarch following advice from the Privy Council. Such companies created in this way are the BBC, the Privy Council. Companies created in this way include the BBC, the Bank of England and the Law Society.

Incorporation by Registration

Today, the majority of companies are incorporated by registration, so called because the process involves registering documents with Companies House. These documents, once registered and authorized by Companies House, bring a company into existence. Section 9 of the CA 2006 provide that the documents are the memorandum of association, an application for registration and a statement of compliance. A statement of compliance states that the statutory requirements regarding registration have been met. In addition, the Small Business, Enterprise and Employment Act 2015 amended the Companies Act 2006 so that companies must also provide the following:

- a statement identifying persons who have significant control over the company, and
- if the company is private, and the promoters have elected to have Companies House keep its statutory registers, then a notice indicating this must be delivered to Companies House upon registration.

The advantages of an incorporated company over an unincorporated company are as follows:

- The main advantage is that the company acquires a corporate (or separate or legal) personality. This means that the company is regarded in law as a person. Whereas humans are natural persons the company is a legal person and can do many things that a human can.
- A company has limited liability, this means that, as the company is a

separate legal entity the members are not usually liable for its debts and liabilities-the company itself is liable. The members liability is limited to the value of their financial investment in the company.

- Whilst members of companies (or partnerships) come and go, companies can last forever as they are separate entities. In the case of *J. H. Rayner (Mincing Lane) Ltd. v. Dept. of Trade and Industry, (1990),* no member is bound to contribute anything more than the nominal values of the share held by him. The Companies Act states, 'Members may come and members may go, but the company can go on forever.'
- Contractual capacity-as the company is a person, and a separate entity, it can enter into contracts with persons inside and outside the company.

Public companies and private companies

Another main area which runs through company law is that of the distinction between the public company and the private company. The majority of companies in the United Kingdom are private companies. One main feature of company law is that, with a few exceptions, the same rules apply to private companies as to public companies.

Brexit itself will not cause any change to the legal status of companies incorporated in and operating within the UK (subject to those changes outlined in Chapter 1). Although a good deal of UK company law is based on EU directives, the Companies Act 2006 and other domestic UK legislation will continue in force as at present unless and until the UK Parliament votes to amend it.

One main feature of a public company is that it must have a minimum subscribed share capital of at least £50,000, paid up to at least 25 percent before it can be incorporated (s586 of the CA 2006). In addition to the payment of the minimum subscribed share capital to at least 25 percent on initial allotment of shares, the whole of any premium must be paid up.

A further distinction between public and private companies is in the name of the company. The Companies Act of 2006 states that a public company must end with suffix "public limited company" or the abbreviation PLC. In Wales the term is cwmni cyhoeddus cyfyngedig with the abbreviation ccc. A private company will end with the term "limited" or the Welsh equivalent cyfyngedig or "cyf".

In addition, another fundamental distinction between the public and private company is that the private company is prohibited from seeking finance from the public by offering shares or debentures. The public company is authorised to seek shares in this way. It is worth noting that most public companies are not listed. Listed companies have to comply with more and more regulations. Currently, in addition to complying with the Companies Act 2006, listed companies are also required to comply with the provisions of Pt V1 of the Financial Services and Markets Act 2000 and a body of rules collectively known as the Listing Regime, which principally consists of (i) The Disclosures and Transparency Rules (ii) the Prospectus Rules and most importantly (iii) The Listing Rules. These latter rules are drafted and administered by the Financial Conduct Authority and impose obligations upon listed companies in relation to the disclosure of information, as well as supplementing the CA 2006 as regards certain areas of internal control.

These rules have the force of law as the FCA is regarded as the 'competent authority' under part V1 of the Financial Services and Markets Act 2000.

Company limited by guarantee

A company limited by guarantee is a private company, very like a private company limited by shares, but it does not have a share capital. It is widely used for charities, clubs, community enterprises and some co-operatives. The vast majority of such companies are non-profit distributing, but they do not have to be. A company limited by guarantee is registered at Companies House, has articles of association, directors, etc., and is subject to all the requirements of the Companies Acts (except those relating to shares). There are no shares and so no shareholders, but such a company does have members who meet and control the company through general meetings. The directors are often called a management committee or council of management, etc. but in law are still company directors and subject to all the rules that affect other directors.

A company limited by guarantee confers limited liability as effectively as a company limited by shares. The articles state that the members guarantee to pay its debts, but only up to a fixed amount each. Usually that sum is £1, and no member can be liable for more than that amount if the company fails. The Companies Act 2006 also outlines other distinctions between companies:

- A private company can operate with one director, in contrast to the public company which is required to have two
- A private company needs only to have one member whereas a public company has to have two (s154 CA 2006).
- The company secretary of a private company can be anyone and that person needs no particular qualifications. There is now no legal requirement for a company secretary of a private company under the CA 2006. The company secretary of a public company must be qualified, holding a recognised qualification in this area in order to hold the post.
- Before a public company can pay a dividend, it must ensure that it has

trading profits and that its capital assets are maintained in value to at least the value of the subscribed share capital plus undistributable reserves. There is no such rule applying to a private company (CA 2006)

- Before a public company can distribute shares in exchange for property it must obtain an independent experts valuation of the property. This requirement does not apply to a private company (CA 2006)
- A public company may not issue shares in exchange for services. This rule does not apply to a private company (CA 2006).
- The Directors of a public company must call an Extraordinary General Meeting (EGM) if it suffers a serious loss of capital. There is no requirement for a private company to do this.
- Proxies in a private company may speak at a meeting. In a public company there is no such right.
- In a private company there are courses of action which may be taken in order to dispense with formalities such as the need to hold an Annual General Meeting, the laying of accounts and the annual appointment of auditors. This is not the case with a public company, which is rigidly bound.
- Private companies may act by unanimous written resolution, in most cases. This does not apply to public companies.
- Where there is a proposal to elect a director aged 70 or over to the board of a public company, special notice is required. There is no such requirement for a private company.
- The minimum age for a company director under the CA 2006 s57, for both private and public companies is 16.

Community Interest Companies

The Companies (Audit, Investigations and Community Enterprise) Act 2004 and regulations made under the Act, establish the legislative framework for CICs. CICs are regulated by the CIC Regulator. A Community Interest Company can be registered in England and Wales, Scotland or Northern Ireland. It is a hybrid between a charity and a profit making company. A Community Interest Company must be set up and run for the benefit of the community. A CIC can only be registered with the consent of the Community Interest Companies Regulator. The application must comply with CIC legislation as well as the usual rules for registration of a company. The CIC Regulator has to be satisfied that the proposed company is being set up to benefit the community and that its articles include all the provisions required of a community interest company. Each year, the CIC must submit a return stating what its activities have been and that these have been of community benefit.

Property management companies

A property management company in England and Wales, Scotland or Northern Ireland is a particular type of company: one set up to hold an interest in a property which is divided into units, each unit being owned separately. A typical example is a large house which has been divided into a number of flats (sometimes called a flat management company), each flat being owned by one or two people. Such a company can also be used for large blocks of flats, housing estates and commercial properties divided into units. A property management company will always be a private limited company. It may be limited by shares or limited by guarantee. People who deal with property management companies professionally tend to have their preferences. It is one of those circumstances where either type of company will work perfectly well. The only significant difference between them is that a company limited by shares has a share capital, owned by its shareholders and a company limited by guarantee does not, but is controlled by its shareholders. If the company is to own the freehold, some people prefer it to be a company limited by shares as this gives a form of ownership between the shareholders (who own the company) and the property (which is owned by the company). On the other hand, with a company limited by guarantee, there is no need to transfer a share when the flat is sold.

The concept of the corporate personality

The principle of the separate legal personality of a company was established in an important early case, *Saloman v A Saloman (1897).* The facts of the case were that Saloman had incorporated his shoe repair business, transferring it to a company. He took all the shares of the company with the exception of six which were held by his wife, daughter and four sons. Part of the payment for transfer of the business was made in the form of debentures (secured loan) issued by the company to Saloman. Saloman transferred the debentures to Broderip in exchange for a loan. Saloman defaulted on payment of interest on the loan and Broderip sought to enforce the security against the company. Unsecured creditors tried to put the company into liquidation. There was a dispute between Broderip and the unsecured creditors over who had priority over payment of the debt. It was argued for the creditors that Salmons security was void as the company was a sham and was in reality the agent of Salomon.

The House of Lords held that this was not the case as the company had been properly incorporated and therefore the security was valid and could be enforced. This case is seen as one of the most important cases in company law as it is from this that many principles of company law flow.

There are certain statutory exceptions to the Salmon principle and they are as follows:

- Section 7 of the Companies Act 2006 provides that if the membership of a public company falls below the statutory minimum of two then the remaining member should after a period of six months grace, be liable for the company's debts and obligations where he or she knew of the situation.
- Section 767 (3) of the Companies Act 2006 provides that where a public company fails to obtain a trading certificate in addition to its certificate of incorporation before trading and borrowing money then the companies directors are liable for any obligations incurred.
- Sections 398-408 of the Companies Act 2006 provides that where a group situation exists (i.e. where there is a holding company and subsidiaries) then group accounts should be prepared. In assessing whether this is the case, clearly the veil is being lifted to see if the holding company/subsidiary relationship exists.
- Section 83 of the Companies Act 2006 provides that if a company officer mis-describes the company in a letter, bill, invoice, order, receipt or any other document then the officer is liable in the event of the obligation not being honored.
- Section 994 of the Companies Act 2006 may involve lifting the veil to determine, for example, the basis on which the company was formed.
- Sections 1159-1160 of the Companies Act 2006 set out the formula for determining if a holding company/subsidiary company relationship exists.
- Section 15 of the Company Directors Disqualification Act 1986 provides that if a director who is disqualified continues to act, he or

she will be personally liable for the debts and obligations of the company.

- Section 122 (1) (g) of the Insolvency Act 1986 provides that a petitioner may present a petition to wind up a company on the just and equitable ground.
- On occasion, this may be based on a situation involving the lifting of the company veil in order to determine the basis of the company formation.
- Section 213 of the Insolvency Act 1986 provides that where a person trades through the medium of a company, knowing that the company is unable to pay its debts, he or she may be held liable for contributions to the companies assets where the company is being wound up. This has a criminal counterpart in s999 (1) of the CA 2006.
- Section 6 of the Law of Property Act 1969 provides that where a person has a controlling interest in a company which is carrying on a business, the business is treated as the controller for the purposes of refusing a renewal of a tenancy issued out of the Landlord and Tenant Act 1954.

In addition to the statutory exceptions to the Salomon principle there are certain judicial decisions which have had an impact. One such decision is that of combating fraud. There are several well-known legal cases that have dealt with fraud.

One such case is that of *Jones v Lipman (1962)* where a vendor decided to sell a piece of land and then changed his mind. This resulted in the would-be purchaser suing for specific performance. In order to avoid this, the vendor transferred the piece of land to a company. The courts held that although the company was another legal entity nevertheless the action was designed to avoid legal action and the courts refused to accept the action of transferring the land and ordered specific performance against the vendor.

Therefore the action of transferring assets from the individual to a company in order to change a legal status is not tolerated if it is seen as fraudulent, as in the case above. There are numerous other examples of a company veil being lifted in order to combat fraud.

Group structures

Group structures are governed by s1159 of the CA 2006. Sometimes the fact that a company is within a group is seen as a reason for identifying it with another company within the group. In *Harold Holdsworth and Co (Wakefield) Ltd v Caddies (1955)* the respondent held an employment contract with the appellant company to serve it as managing director. The House of Lords held that the appellant company could require the respondent to serve a subsidiary company.

A fundamental case in this area is *DHN Food Distributors Ltd v Tower Hamlets London Borough Council (1976)*. This case concerned compensation for compulsory purchase. The company operating the business was the holding company and the premises were owned by the companies wholly owned subsidiary. Compensation was only payable for disturbance to the companies business if the business was operated on land owned by the company.

In this case, Lord Denning said:

"In many respects a group of companies are treated together for the purposes of accounts, they are treated as one concern. This is especially the case when a parent company owns all the shares of the subsidiary-so much so that it can control the activities of the subsidiaries. These subsidiaries are bound hand and foot and must do just what the parent company says."

Companies and crimes and negligence

Companies, as any individual, can commit crimes, although there are certain obvious exceptions, such as rape or murder. A company can, however, commit manslaughter. In December 1994, OLL Limited became the first company in England to be convicted of manslaughter. This arose from the death of four young people in a canoeing accident in Lyme Bay which was organised by the company. In the case, *Kite v OLL Ltd*, the managing director of the company that organised the trip was imprisoned for manslaughter and the company fined £60,000.

The Law Commission reported on the law of corporate manslaughter in consultation paper number 135 (1994). They recommended a new offence based on whether the companies conduct fell significantly below what could reasonably be expected of it in the context of the significant risk of death or injury of which it should have been aware. In a later report (Law Commission Paper 237) Legislating the Criminal Code, Involuntary Manslaughter (1996) the Law Commission, in its final report, called for a new offence of corporate killing comparable to killing by gross negligence. It is imperative that at least one person should be recognised and identified as the directing force of the company causing death by gross negligence when acting as the company.

One other case of a company being convicted of manslaughter, was that of *Jackson Transport (Ossett) Ltd.* The company concerned was a medium sized company employing about 40 people. A person was killed in May 1994 while he was cleaning behind a tanker containing chemicals. Mr Jackson, the owner, ran the business himself and he and the company was convicted of manslaughter. Companies may also commit strict liability offences. This is important in areas such as pollution and food safety. There is however, a diligence defence and if the company can demonstrate the practice of diligence, or that lack of diligence was on the part of a person who was not the true embodiment of the company, it will escape liability.

The Corporate Manslaughter and Corporate Homicide Act 2007

The Corporate Manslaughter and Corporate Homicide Act 2007 is an Act of the Parliament of the United Kingdom that seeks to broaden the law on corporate manslaughter in the United Kingdom. The Act created a new offence respectively named corporate manslaughter in England and Wales and Northern Ireland, and corporate homicide in Scotland.

****

4.2

The Constitution of a Company

The Companies Act 2006 significantly altered the form and content of the corporate constitution. Prior to the passing of the CA 2006, a companies constitution consisted primarily of the memorandum of association and the articles of association. Section 17 of the CA 2006 now provides that a company's constitution will include:

1. the company's articles, and
2. resolutions and agreements affecting the company's constitution

Under the Companies Act 2006, the importance of a company's memorandum of association has been reduced to a mere historical record. Constitutional provisions are to be contained within the Articles of Association instead. The memorandum is a document that needs to be submitted as part of the incorporation process and will not be capable of amendment. The information that was contained within the memorandum will now be provided to the registrar in an application for registration under s9 of the Companies Act 2006.

The application for registration must contain the following::

- The name of the company (s9) (2) of the Companies Act 2006.
- If the company is a public company a statement indicating this s9 (2).
- A statement that the registered office of the company is situated in England and Wales, in Wales or in Scotland s9 (7).

The application must also contain:

- A statement of initial shareholding
- A Statement of share capital
- A Statement of guarantee
- A Statement of proposed officers
- A Statement of compliance

Objects clauses and *ultra vires*

By virtue of s31 of the CA 2006 unless a company's articles specifically restrict the objects of the company, its objects are unrestricted. If the company does decide to amend its objects, then this change must be made by amendment to the articles. This is stated in s40 of the CA 2006. The effect of the law is to effectively abolish *ultra vires.* However, there are still occasions where a challenge could arise. These are where a director or connected person is involved or a third party acted in bad faith. A challenge could also arise if an injunction is sought to prevent directors acting, or to allege a breach of duty after events. S 239 of the CA 2006 now only requires ordinary resolutions to ratify any breaches of duty by directors. However, the votes of any director or person involved in the breach of duty will not count. S 41 (3) of the CA 2006 makes any directors involved liable to account for the transaction and to indemnify the company whether they knew they were exceeding their powers or not.

The position at common law

The old case will still be applicable in certain limited circumstances. Prior to statutory reform, at common law, contracts that were outside the scope of the company's objects were held to be *ultra vires* and void.

Before statutory intervention therefore the question was simple: if the objects clause covered the relevant contract it was valid. If it was outside the scope of the company's permitted range of activities it was void and unenforceable. There are several cases which serve to highlight the nature of the above. One such case is that of Payne and Co Ltd (1904) where a company borrowed money which was then used for purposes outside of the objects of the company. The lender was able to enforce the loan because he did not know the purpose of the loan.

In *Re John Beauforte Ltd (1953)* a different decision was reached on the basis that a supplier to the company provided coke. The company could have been using the coke for internal purposes as it was engaged in the manufacturer of veneered panels. The order was placed on notepaper showing that the company was engaged in this business and the courts held that the combination of constructive notice of what the company could do and the actual notice of what it was doing was fatal to the suppliers claim.

Statutory intervention

Article 9 of the first EC directive on company law provided as follows:

- Acts done by the organs of the company shall be binding upon it even if those acts are not within the objects of the company, unless such acts exceed powers that the law confers or allows to be conferred on those organs.

Since that first article, company law has developed and now the Companies Act 2006 has amended the law on ultra vires and objects clauses.

The Prentice Report (reform of the ultra vires rule, a consultative document (1986) (par 50) put forward the following recommendations in relation to the reform of the ultra vires rule:

- A company should have the capacity to do any act whatsoever

- A third party dealing with the company should not be affected by the contents of any document merely because it is registered with the registrar of companies or with the company.
- A company should be bound by the acts of its board or an individual director.
- The third party should be under no obligation to determine the scope of the authority of a company's board or individual director, or the contents of the company's articles or memorandum.
- A third party who has actual knowledge that a board or an individual director do not possess the authority to enter into a transaction on behalf of the company should not be allowed to enforce against the company but the company should be free to ratify this. The same result should obtain where a third party has knowledge that the transaction falls outside of the company's objects, but in this case ratification should be by a special resolution.
- Knowledge in this context will require understanding, and it will only be the knowledge of the individual entering into the particular transaction that will be relevant
- The proposal (in relation to third parties) should be modified where a third party is an officer or director of the company and in this situation constructive knowledge should be sufficient to render the transaction unenforceable and for this purpose constructive knowledge should mean the type of knowledge which may reasonably be expected of a person carrying out the functions of that director or officer of the company.
- In consequence of the recommendations of the Prentice Report the Companies Act of 1989 amended the law on ultra vires and objects clauses.

The Companies Act of 2006-provides that the validity of an act done by a company shall not be called into question on the ground of lack of capacity by reason of anything in the company's memorandum. A transaction can thus be enforced by an outsider or the company.

A member may, however, restrain the company from entering into a transaction which is outside the company's objects. This power to restrain the company can only operate where the company has not entered into a binding transaction to perform the act.

If the directors exceed limitations on their powers then they are in breach of their director's duties. Even if the directors conclude a contract outside of the objects clause, and a member has not succeeded in restraining this, the company may be able to sue their directors for breach of duties (Companies Act 2006). It is open to the company to ratify what has been done by special resolution. The company may also ratify by a separate special resolution the breach of the director's duties thereby putting the matter outside of litigation.

S.40 (1) of the CA now provides that where a person deals with a company in good faith the power of the directors to bind the company shall be deemed to be free of any limitation under the company's constitution. The outsider is not to be regarded as in bad faith by reason only by his knowing that the transaction was outside of the director's powers.

Further, this section provides that:

...a party to any transaction with a company is not bound to enquire as to whether it is permitted by the companies memorandum or as to any limitations on the board of directors to bind the company or to authorise others to do so.

The wording under sections s.40 (1) will protect outsiders in most circumstances. The CA 2006 builds on these provisions, which extends to other officers acting on behalf of the company.

This provides that:

... a person shall not be taken to have notice of any such matters merely because of its being disclosed in any document kept by the registrar of companies (and thus available for inspection) or made available by the company for inspection.

The rules governing company names

The first clause in the company's memorandum should be the name of that company. The statutory provisions relating to company names are set out in The Companies Act 2006. These provisions are as follows:

- Section 58 of the CA 2006 provides that the name of a public company must end with the word "PLC" or the Welsh equivalent as mentioned. A private company limited by shares or guarantee should end with "Limited" or the abbreviation Ltd or the Welsh equivalent as mentioned.
- In certain cases, a private limited company may be permitted to omit the word "limited" from the end of its name. The Companies Act 2006 permits companies to omit the word limited on satisfying certain conditions. The company concerned must be a private limited company and have as its objects the promotion of science, commerce, art, education, religion, charity or any profession and anything incidental or conducive to any of these objects and must have a requirement in its constitution that its profits or other income be applied in promoting these objects. The constitution must also prohibit the payment of dividends to its members and require all of the assets which would otherwise be available to its members

generally to be transferred on its winding up to another body with similar objects or to a body the objects of which are the promotion of charity and anything incidental.

- Section 53 of the Companies Act 2006 prohibits the use of certain names. The words public limited company, limited and unlimited can only be used at the end of a company name as may be the Welsh equivalents.
- The name must not be the same as a name already registered at Companies House. (s 66 CA 2006)

S 55 of the CA 2006 states that there are certain words and expressions, which require the prior permission of either the Secretary for State or some other designated body. There is a list of the words specified in regulations made under s55 of the Companies Act. If the name of the company implies some regional, national or international pre-eminence, governmental link or sponsorship or some pre-eminent status, then consent may be required.

- The choice of company name is limited by other considerations. If the name is a registered trademark the person who owns the trademark may take action to prevent the use of the name under the Trades Mark Act 1994.
- The use of a name which is already used by an existing business (whether sole trader, partnership or company) or a name which is similar to that of an existing business such that it appears to the public that there is a link between the two businesses may be subject to legal action, such as an injunction to restrain the company from further use.

Change of name

Section 77 (1) of the Companies Act 2006 provides that a company may change its name by special resolution in general meeting. There are other provisions relating to change of name, that is if the Secretary of State or Companies House gives a direction that the company must do this. This will usually happen in a situation where the original name was misleading or that the name itself is deemed to be of potential harm.

The articles of association of a company

The articles of association is now the most important document to be submitted to the registrar (CA 2006 s 18). The articles tend to regulate the internal workings of the company and typically cover such issues as the balance of power between the members and the directors, the conduct of general meetings, and certain issues pertaining to shares and distribution of assets.

Although a company must have articles of association, the contents of the articles are not laid down by the 2006 CA. Under s 20 of the 2006 CA, a limited company doesn't have to register articles. If they are not registered then model articles drafted under the Companies (Model Articles) Regulations can be adopted. Section 21 of the Companies Act 2006 allows a company to alter its articles by special resolution. However, the power to alter the articles of a company is restricted by the following:

- The company cannot alter its articles in a way which would lead to contravention of the 2006 Companies Act.
- Any alteration of the company's articles which would lead to a difference between, or a clash between the memorandum is void.
- If an alteration of the articles is proposed which conflicts with an order of the court then this would be automatically void.
- If the proposed alteration of the articles leads to an alteration of the class rights then special procedures need to be followed in addition to

a special resolution being passed. A company must follow a regime which is appropriate to the variation of class rights which is set out in s121 of the 2006 Companies Act.

If a change of articles involves a variation of class rights then this procedure must be followed. If a company has more than one class of shares then questions of variations of class rights sometimes arise. Once it has been determined that there is more than one class of share in the company then the next question for determination is whether there has been a variation of rights attached to those shares. Once it has been established that there has been a variation of class rights then the rules that have to be followed to carry the variation into effect are dependent upon whether the company has a share capital or not. If the company has a share capital then the rights may be varied:

a) in accordance with provision in the company's articles for the variation of those rights; or
b) where the company's articles contain no such provision, if the members of that class consent to the variation in accordance with this section.

The consent required for the purposes of this section on the part of the members of a class is-

a) consent in writing from at least three quarters of the members of the class, or
b) a special resolution passed at a separate general meeting of the members of that class sanctioning the variation.

If class rights are varied, dissentient minorities have special rights to object to the alteration. They must satisfy certain conditions. The dissenters must hold no less than 15% of the issued shares of the class and must not have voted in favour of the resolution (s 633 of the CA 2006). They may then object to the variation within 21 days of consent being given to the resolution.

If the class rights are varied under a procedure set out in the memorandum or articles of association of the company or if the class rights are set out otherwise than in the memorandum or articles are silent on variation, then dissentient minorities have special rights to object to the alteration.

They must satisfy certain conditions:

- The dissenters must hold no less than 15 percent of the issued shares of the class and must not have voted in favour of the resolution. They may then object to the variation within 21 days of the consent being given to the resolution. On occasions, their objections may be upheld by the courts (s 623 CA 2006).

'Bona Fide for the benefit of the company as a whole'

In addition to the various statutory restrictions considered above, the power to alter a company's articles is subject to the overriding principle that any alteration must be bona fide for the benefit of the company as a whole. One case that illustrates this is *Allen v Gold Reefs of West Africa Limited (1900).* In this case, the company's articles originally provided:

.....that the company shall have a first and paramount lien for all debts obligations and liabilities of any member to and towards the company upon all shares (not being fully paid) held by such member...........

The alteration proposed was to delete the words 'not being fully paid' to provide the company with a lien over any shares of a member where a debt was due from that member. The alteration was challenged. Lindley MR said as follows:

" Wide, however, as the language of s50 is (now section 21 of the CA 2006) the power conferred by it must, like all other powers, be exercised subject to those general principles of law and equity which are applicable to all powers conferred on majorities and enabling them to bind minorities stock. It must be exercised not only in the manner required by the law, but also bona fide for the benefit of the company as a whole, and it must not be exceeded. These conditions are always implied and are seldom, if ever, expressed. But, if they are complied with, I can discover no grounds for judicially putting other restrictions on the power conferred by the section and those contained within it"

.

In the instant case the Court of Appeal held that the power had been exercised *bona fide*.

The constitution as a contract

The courts have long held that a companies articles form a contract between a company and its members, and between the members themselves as in the case *Tavarone Mining Co (Pritchards Case) 1873.* Section 33(1) of the CA 2006 expands upon this by stating that:

The provisions of a company's constitution binds the company and its members to the same extent as if they were covenants on the part of the company and of each member to observe those provisions.

Accordingly, the company's constitution forms what is known as the 'statutory contract' and imposes obligations upon:

- the company when dealing with its members

- the members when dealing with the company
- the members when dealing with each other.

The statutory contract

The statutory contract created by s33 is unusual in that differs from a standard contract and is not subject to standard contractual rules. One cardinal rule that does apply to the statutory contract is the doctrine of privity of contract. The statutory contract is formed between a company and its members - persons not party to the contract are therefore not permitted to enforce the rules of the constitution. One case that demonstrates this is *Eley v Positive Government Security Life Assurance Co (1876)* where Eley, a solicitor drafted the defendant company articles, which were then registered. The articles provided that Eley would act as the company solicitor and could not be removed unless guilty of misconduct. Soon after, the company ceased to employ Eley and employed another solicitor and Eley alleged that the company had breached the terms of contract. Eley lost the case as Eley was not party to the statutory contract and therefore could not sue.

The contract between the company and its members

As the constitution forms a contract between the company and its members, it follows that both parties can enforce compliance with the terms of the constitution against the other. In the case of *Hickman v Kent or Romney Marsh Sheepbreeders Association (1915)* the company's articles provided that any dispute between it and a member should be referred for arbitration before any legal proceedings were initiated. The company purported to expel one of its members (Hickman) from its organisation but, instead of referring the dispute to arbitration, Hickman petitioned the High Court for an injunction restraining his expulsion. It was held that the articles formed a contract between the company and its members. The company was therefore permitted to enforce the terms of the articles and require disputes to be referred to arbitration. The High Court stayed Hickmans legal proceedings and he was subsequently expelled.

Member enforcing compliance of a term of the constitution

A member can enforce compliance of a term of the constitution against the company, as occurred in the case of *Pender v Lushington (1877)* where the company's articles provided that its members would have one vote for every ten shares up to a maximum of 100 votes. Consequently, members with over 1,000 shares would not have voting power commensurate to their shares.

To avoid this, members with over 1,000 shares (of which Pender was one) transferred some of their excess shares to several nominees, thereby unlocking the votes within them. The company's chairman (Lushington) refused to accept the nominees votes and Pender alleged that his votes were improperly rejected. Penders action succeeded. The shares were properly transferred and registered to nominees so refusing to accept their votes constituted a breach of the articles.

It is important to note that not all the terms of the constitution can be enforced this way. As Buckley LJ stated in *Blagood v Henderson's Transvaal Estates Ltd (1908):*

'...the purpose of the constitution is to define the position of the shareholder as shareholder and not to bind him in his capacity as an individual'.

*

The contract between members themselves

Just as the constitution forms a contract between the company and its members, so too does it form a contract amongst the members themselves. Accordingly, a breach of the statutory contract by a member can be enforced by another member, providing that the provision breached concerns a members rights.

In the case *Rayfield v Hands (1960)* the company's articles provided that, if a member wished to sell his shares, he should inform the directors, who would then purchase the shares between them. Rayfield wished to sell his shares and so notified the directors, but the directors refused to purchase his shares. The directors were all members of the company, and so Rayfield sought an order requiring the directors to purchase his shares.

The court ordered that the directors should purchase Rayfields shares. As the company was a quasi-partnership, the article provision affected the directors in their capacity as members. Accordingly, the provision concerned a membership right and formed part of the statutory contract.

The capacity of a company

As the company is a legal person, it can enter into contracts in much the same way as natural persons can. However, historically, the company's ability to enter into contracts was subject to a significant limitation. Prior to the passing of the CA 2006, all companies were required to state in their memoranda the objects or purposes for which the company was set up (this is known as the 'objects clause'). The objects clause serves to limit the contractual capacity of the company and if a company entered into a contract that was outside the scope of its objects clause, the company would be acting *ultra vires* (beyond ones powers) and the contract would be void. (*Ashbury Railway Carriage and Iron Co Ltd v Richie, 1875*)

This restriction on a company's capacity was introduced to protect a person who provided a company with capital, namely members and creditors. Such persons provided capital on the expectation that the company would pursue lines of business for which it was set up and not for activities outside of the company's remit.

The abolition of the requirement to include an objects clause

The requirement of an objects clause has been abolished by the CA 2006 (although companies can still include an objects clause if they wish and such companies will accordingly have unrestricted objects (CA 2006 s 31.(1)). For those companies incorporated before the passing of the CA 2006 a special resolution by company members can delete existing objects clauses, thereby acquiring unrestricted capacity

Alteration of the articles

As a company, or the markets that it operates in evolves, it may be necessary for it to alter its articles. Section 21 (1) of the CA 2006 provides that a company may amend its articles by passing a special resolution and, in certain cases, the courts also have the power to amend the articles. The Courts also recognise that if all members agree to an amendment to the articles, this will be effective even if no resolution was passed (*Can v Jones 1980*). It has also been held that agreement to amend can be inferred from the members conduct.

However, it should be noted that the ability to alter the articles is not limitless and both statute and common law impose restrictions on a company's ability to alter its articles.

Entrenched article provisions

A company cannot make its articles unalterable (*Walker v London Tramways co (1879*). However, the CA 2006 s.22 introduced the ability to entrench company article provisions, making it more difficult to alter. This could be done by requiring additional conditions to be met.

In order to prevent abuse the Act imposes several safeguards, including:

- Entrenchment will not prevent alteration where all of the members agree to an alteration, or where the court orders an alteration to be made.
- If a company wishes to entrench an article provision after the company has been formed, it can only do so with the agreement of all the members of the company.

****

4.3

Company Finance

The role and definition of the promoter

Although there is no statutory definition of a promoter, case law has developed a definition. In the case *Twycross v Grant (1877)* a promoter is defined as "one who undertakes to form a company with reference to a given project and to set it going, and who takes the necessary steps to accomplish that purpose."

In *Emma silver Mining Co v Grant (1879)* Lord Lindley stated that the term had no very definite meaning. Whether or not a person is a promoter is a question of fact. Promoters are quite often a company's first directors. The importance of establishing whether a person is a promoter lies partly in locating liability for acts done on behalf of or in connection with the company to be formed, for example, for statements in prospectuses. Not yet being in existence, the company cannot be liable. Promoters are not necessarily partners with each other (*Keith Spicer and Mansell (1970)*). Mainly it rests in deciding whether a person owes promoters fiduciary duty to the company.

Liability of a promoter

A promoter may become liable to third parties for misrepresentation or perhaps as the partner of another promoter under agency principles in partnership law. The traditional area of liability to the company is for breach of the fiduciary duties he owes it during his time of promotion.

Equity will not allow the promoter to take advantage of his privileged position in relation to the unborn company. He must make full disclosure to it, when formed, of his interest in any transaction and must not profit from his position without the company's free consent. Otherwise, he must account personally for profits made and hold on constructive trust any property received which came to him by virtue of being a promoter.

A promoter must disclose fully the extent and the nature of his interest and profit. The duty cannot be avoided by setting up a company with a board of directors which cannot and does not "exercise an independent and intelligent judgment on the transaction" and disclosing merely to that board.

In *Erlanger v New Sombrero (1878*) a syndicate headed by Erlanger, a French banker, acquired for £55,000 a lease of an island in the West Indies with phosphate mining rights. Erlanger then arranged for the syndicate to set up a company and to appoint its first directors, who were in reality puppets. The lease was sold, through a first party nominee, to the new company for £110,000 and within days of the company being established, the sale and purchase were ratified by the directors. The full details were not disclosed to members of the public who became shareholders. After the initial phosphate shipments proved unsuccessful, the true circumstances were revealed and the shareholders replaced the board of directors. It was held that the sale of the lease should be rescinded, the lease to be returned to the syndicate, which had to repay the purchase price to the company. The directors should not contribute to disadvantaging the shareholders.

Disclosure to the members would be effective if they acquiesced (*Lagunas Nitrate v Lagunas Syndicate (1899)* but not if an undue advantage over investors remained e.g. if the original members comprised or were otherwise under the influence of the promoters (*Gluckstein v Barnes) (1990).*

Remedies

The company may be able to rescind contracts entered into consequent upon non-disclosure or misrepresentation by a promoter unless one of the bars to rescission has become operative i.e. affirmation (unless this amounts to ratification of breach of duty by way of fraud on the minority: *Atwool v Merryweather (1867*); lapse of time; intervening third party rights; inability to make restitution integrum; and the courts discretion to award damages in lieu of rescission (Misrepresentation Act 1967 s2 (2)).

Breach of fiduciary duty may result in liability to account and/or imposition of a constructive trust. But promoters should be able to retain expenses incurred in acquiring property in such cases *(Bagnall v Carlton (1877))*.

Remuneration and expenses

The promoter does his work and incurs expenses by the nature of his position, at a time before the company has become legally capable of acting. The company cannot therefore enter into a binding contract with him to pay him, nor can the company when formed validly ratify such an agreement made when it did not exist (retrospectively validate). The practical solution is for promoters to secure the insertion in the articles of a provision enabling the directors to pay promoter's expenses plus reasonable remuneration, which provision will be valid if full disclosure is made.

Pre–incorporation contracts

Similar difficulties arise with contracts purporting to be made between the company and third parties before incorporation. The company will not normally be bound by preliminary contracts. Nor will the promoter be liable for breach of implied warranty of authority if no implication can be made, the third party knowing the true facts. The company may be liable apart from contract, to pay a reasonable amount for benefits actually received, or for conversion, for refusing to permit the third party to retake goods delivered. Rather than attempt to bind a company, a promoter might contract personally with a third party and forward benefits received to the company when formed, under a separate contract, subject to full disclosure.

He might make the company liable on his original contract by assignment.

Under The Companies Act 2006 s 21:
"A contract that purports to be made by or on behalf of a company at a time when the company has not been formed, has effect, subject to any agreement to the contrary, as one made with the person purporting to act for the company or as an agent for it, and he is personally liable on the contract accordingly."

The company's agent will be personally liable whether he purports to act on behalf of the company or signs the contract in the company's name alone, and he may be personally liable as both parties know the company is about to be formed and is not yet at the stage of being formed (*Phonogram v Lane (1981*). However, a person carrying out the affairs of an existing company under a new name which has not yet been registered will not be personally liable. Such a company is not one which has not been formed (*Oshkosh B'Gosh v Dan Marbel (1988).*

Trading certificate

A public company initially registered as such cannot commence business until the registrar receives a declaration that the nominal value of the allotted share capital meets the authorised minimum and, satisfied that it is, issues a trading certificate, (Companies Act 2006). This provision can be avoided by registering as a private company and registering as a public one.

Rules relating to payment for shares

The following matters should be checked where shares are to be issued by a public or private company:

- Does the company have sufficient authorized share capital for the issue?

This may be checked by looking at the company's memorandum. If necessary, the authorized capital may be increased.

- Do the directors have authority to allot the shares? See s.549 of the CA 2006. However, a private company may pass an elective resolution that s.549 is not to apply to that company, since, normally, authority under s.551 of the CA 2006 can only last for a maximum period of five years, unless renewed.
- Do pre-emption rights apply? Section 561 of the CA 2006 makes statutory provision for pre-emption on second and subsequent issues of shares. This may be excluded by a private company in its constitution. It may be excluded by both private and public companies by special resolution.

The rules for payment for shares are based upon the Second EC Directive on company law. They are incorporated into the CA 2006. Section 582 (1) of the CA 2006 requires that shares should be paid up in money or money's worth. Section 582 (1) of the CA 2006 provides that a public company cannot accept an undertaking from a person to do work or perform services for shares. Section 580 of the CA 2006 requires that shares cannot be issued at a discount. This applies to both public and private companies. There are, however, exceptions to this principle:

- Shares may be issued to underwriters at a discount of up to 10 per cent (s. 553 of the CA 2006)
- Shares may be issued in exchange for services that happen to be overvalued in a private company. Shares may not be issued in exchange for services in a public company.
- Shares may be issued in exchange for property which is overvalued in a private company. In a public company, there is a need for an independent expert valuation of the property concerned (s.593 CA 2006).

In a public company shares must be paid up at least one quarter of their nominal value plus the whole of any premium (CA 2006 s 586)

A public company cannot issue shares in exchange for a non- cash consideration which may be transferred more than five years from the date of allotment (s. 587 (1) CA 2006). Where shares are issued at a premium (that is above their nominal value) in either a public or private company, the whole of the premium is placed in a share premium account. This is treated as if it were ordinary share capital for most purposes. It cannot be used to pay up a dividend. However, it may be used to pay up a bonus issue of shares (s.610 CA 2006).

Small Business, Enterprise and Employment Act 2015: abolition of bearer shares

The Small Business, Enterprise and Employment Act 2015 received Royal Assent at the end of the last Parliament. The changes to bearer shares came into force in May 2015.

The key provisions

From 26 May 2015, the issue of new share warrants to bearer (also known as bearer shares) is not permitted. 26 May 2015 was the "commencement date" in a strict nine month timetable during which the holders of bearer shares had the right to surrender the warrants for conversion into registered shares. Companies with bearer shares in issue must have given various notices to the holders (including putting notices in the Gazette) informing them of their right to convert the bearer shares and the consequences of not doing so. The first notice must have been given within the period of one month following the commencement date.

Companies are obliged to apply to court to cancel bearer shares if they were not surrendered for conversion within the surrender period and pay into court the amount of share capital (nominal and premium) paid up on the bearer shares to be cancelled, plus any accrued dividends.

The supervision and control of investments

The Financial Services and Markets Act 2000 is an Act of Parliament that created the Financial Services Authority (FSA) as a regulator for insurance, investment business and banking, and the Financial Ombudsman Service to resolve disputes as a free alternative to the courts.

The Act was considerably amended by the Financial Services Act 2012 and the Bank of England and Financial Services Act 2016 and provides for a regime to protect investors. The Act provides statutory regulation and self-regulation by the market. Deposit taking businesses are regulated by the Banking Act 1987.

Dissolution of the FSA

In the aftermath of the financial crisis of 2008, government officials decided to revise the regulatory structure of the financial markets in the

U.K, passing the Financial Service Act 2012 and dissolving the FSA beginning in April 2013. In order to continue with the financial regulation needs, two new agencies were created: the Financial Conduct Authority and the Prudential Regulation Authority of the Bank of England.

Replacing the Financial Services Authority

The Financial Conduct Authority was established to regulate financial markets, providing protection for consumers and encouraging market integrity in the U.K. financial system, and facilitating competition in order to better serve the interests of consumers.[9] An independent public body, the Financial Conduct Authority, is funded by fees from the 58,000 firms the agency regulates. The Prudential Regulation Authority's responsibilities include the regulation of banks, credit unions, insurance firms, and investment firms. The Prudential Regulation Authority is part of the Bank of England, which in turn is owned by the government of the U.K. and is governed by Parliament.

The conduct of investment business

Subject to certain exceptions, the issue by or approval of an authorised person is necessary for the issue of an investment advertisement, which is an advertisement inviting people to enter into an investment agreement. An investment agreement is one involving dealing or advising on investments, though not involving employee share schemes, sales of shares in private companies carrying over 75 percent of voting rights or where the terms of the transaction are uniform for all such transactions in the investment. It is an offence knowingly or recklessly to make a misleading statement and to induce another to enter into, decline or refrain from exercising rights under an investment agreement, and without reasonably believing that he would not be so, to be involved in conduct creating a false impression as to the markets regarding investments and inducing a person to deal or refrain from dealing in those investments.

On the Secretary of States application, the court may issue an injunction to prevent contravention of these provisions and order restitution of benefits.

The Securities market

For securities listed, or to be listed on the Stock Exchange it is necessary to comply with the requirements of the Financial Services and Markets Act 2000 as amended. It empowers the Council of the Stock Exchange to make rules for this purpose, including provisions for rectification for non-compliance with the rules. These rules on Admission of Securities to Listing (The Yellow Book) contain continuing disclosure requirements. Additional to information required by the yellow book, the submitted listing particulars must contain such information as investors and their advisors would reasonably expect to make an informed assessment of the present and anticipated future rights and financial status of the securities and copies must be delivered to the registrar. Where listing particulars are to be published in connection with an application for listing, no other advertisement should be issued without the approval of the Stock Exchange.

A person acquiring relevant securities is entitled to be compensated by persons responsible for misleading particulars for loss suffered by reliance on the information unless they reasonably believed the statements or any detail were properly omitted but shareholders have no right to challenge cancellations of listing by judicial review *(R v Stock Exchange ex p Else (1992))*.

Unlisted securities

Unlisted shares are regulated by the Public Offers of Unlisted Securities Regulations 1995, which amended the Financial Services Act 1985.

Companies which are inadmissible to the Official Listed Market may apply for admission to the Alternative Investment Market (A.I.M.). A person may not be responsible for the issue of an advertisement offering securities to be admitted to an approved exchange (R.I.E.) without the approval of the exchange and the delivery to the Registrar of a prospectus. Similarly, a prospectus must be registered if the person is responsible for the issue of an advertisement for securities which is a primary offer (i.e. one inviting the initial subscribing for or underwriting of securities) or a secondary offer (i.e. by a person who has acquired shares from a purchaser) though the Secretary of State can make an exemption in cases where the general public is unlikely to require the relevant information.

Prospectuses must contain information prescribed by rules made by the Secretary of State and must contain all such information as investors and their professional advisors would reasonably expect to make an informed assessment of the present and anticipated rights and financial status of the securities. Advertisements may not be issued for securities in private companies.

Subsequent dealings

A subsequent purchaser of securities on a market governed by the above rules should be protected by the securities having to comply with the rules governing the market. In addition, the ordinary law will also provide protection.

Criminal penalties and civil liability

The Financial Services and Markets Act 2000, as amended b y the Financial

Services Act 2012, imposes a criminal liability for contravention of certain provisions. In addition it is an offence fraudulently or recklessly to induce someone to deposit money with any person (Banking Act 1987 s35).

Under the Theft Act 1968 s19 a company officer causing or contributing to publication of a statement knowing it to be false or misleading, with intent to deceive members or creditors, may be imprisoned.

Civil liability

Whether on a first issue of or a subsequent dealing with shares, a person relying on a false statement may have a remedy against the company or the individual responsible. The following rules also apply:

- A person subscribing for or purchasing shares on the basis of misrepresentation may rescind the contract. The remedy is subject to the usual bars and to the courts discretion to award damages in lieu.
- Damages for breach of contract are unlikely to be available against the company, mainly because of the rules governing the maintenance of capital and equal rights of membership, but such damages might be claimed from a transferor of shares.
- A person intending to rely and actually relying on a false representation made knowingly or without belief in its truth or recklessly may sue for damages for deceit, but a purchaser of shares in the market cannot sue if the representation is made as an inducement only to original subscribers unless it is also meant to mislead subsequent purchasers or is reactivated by a later statement.
- A defendant issuing a prospectus may be liable for damages for negligence to a subsequent purchaser of the companies shares on the unlisted securities market if the defendant intended subsequent purchasers to rely on the prospectus.

- At least before liquidation begins, a person is now no longer debarred from obtaining compensation from a company simply by virtue of his status as a holder for applicant, or subscriber for, shares. The Financial Services and Markets Act 2000, as amended by the Financial Services Act 2012 entitles a person to receive compensation for loss caused by false listing particulars and prospectus without having to relinquish his membership.
- A person acquiring securities on the basis of a false statement in listing particulars or a prospectus may claim compensation from persons responsible subject to defences of reasonable belief, ignorance or disclaimer.
- Damages for breach of statutory duty might be recoverable for omission of statutorily required details from prospectuses and courts have a discretion to award compensation in criminal proceedings.

The raising and maintenance of capital-statement of capital

Companies can raise capital to finance activities in a number of ways. The deferral of payments, through the acquisition of items on hire purchase or lease terms is one way. For the raising of substantial sums a company will need to obtain loans at preferential rates and will, more often than not, issue debentures, a form of promise to pay at a fixed rate of interest. Debentures can be attractive, depending on interest rates and tax advantages.

Companies will issue shares to raise capital. The definition of a share is contained within the Companies Act 2006 Section 540 (1) which defines a share as a 'share in the company's share capital'. This is a very sparse definition. Section 541 of the CA 2006 goes on to define a share as an item of property. A share has no physical existence (other than a share certificate) but confers a number of rights and obligations upon the holder and provides evidence of the existence of a contract between the shareholder and the company. One main fact to note is that share ownership does not give the shareowner a proprietary right over a company's assets, as was demonstrated in the case of *Borland's Trustee v Steel Bros and Co Ltd (1901).* The assets of a company belong to the corporate entity.

Share classes

Although most companies will have only one class of share, giving shareholders equal rights if the articles so authorise, a company is free to issue different classes of shares that confer differing rights on the shareholder.

Common examples of classes of share classes include:

- Ordinary shares-this is typical where the company has one class of share. Ordinary shareholders will typically have the right to vote at general meetings, the right to a dividend and the right to a share in surplus capital once all creditors have been paid and the company is wound up.
- Preference shares-these normally provide the holder with preferential claims on any surplus assets on winding up and/or entitle the owner to a predetermined fixed percentage dividend before anything is paid to the ordinary shareholder.
- Deferred shares-these shares typically provide that the holders are not entitled to a dividend or surplus assets on liquidation unless the ordinary shareholders have first been paid. These types of shares are very rarely issued these days.
- Redeemable shares-offer their holders temporary membership and

can be bought back by a company, usually upon the company or holders insistence.

The rights that are attached to the differing classes of shares are known as 'class rights. The Companies Act 2006 provides that a variation of class rights will only be effective if strict formalities are complied with. The courts distinguish between an alteration that affects a class right (which may amount to a variation) and an alteration that merely affects the enjoyment of a class right (which will not amount to a variation) This was illustrated in *White v Bristol Aeroplane Co Ltd (1953*).

Another important case is that of *Re Mackenzie and Co Ltd (1916)* where the company issued preference shares with a nominal value of £20 each The shares entitled the owners to a 4% dividend. However, the articles were amended to reduce the nominal value of the shares to £12, thereby reducing the dividend. The courts held that the alteration of the articles did not constitute a variation of class right, as the right remained the same, i.e. 4% paid up, it just affected the value of the share. Providing the right remained the same the fact that the alteration to the articles renders the right less valuable will prevent the alteration amounting to a variation.

Sections 630 and 631 of the CA 2006 provide that class rights can only be varied in one of two ways - if the company's articles contain a clause stating how class rights can be varied the variation will be valid if it complies with that clause. In addition if the company's articles do not contain such a clause, then a variation will be valid if it is approved in writing by the holders of three quarters in nominal value of the issued shares in question or approved by the passing of a special resolution at a meeting of holders of that share.

When voting on a variation to a class right the shareholders must exercise their vote for the dominant purpose of benefiting the class as a whole. This was illustrated in *British America Nickel Corp Ltd v MJ O'Brien Ltd (1927)*.

Share capital can be nominal, in other words the amount of money the company's memorandum entitles the company to raise. This can comprise issued share capital and un-issued share capital. Paid up capital represents the money actually received from shares sold and uncalled capital the amount owed.

Reserve capital is uncalled capital which the company has resolved only to call up on liquidation (Companies Act 2006). Shares may be issued at a premium (for more than their nominal value. If so the extra value must be transferred to a share premium account. Profits undistributed as income are kept in a reserve fund.

The liability of members of limited companies is limited to the nominal value of their shares. The nominal value of a public company's share capital must not be less than the authorised minimum, currently £50,000 (Companies Act 2006). One quarter of the value of all issued shares of a public company plus any premiums must be paid up. Shares must not be issued at a discount although debentures may.

A commission may be paid to underwriters. Shares may be allotted for money or moneys worth. If shares are allotted for moneys worth, the consideration for allotment must be valued by an expert, whose report must be made to the company and made available to the allotee. Capital cannot be returned to members by the company. In general a company cannot acquire its own shares, subject to some exceptions (CA 2006 s 658).

A company must not provide financial assistance to another to acquire its or its holding company's shares. There are unconditional exceptions to this principle in s 681 of the CA 2006:

a) a distribution of the company's assets by way of a dividend lawfully made, or a distribution in the course of a company's winding up;
b) an allotment of bonus shares;
c) a reduction of capital'
d) a redemption of shares;
e) anything done in pursuance of an order of the court sanctioning compromise or arrangement with members or creditors;
f) anything done under an arrangement made in pursuance of s 110 of the Insolvency Act 1986;
g) anything done under an arrangement made between a company and its creditors that is binding on the creditors by virtue of Part 1 of the Insolvency Act 1986.

There are further exceptions for public companies in s 682 of the CA 2006:

- Companies may reduce their capital by passing a special resolution to this effect and obtaining the consent of the court to the reduction (s 641 (1) of the CA 2006)
- If a public company suffers a serious loss of capital (net assets worth half or less of called up share capital) then a general meeting is required to be called to alert the shareholders within 28 days of discovering that the loss of capital has occurred. The meeting should take place within 56 days (s 656 of the CA 2006).

Dividends to shareholders

S 820 of the CA 2006 applies to 'every description of a company's assets to its members, whether in cash or otherwise'. Section 830 (2) of the CA 2006 provides that distributions can only be made out of profits available.

Section 831 of the CA 2006 applies to public companies. It requires the public company to maintain the capital side of its account in addition to having available profits. Therefore, if the company's net assets are worth less than the subscribed share capital plus undistributable reserves at the end of the trading period, that shortfall must first be made good out of distributable profits before a dividend can be made. If a dividend is wrongly paid, a member may be liable to repay it under s 847 of the CA 2006.

Directors who are responsible for unlawful distributions can be held liable for breach of duty. If the directors have relied on auditors in recommending a dividend, then the auditors may be liable.

Changes made by the The Small Business, Enterprise and Employment Act 2015

From June 2016, the Statement of Capital was simplified. The changes removed the requirement to show the amount paid up and unpaid on each share. Instead, director(s) now need to show the aggregate amount unpaid on the total number of shares. This figure is more useful for shareholders and creditors as it shows money which is still due to the company.

Before the SBEE 2015, a statement of capital needed to be provided every year on the annual return. Tt can now simply be shown on the confirmation statement that there have been no changes for that year. Director(s) will only need to provide a full statement of capital where changes have been made during the year. This will avoid having to provide duplicate information to the registrar.

Becoming a shareholder

A person can become a shareholder by subscribing to a company, as per its memorandum or having shares transferred to him by an existing shareholder. Companies must keep a register of the class and extent of the company's shareholdings. A share is an item of property and usually freely transferable. It gives the holder an interest in the company measured by a sum of money and entitling him to the rights contained in the articles of association. The value of the shares is generally their market price although a large number whose votes confer more may have a greater value.

Shareholders would usually have equal rights but companies can issue various classes of shares depending on the articles of association. The nominal value of a share specifies the maximum liability of a member of a company. A share in a public company must be paid up by at least 25 percent but the company can make calls on the holder up to its unpaid value.

The articles may give the company a lien over the share for calls on the holder up to the unpaid value. They often empower it to forfeit the share for unpaid calls. A lien is an equitable charge on the share. It becomes effective on a specified event. Thus, a different equitable interest of which the company has interest overrides a lien for debts due from the member (which it could set off against dividends) if the member only becomes indebted after the interest arose.

Under the Companies Act 2006, a company must, within two months of the allotment of shares or debentures or within two months of the lodging of a transfer of such securities, complete certificates, unless it is otherwise provided in their original issue, or it is not entitled to a certificate by virtue of the Stock Transfer Act 1982 (governing transfer of securities through a computerized system), or the allotment is to or the lodging of transfer is with a Stock Exchange nominee, or it is excused under The Uncertificated Securities Regulations 2001.

Transfer and transmission of securities

Formal documentation is usually necessary for the transfer of shares. However, the Secretary of State has been authorized to provide by regulation for title to securities to be evidenced and transferred without a written instrument. Otherwise, shares are freely transferable. Articles of association may restrict transfer in which case a refusal to register must be made within two months of its being lodged and must not be made in bad faith. The seller should transfer his share certificate to the buyer so that the company will readily consent to registering him as a member. If the seller only transfers part of his holding, he should deposit his share certificate with the stock exchange (if PLC) or the company, which will issue a certificate of transfer. Fully paid registered securities may be transferred by a stock transfer form approved under the Stock Transfer Act 1963. For a transfer to be registered by the company, unless the transfer is exempted by the Stock Transfer Act 1982, an instrument of transfer must be delivered to the company by either the transferor or the transferee.

Insider dealing

In recent years in particular, there has been controversy over the use of confidential information affecting the values of securities which is taken into account by the person in possession of it in deciding whether to buy or sell shares so as to make a profit. Insider trading, which is the use of knowledge by people on the inside of companies, is seen as commercially immoral. However, it is extremely difficult to prevent. The only real deterrent is to impose criminal sanctions and to increase the powers of the various regulatory bodies.

The Stock Exchange requires listed companies to adopt its Model Code for Securities Transactions for Directors and to secure compliance with it.

The Code warns directors to avoid insider dealing and requires them to refrain from dealing within two months before announcement of the company's results and to notify the company of such dealings.

The common law position in relation to insider dealing is based on *Percival v Wright (1902)*. Shareholders offered to sell shares to directors who knew their true value was greater because of an impending takeover bid, which information their confidential obligations to the company forbade them to disclose. For that reason, it was decided that the shareholders could not rescind the contract. The directors had no general duty to the shareholders to disclose price sensitive information to them. The Companies Act 2006 imposes a statuary prohibition by making it a criminal offence for a director to purchase an option to buy or sell quoted shares or debentures to a company in his group. This liability is extended to his wife and children unless they had no reason to believe he was a director.

The Companies Act also enacts requirements for disclosure and publicity. A director must disclose to the company details concerning the acquisition or disposal of any beneficial interest to himself, his wife or children in the group. If the shares are quoted the company must pass the information on to the stock exchange which may publish it. Any shareholders knowingly acquiring or disposing of a notifiable interest in voting shares (5 percent) in a public company must notify the company, which must keep a register of such interests.

There is also some administrative control. Under the CA 2006, the Secretary of State can appoint inspectors to investigate suspected breaches of the various areas of the Companies Act.

*

The Criminal Justice Act 1993 Part V

If an individual knowingly has information which is insider information, then he commits an offence if:

- Where the acquisition or disposal occurs on a regulated market, or where he acts or relies on a professional intermediary, he deals price affected securities.
- He encourages another person to deal in such securities knowing or having reasonable cause to believe that the acquisition or disposal occurs on a regulated market, or that the person dealing acts as or relies on a professional intermediary.
- He discloses the information to another person other than in the proper performance of his employment, office or profession.

The offence is punishable by a fine and/or up to seven years imprisonment. The Act has other provisions which provide for further sanctions and defenses.

Borrowing money

In addition to issuing shares a company can raise finance by borrowing money. This is usually done in the longer term by issuing debentures. A Company may create a debenture fund and issue certificates for parts of the fund. The rights of debenture holders are fixed by the contract governing the loan. This is incapable of being altered even if, along the way, the articles are altered. Any attempted alterations represent a breach of contract.

Charges

Any form of security interest (fixed or floating) other than an interest arising by operation of law, is for the purposes of the Companies Act 2006 (Registration of charges) known as a charge.

Fixed and floating charges

A company can create a fixed charge over part of its property for the amount of the loan. Where a fixed charge is inappropriate, i.e. over fluctuating assets, a floating charge over the whole or part of the company's assets can be made. The value of the charge as security depends on the assets in the company's possession at the time.

A charge must be registered within 21 days of its creation or the acquisition of property subject to it. The company and any officer at fault may be fined for non-registration. The court has discretion to extend a registration period. The Companies Act 2006 lists the registrable charges, including those on land, goods, intangible moveable property, i.e. intellectual property, for securing issues of debentures and floating charges. Not every charge is registrable, this very much depends on the nature of the charge.

Effects of non-registration

Where a registrable charge created by the company is not registered, the security is void against an administrator or liquidator of the company and any person who for value acquires an interest in or right over property subject to the charge where the beginning of insolvency proceedings, or acquisition occurs after the charge's creation. Where the registered particulars are not complete or accurate the charge is void, unless a court orders otherwise.

A registered charge, in general, gives the chargee a prior right, according to its terms, over a subsequent charge and any previous unregistered charges. But a subsequent floating charge can be created over a particular part of the assets covered by a previous floating charge over the wider category. A later fixed charge will gain priority over a previous floating charge covering the assets in question. In either case this is because floating charges are created with knowledge of the possibility of subsequent dealings with assets.

Unregistered chargees may prove in a company's liquidation as unsecured creditors and rank in priority as such. Fixed chargees can simply enforce their security according to the terms of the charge. The rights of floating chargees are, however, postponed to those entitled to preferential payments on a winding up.

A floating charge created within 12 months of the onset of insolvency (24 months if in favour of a person connected with the company) or between the presentation of a petition for and the consequent making of an administration order is, unless the charge is not connected with the company and the company was solvent immediately after its creation, void except to the amount of any consideration provided simultaneously with or subsequent to its creation, plus interest.

****

4.4

Company Management-The Role of Directors

Definition of a director

The Companies Act 2006 does not provide a clear definition of what a director is. However, it does state who is included within the office of director with s 250 of the Act stating that a director includes 'any person occupying the position of director, by whatever name called'. The word 'person in s 250 indicates that a director can be a natural person or a body corporate. However, there are concerns regarding the use of corporate director with the government preferring individual directors as being more transparent and accountable.

A good example of a case that highlights issues that arise with establishing liability in cases involving corporate directors is that of *Revenue and Customs Commissioners v Holland (2010*) in which the defendant was able to avoid liability through a complex web of 42 companies, all of which has one common corporate director.

The Small Business, Enterprise and Employment Act 2015 largely abolishes corporate directors by inserting s 156A into the CA 2006 which provides that '[a] person may not be appointed a director of a company unless the person is a natural person'.

Shadow directors

A person who has neither been appointed as a director, nor acts as a director, may be treated as a director if he is a 'person in accordance with whose directions or instructions the directors of the company are accustomed to act' (CA 2006 s 251(1)) other than where that advice is given in a professional capacity. (CA 2006 s 251(2)). Such a person is known as a 'shadow director'. In practice, determining whether a person is a shadow director can be difficult. In several cases, the courts have provided guidance. Firstly *The Secretary of State for Trade and Industry v Deverell (2001)* and secondly *Ultraframe (UK) Ltd v Fielding (2005*). A summary of the findings of these eases are:

- it is not necessary for the shadow director to give directions/instructions over the whole field of the company's activities;
- whether a communication amounts to a direction/instruction is to be interpreted objectively;
- it is not necessary to show that the *de jure* directors acted in a subservient manner A *de jure director* (meaning a director from law) is a director who is properly appointed to the board and registered with Companies House.
- it is insufficient that some of the *de jure* directors follow the directions/instructions-it must be demonstrated that a governing majority of the board were accustomed to following the directions/instructions;
- as the *de jure* directors must be accustomed to the directions/instructions, it follows that, initially, a person who gives directions/instructions will not be a shadow director; and
- the mere giving of directions/instructions is insufficient-it must also be shown that the directors acted on such directions/instructions.

Historically, the courts held that a shadow director could not also be a *de facto* director and vice versa. A *de facto* director (meaning a director in fact or in reality) is someone who has not been properly appointed and notified to Companies House as a director but who nevertheless acts as a director and holds themselves out to third parties as a director. Sometimes (but not always) they will have the word 'director' as part of a job title. However, the courts have now acknowledged that a person can be both a de fact director and shadow director. This was held in *Secretary of State for Business, Innovation and Skills v Chohan (2013).*

Appointment of directors

All private companies must have at least one director and every public company must have at least two directors. (CA 2006 s 154). The directors are appointed on incorporation and thereafter, the powers to appoint directors will be a matter for the articles, but where the articles are silent on this issue the power to appoint directors is vested in the members and is usually exercised by ordinary resolution, or by a decision of the directors.

Whilst anybody can act as a director, certain types of person are prohibited by statute from being appointed (e.g. a company's auditor)

Diversity

The need to improve board diversity has long been recognised among larger companies. Lord Davies 2011 report *Women on Boards* highlighted the issue.

The report recommended that FTSE 100 companies should aim for a minimum of 25% female representation by 2015. This was successfully reached and a new voluntary goal has been set by the Hampton-Alexander Review which is that the FTSE 350 companies should aim for 33% female representation by 2020. The outcome is still awaited as we write in 2021.

The Board of directors

The directors of a company are collectively known as the 'board'. Much of a company's power is concentrated in its board, which exercises its powers in board meetings (not to be confused with general meetings of the company). the procedures relating to board meetings are contained within its articles and decisions of directors are only valid if made at a board meeting unless all the directors agree to, or acquiesce to, the decision. This was demonstrated in Charterhouse Investment Trust Ltd v Tempest Diesels Ltd (1986)

The law does not require that all directors must be present at a board meeting but decisions of directors will only be valid if a quorum can be obtained. The make up of the quorum will be contained in the articles.

The duties of a director

Director's duties can be split into two parts – the director's duty of care and skill and the director's fiduciary duties. The rules governing directors duties are now codified in the CA 2006 s171-177.

The CA 2006 provides that:

- The matters to which the directors of a company are to have regard in the performance of their functions include the interests of the company employees in general as well as the interests of the members.
- Accordingly, the duties of this section imposed on the directors of a company is owed by them to the company (and the company alone) and is enforceable in the same way as any other fiduciary duty owed to a company by its directors.

Section 247 of the Companies Act 2006 permits a company to make payments to its employees on ceasing to trade or on transferring the business. Previously, this had been ultra vires where there was no business that was capable of being benefited.

The duty of care and skill

The duty of care and skill, owed to a company by its directors has traditionally been interpreted in such a way that places a very modest burden on the shoulders of its directors. However, under the CA 2006 the general duties of directors has been placed on a statutory basis. This can be found in s 170 of the CA 2006. Section 170 (3) states that:

....the general duties are based on certain common law rules and equitable principles as they apply in relation to directors and have effect in place of those rules and principles as regards the duties owed to a company by a director.

S. 170 (4) of the CA 2006 states that:

The general rules shall be interpreted and applied in the same way as common law rules or equitable principles, and regard shall be had to the corresponding common law rules and equitable principles in interpreting and applying the general duties.

The leading case is *Re City Equitable Fire and Insurance Co Ltd (1925).* In this case there had been a serious shortfall of funds and the managing director was convicted of fraud. The liquidator also wanted to implicate three other directors in the fraud. The judge in the case, Romer J set out three basic propositions which constituted the duties of directors:

" A director need not exhibit in the performance of his duties a greater degree of skill than may reasonably be expected from a person of his knowledge and experience. A director of a life insurance company, for instance, does not guarantee that he has the skill of an actuary or a physician. In the words of Lord Lindley, MR, " If the directors act within their powers, if they act with such care as is reasonably to be expected from them having regard to their knowledge and experience, and if they act honestly for the benefit of the company they represent, they discharge both their equitable and their legal duty to the company" (*Lagunas Nitrate Co v Lagunas Syndicate (1899).*

Although the above statement, summing up director's duties, puts forward the notion of a somewhat limited duty of care there are indications that the nature of care and skill is changing somewhat. Section 214 of the Insolvency Act 1986 provides for an objective standard of care in relation to directors and shadow directors where the company is insolvent and they ought to have recognised that fact. In *Norman v Theodore Goddard (1991)*, Hoffman J accepted that the standard applied in s214 applied generally in relation to directors. The second proposition put forward by Romer J in Re City Equitable relates to the attention that has to be paid to the affairs of the company and states:

" A director is not bound to give continuous attention to the affairs of a company. His duties are of an intermittent nature to be performed at periodic board meetings and meetings of any committees of the board upon which he happens to be placed. He is not, however, bound to attend all such meetings, though he ought to attend whenever, in the circumstances, he is reasonably able to do so."

The third proposition set out by Romer J is as follows:

" In respect of all duties that, having regard to all the exigencies of business and the articles of association, may properly be left to some official, a director is, in the absence of grounds for suspicion, justified in trusting that official to perform such duties honestly."

Fiduciary duties

The term "fiduciary duties" describes the other duties owed by directors to their company. Both statute and case law heavily govern this area. While, as seen above, there is little expectation of a director in relation to care and skill, there is great expectation in relation to honesty and integrity.

The Companies Act 2006 s 182 (1) requires directors to make disclosures. There is a requirement for a director to disclose any interest that he has between himself and the company. The provision also covers connected persons, such as family, another company with which the director is associated controlling more than 20 percent of the voting capital, a trustee of a trust whose beneficiaries include the director himself or a connected person, a partner of a director or of a connected person. The Companies Act 2006 further elaborates. A shadow director is also required to comply with The CA 2006 s 182 as well as a director. Disclosure should be to the full board. Mere compliance with the section does not entitle a director to keep any profits. In order to keep any profits, the director must be able to rely on a provision in the company's constitution or have his retention of the profit ratified by the company in general meeting.

Some contracts require prior authorisation by the company in general meeting. Section 190 (1) of the Companies Act 2006 applies to what are termed substantial property transactions. If the director or a shadow director is to sell or purchase from the company one or more non-cash assets that are substantial, then prior approval in general meeting is needed. A transaction is substantial if the market value of the asset exceeds the lower of £100,000 or 10 percent of the company's net asset value.

Transactions worth less than £2,000 are never substantial. Section 190

(1) also applies to connected persons.

Section 323 prohibits a director or shadow director of a company from buying options on shares or debentures of the company or its holding company or its subsidiaries. The penalty for infringement is a fine or imprisonment. The Companies Act 2006 requires a director or shadow director to notify the company of any interest in the shares or debentures of the company or subsidiaries.

A director must not place himself in a position where his interests conflict with the company's interests. The leading case here is *Regal (Hastings) v Gulliver 1942*. Regal owned a cinema in the town of Hastings and wished to acquire two other cinemas in the area, at the suggestion of the company solicitor. The company did not have funds for the purchase and it was suggested that the solicitor, the directors and the company itself should put up the money. This was successful, improving the finances of the company. The company was sold as a going concern, to a purchaser who bought the company's shares. The company, under new management then began an action against the erstwhile directors for damages in respect of the profit that they had made on the sale of their shares. It was established that the directors had acted from prudent financial motives and there was no damages due. The House of Lords thought different and held that the directors had acquired the shares in exploitation of their position as directors. They had not obtained the consent of the company and had to reimburse the company.

The same principle has been established in later decisions. However, not every case of a director taking an opportunity that has come by way of the company will be committing a breach of duty. If the company has turned down the opportunity without any proper influence from the director and the director takes it up subsequently, there is no reason why the director cannot retain the profit. A number of high profile cases have borne this out, for example, *Peso Silver Mines v Cropper, (1966) and Island Export Finance Limited v Umunna (1986).*

A related area is the question of competition. To what degree is the director of a company able to compete with the company of which he is a director, either through another company or a partnership or trading as a sole trader. The case of *London and Mashonaland Exploration Co Ltd v New Mashonaland Exploration Co Ltd (1891)* has found that it does not involve a breach of duty. However, in spite of the above case, the position of a director competing against his company is untenable. If a director is director of two companies in this situation then clearly he would be in breach of duty to one or another company.

There are areas of law which indicate that competition is not permissible. In *Hivac Ltd v Park Royal Scientific Instruments Ltd (1946) s*enior employees engaged on sensitive work in wartime were not able to compete with their employer. However, the fact that it was wartime makes this decision rather special. Thus, director's powers must be exercised in a fiduciary way. The overall duty is one of trust, which must be borne out by integrity.

Directors personal liability

Directors may be liable in contract for:

- Breach of warranty of authority.
- A collateral guarantee.
- Pre–incorporation contracts under The Companies Act 2006.

Tort

Directors may be liable in tort:

- For fraud in relation to listing particulars and prospectuses.

- For negligent misstatement in relation to listing particulars and prospectuses.
- For a breach of personal duty and care.

Statute

Directors may be liable under statute:

- For misstatements or omissions in listing particulars (s.150 of the Financial Services Act 1986) as amended.
- For improper use of the company name (The Companies Act 2006).

Directors may be liable under other legislative provisions including:

- Section 213 of the Insolvency Act 1986 in relation to fraudulent trading.
- Section 214 of the Insolvency Act 1986 in relation to wrongful trading.
- Section 216 of the Insolvency Act 1986 in relation to Phoenix Companies under prohibited names.
- Under other legislation particularly health and safety and the environment, such as the Health and Safety at Work Act 1974, the Control of Pollution Act 1974 and the Water Industry Act 1991.

Limiting liability of directors

The Companies Act 2006 prohibits the exclusion of directors from liability but makes it possible to provide insurance for directors. The Companies Act 2006 allows courts to relieve directors of liability if thought that they have acted reasonably and honestly.

The role of the company secretary

The Company secretary is one of the principal officers of the public company. As stated there is now no requirement for a private company to have a secretary. The company secretary is the agent through whom most of the company's administrative work is done.

The following are some of the company secretary's responsibilities:

- Preparation and keeping of minutes (s248 CA 2006)
- Dealing with share transfers and issuing share and debenture certificates
- Keeping and maintaining the register of members and debenture holders s113 (1) and 743 (6) of the CA 2006..
- Keeping and maintaining the registers of directors and secretarys 804 2006 CA.
- The registration of charges and maintaining the company's register of charges. S 860 to 876 CA 2006.
- Keeping and maintaining the register of directors share interests s 809 2006 CA.
- Keeping the records of the director's service contracts s 328 CA
- The collation of directors interests that have to be disclosed.
- Keeping and maintaining the register of material share interests. S 808 (1) CA 2006
- Sending notices of meetings, copies of accounts etc.
- Keeping the company's constitution up to date.
- Preparation and submission of the annual return.
- Filing of returns and documents.
- Preparation of returns required by government departments.
- Witnessing documents together with a director.
- Payment of dividends and the preparation of dividend warrants.

These are most of the duties but there are other matters, such as employment issues, which may become the responsibility of the company secretary. In a Public Limited Company the Companies Act 2006 requires the secretary to hold a recognised professional qualification before taking up such a post.

The role of company auditors

Every company must appoint auditors, except dormant companies and private companies which are exempt from the audit requirements (Companies Act 2006). An auditor may be removed by ordinary resolution of the company. Special notice must be served and the auditor can make representation and seek compensation.

An auditor may resign from office under the Companies Act 2006, circulating a statement as to why and setting out any irregularities which he thinks should be brought to the attention of the board. When an auditor does deposit a statement of circumstances, which he wishes to bring to the attention of members or creditors, he may deposit a requisition with the statement requiring the company to call an extraordinary general meeting. The auditor who is removed or who has resigned may attend the meeting to appoint new auditors. The auditors have a duty to audit company accounts (s485-520 of the Companies Act 2006). The auditor has to be particularly rigorous.

The duties of an auditor have been outlined by Lord Denning:

- First the auditors should verify the arithmetical accuracy of the accounts and the proper vouching entries in the books.
- Secondly, the author should make checks to test whether the accounts mask errors or even dishonesty.
- Thirdly, the auditor should report on whether the accounts give to the shareholders reliable information respecting the true financial position of the company (Lord Denning in *Foment (Sterling Area Ltd v Selsden Fountain Pen Company Limited (1958))*

Auditors liabilities

An auditor is required to investigate suspicious circumstances. In *Re Thomas Gerrard (1967)* it was noted that:

"The standards of reasonable care and skill are from the expert evidence more exacting than those which prevailed in 1896" (*Re Kingston Cotton Mill)*.

In this case, in addition to an overstatement of stock, there had been fraudulent practice in changing invoice dates to make it appear that client's owed money within the accounting period when, in fact, it was due outside of it, and to make it appear that suppliers were not yet owed money for goods when such liability did exist. The auditors in this case were held liable. Liability may arise in contract. The auditor will be liable for failing to perform properly what he has undertaken to do. The other party to the contract – the company – is the only person who can sue the company under this head of liability.

An auditor may be liable in negligence to his client or in the tort of negligent misstatement to third parties. An auditor may also be liable for a winding up for misfeasance or breach of duty to the company (section 212 of the Insolvency Act 1986). Where this has occurred the court will order compensation as it thinks appropriate.

The Small Business, Enterprise and Employment Act 2015

The Small Business, Enterprise and Employment Act received Royal Assent in March 2015. Significant changes have been made to the adminsitartion of companies in particular the maintenance of records. Outlined below are the main changes, although not in date order.

People with significant control (PSC) register

Companies, LLPs and SEs need to keep a register of people with significant control ('PSC register') from **6 April 2016**. A PSC is anyone in a company, LLP or SE who meets one or more of the conditions listed in the legislation.

This is someone who:

- owns more than 25% of the company's shares
- holds more than 25% of the company's voting rights
- holds the right to appoint or remove the majority of directors
- has the right to, or actually exercises significant influence or control
- holds the right to exercise or actually exercises significant control over a trust or company that meets one of the first 4 conditions.

Protecting PSC information -

From 6 April 2016 The PSC's usual residential address won't be available on the public register, and the day of birth will be suppressed. All other PSC information will be available on the public register, much like directors and members details are currently held. In some exceptional cases, it may be that a PSC is at risk of violence or intimidation. For example, this might be because they're linked to a company that might be targeted by activists due to its activities. In these cases, directors may apply to have their details protected, so they aren't available to credit reference agencies.

If protection is granted the directors still need to send PSC information to companies house when it's required (for example on the confirmation statement), and the information will still be available to the police.

*

Filing PSC information

This information now needs to be filed with companies house on incorporation and updated when directors submit later 'confirmation statements'. It's a criminal offence to not provide this information.

Confirmation statement - June 2016

From 30 June 2016, the annual return was replaced. Instead, directors now file a confirmation statement at least once a year. They need to check and confirm the company information that is held for the company and let companies house know if there are any changes. To complete the confirmation statement a director needs to:

- check the information held on the registered office, directors and location of registers – if there's been any changes, there is the need to complete a separate form before filing the confirmation statement
- check and if necessary update the shareholder information, statement of capital and the standard industry classification (SIC code)
- check and confirm the record is up to date
- pay the fee to file online or by post

The due date for the confirmation statement is usually a year after the incorporation of the company or the date directors filed the last annual return.

Statement of capital – from June 2016

As stated in the previous chapter dealing with shareholders, statement of capital will be simplified. The changes remove the requirement to show the amount paid up and unpaid on each share. Instead, directors now need to show the aggregate amount unpaid on the total number of shares. This figure is more useful for shareholders and creditors as it shows money which is still due to the company. Directors can now simply show on the confirmation statement that there have been no changes for that year. Directors will only need to provide a full statement of capital where changes have been made during the year. This will avoid having to provide duplicate information to the registrar.

Accelerated strike-off – from 10 October 2015

The time it takes to strike a company off the register if it's not carrying on business or operation has been reduced. The accelerated strike-off process aims for the right balance between removing a defunct company from the register and allowing creditors time to register an objection. Under old legislation, if no objection was received, the company was struck off not less than 3 months after publication of a notice in The Gazette. Under the new timescales, the company is struck off not less than 2 months from publication of the Gazette notice.

Date of birth -from 10 October 2015

It's always been a requirement of the Companies Act 2006 for directors to provide a full date of birth. Companies House is now giving more protection by suppressing the day of birth on the public record. The full date of birth still needs to be provided to Companies House, but won't be shown in full on their data products or on images or new filings. The full date of birth will only be disclosed in exceptional circumstances (for example to credit reference agencies, or to the police). This procedure is similar to how residential addresses are protected.

Consent to act as an officer -from 10 October 2015

For newly appointed officers, companies house has added a statement to the relevant appointment and incorporation forms (paper and electronic) that the person has consented to act in their relevant capacity. Companies are required to agree to this statement. This replaced the previous consent to act procedure of providing a signature on paper forms and personal authentication on electronic filings.

As part of this, Companies House wrote to all newly appointed directors to make them aware that their appointment has been filed on the public register and explained their general legal duties. See also the new director disputes procedure.

Director disputes -from April 2016

This measure provides a simpler way to get falsely appointed directors' details removed from the register. If an appointed director didn't consent to act in their appointment, they can apply to have the notification of their appointment removed from the register. When an application is received, the company in question will be asked to provide evidence the director 'consented to act' in their appointment. If sufficient evidence isn't provided, this will result in the director's appointment being removed from the register. This proof might be that the company has retained a statement from the director that they have 'consented to act'.

Registered office address (ROA) disputes - from April 2016

This will help when a company is using an address for its registered office without authorisation. Where a complaint is received that a company or a limited liability partnership (LLP) is wrongly using an ROA, Companies House will investigate. If the registrar is satisfied that a company or LLP is not entitled to use an address, they'll be able to change the ROA of that company or LLP to the 'default' address.

Default addresses

The registrar can nominate a default address for each jurisdiction (England and Wales, Scotland or Northern Ireland). Any post sent to a company at the default address will be held at the relevant Companies House office. Companies House offices won't receive packages or bailiff visits for companies whose ROA has been changed to a default address.

Evidence of ROA

Acceptable evidence that a company has the right to use an ROA might be a document that shows it's a building the company owns, one they rent, or an agreement from the owner that they are allowed to use the address as an ROA. The registrar will consider any evidence sent and advise both the company and the applicant of the outcome. If the registrar can't come to an appropriate decision, it may be referred to the courts.

Company registers – from June 2016

Private companies will be able to opt to keep certain information on the public register, instead of holding their own statutory registers.

This will apply to registers of:

- members
- directors
- secretaries
- directors' residential addresses
- people with significant control (PSC)

This is voluntary, and a company can continue holding its own registers if preferred.

Directors misconduct - from October 2015

From October 2015, new offences were added to the current regime that individuals can also be disqualified for.

These are:

- 'disqualification for certain convictions abroad'
- 'disqualification of persons instructing unfit directors'
- The conduct of people instructing unfit directors can also be taken into consideration. If a director has been deemed unfit due to someone exercising control over the director, they could also be disqualified.

Bearer Shares-from 26 May 2015

Share warrants to bearer (known as 'bearer shares') were abolished. These were shares issued by a company, but assigned to a warrant, rather than a registered owner. The warrant allowed the bearer holder to claim any ownership or rights attached to those shares. As the owner's details did not need to be entered into the register of members, it was sometimes difficult to establish ownership of those shares. All shares must now have a designated owner.

If a company has bearer shares

If this affects a company, the bearer shareholders have 9 months (from 26 May 2015) to surrender their warrants voluntarily. These can then be converted into registered shares, and the bearer shareholder will enter their name into the register of members. A company should take steps to ensure bearer shareholders know their rights to surrender their warrants, and the consequences if they don't.

Consequences of not surrendering share warrants

If the share warrants haven't been surrendered within 7 months (from 26 May 2015), all rights are automatically suspended. Bearer shareholders can't vote or claim dividends from the shares. They will also be unable to transfer the warrant, as any transfers made after the 7 month period are void. If the share warrants haven't been surrendered within 9 months, the company has to make an application to the court to have them cancelled.

****

Chapter 5

Business Law-Intellectual Property

Introduction and Summary

Intellectual property is an area of law which is complex and rapidly changing. *Intellectual property rights* is the overall term used to describe the various rights that afford protection to creative and innovative endeavour. There are several main rights, described in more detail throughout the book, including the following:

- Patents. This is a statutory property right that gives the patent holder the exclusive right to use certain inventions. A patent can be obtained by application to the Intellectual Property Office. Many people or organisations will use an agent to obtain a patent but it can be done on a do-it-yourself basis more cheaply. A patent will typically last up to twenty years.
- Trademarks. A registered trademark is, like a patent, a statutory right and gives the exclusive right to use a distinctive sign in relation to either a product or service. The sign can be a name, a symbol, aroma, jingle etc. A trademark can be obtained via an application to the Intellectual Property Office. A trademark may be renewed indefinitely. Again, agents are used in the process but it can be carried out on a DIY basis.
- Copyright and moral rights. Copyright is a statutory right subsisting in original literary, dramatic, musical and artistic works and in sound recordings, films, broadcasts, cable programs and

the typography of published editions. Owners of copyright will have economic rights within their works, including the important right to prevent unauthorised copying and adaptation. Moral rights are rights that authors retain in their works, irrespective of who owns the economic rights. Copyright varies according to its life span, usually the life of an author plus seventy years. Moral rights are personal to the author and arise automatically.

- Breach of confidence. The action for breach of confidence can be used to protect certain categories of confidential information, such as commercial information against unauthorised use or disclosure. The origins are contractual or equitable and the duration is indefinite or until the information is released into the public domain.
- Passing off. Goodwill is a form of property constituting the markets perception of the value and quality of a business and its products. This can be protected against interference or damage by what is known as 'passing off'. This is a tort that may be used in preventing a trader from making misrepresentations, which damages the goodwill of another trader. Again, this is indefinite but ceases when the goodwill of a particular enterprise ceases.
- Design law. Certain aspects of the appearance of articles, aesthetic or non-aesthetic are protected via a combination of the registered design system, the design right (an unregistered design system) and aspects of copyright law. A registered design is the exclusive right to use certain features of a range of products. A design right is the right to prevent the copying of aspects of the shape or configuration of an article, such as a certain type of car. An unregistered design right will last up to fifteen years. A registered design, which can be granted upon application to the

Intellectual Property Office, can last up to twenty-five years, but must be renewed at 5 yearly intervals.

Infringement of intellectual property rights

The holder of an intellectual property right has to be in a position to enforce his or her rights if there is found to be an infringement of the IPR. In the main, civil remedies are available. However, certain infringements constitute a criminal offence. Remedies available after trial are known as final remedies. Interim remedies are also available, which are remedies awarded during trial. In relation to final remedies, financial remedies may take the form of damages or an account of profits.

Examples of IP infringement include when someone:

- Uses, sells or imports a patented product or process
- Uses all or some of another's work under copyright without their permission
- Makes, offers or sells someone's registered design for commercial gain
- Uses a trade mark that's identical or similar to one another has registered

The following steps can be taken:

- Get the other party to stop using IP or come to an agreement with them, for example license the IP.
- Use mediation or another type of dispute resolution.
- Take legal action if parties can't resolve the dispute by other means.

Report IP crime

It can be a criminal offence to copy or use copyright material and registered trademarks and designs without permission. Suspected IP crime should be reported to Trading Standards by contacting Citizens Advice.

Get help and advice

An intellectual property (IP) professional can give legal advice on a dispute, or act on someone's behalf. An IP professional can be found through organisations including:

- The Chartered Institute of Patent Attorneys
- The Chartered Institute of Trademark Attorneys
- The Law Society (England and Wales)
- The Law Society of Scotland
- The Law Society of Northern Ireland

Contact the Intellectual Property Office (IPO)

A person can contact IPO for:

- an opinion on whether their patent or supplementary protection certificate is being infringed - it costs £200
- to start legal proceedings over some types of IP dispute
- general advice on IP

Come to an agreement

If someone is using a person's IP without their permission they can contact them and ask them to stop.

Make a deal

A person can offer to make a deal with the other party, which is usually cheaper and quicker than going to court. They can also come to a Coexistence Agreement with someone who has a similar trade mark. A coexistence agreement is a legal agreement whereby two parties agree to trade in the same or similar market using an identical or similar trade mark.

Use a mediator

A person can use a mediator if they can't come to an agreement over an intellectual property (IP) dispute. Mediation is a way of resolving disputes without going to court. It's cheaper and quicker than taking legal action and the outcome is usually beneficial to all parties. Mediators provide an independent view on a dispute. They can't make a decision for another person, but they can help to find a solution that both parties accept. Discussions with a mediator are confidential and can't be used in court later if the dispute isn't resolved. Mediation can be used in most IP disputes including those about infringement, licensing, and patent entitlement.

IPO mediation service

The Intellectual Property Office (IPO) has its own mediation service. What someone will pay for mediation depends on how much time they need and the approximate value of the claim.

Other mediators

Civil Mediation Council (England and Wales)-Scottish Mediation Network-Northern Ireland Mediation.

Take legal action

A person can file legal proceedings either through the Intellectual Property Office (IPO) or through the courts. Some types of proceedings can only be filed through one or the other. A court will expect a person to have tried to resolve their dispute - possibly using mediation before starting legal proceedings.

File through the courts in England and Wales

The court to go to depends on the nature, complexity and value of a claim.

Claims below £10,000

A person can use the Intellectual Property Enterprise Court (IPEC) small claims track if their claim is for less than £10,000 and for infringement of one of the following:

- copyright
- passing off
- trade marks
- breach of confidence
- unregistered design rights

A lawyer isn't needed to use the IPEC small claims track.

Claims up to £500,000

A person can take a case for any IP right to the Intellectual Property Enterprise Court (IPEC) if they do not wish to claim more than:

£50,000 for legal costs

£500,000 for damages

If someone is claiming more than £500,000 in damages

They use the Chancery Division of the High Court of England and Wales - there are no limits to legal costs or damages they can claim.

File through the courts in Scotland

Court of Session should be used if a claim is complex or valuable - there are no limits to legal costs or damages one can claim.

File through the courts in Northern Ireland

A person can use the Chancery Division of the High Court of Northern Ireland if their claim is complex or valuable - there are no limits to legal costs or damages one can claim.

Artificial Intelligence and intellectual property rights-Overview

In the last few years, there has been a rash of court cases concerning intellectual property and Artificial intelligence, straddling all areas of IP, such as copyright, trademarks, patents, design law and the area of music. Most cases concern unauthorized use of some areas of IP by creators of artificial intelligence. The generation of contents that bypasses the rights of the original creators.

In particular, the debate on artificial intelligence and intellectual property is in the limelight thanks to the recent news from jurisdictions such as Australia and South Africa concerning patent applications for an AI-generated invention.

In chapter 2, dealing with patents, we have outlined a key case which changed the assumptions in this area. This is the case of Emotional Perception AI Ltd v Comptroller General [2026].

Government review of AI

Sir Patrick Vallance completed a review on pro-innovation regulation for digital technologies. It recommended that the government should clarify the relationship between intellectual property and generative AI. The government published a response on 15 March 2023, accepting this recommendation.

The government is now working with users and rights holders on a code of practice on copyright and AI. The code of practice aims to make licenses for data mining more available. It will help to overcome barriers that AI firms and users currently face and ensure there are protections for rights holders. This ensures that the UK copyright framework promotes and rewards investment in creativity. It also supports the ambition for the UK to be a world leader in research and AI innovation.

The Intellectual Property Office invited industry representatives from the technology, creative and research sectors to form a working group. These sectors will help to ensure a balanced and pragmatic code of practice. It will enable both the AI and creative sectors to grow in partnership.

Detail of outcome-The Government stated:

The Government sought evidence and views on a range of options on how AI should be dealt with in the patent and copyright systems. This response sets out the conclusions of that process.

Three specific areas were covered:

1. Copyright protection for computer-generated works (CGWs) without a human author.
2. Licensing or exceptions to copyright for text and data mining (TDM), which is often significant in AI use and development.
3. Patent protection for AI-devised inventions.

For computer-generated works, we plan no changes to the law. There is no evidence at present that protection for CGWs is harmful, and the use of AI is still in its early stages. As such, a proper evaluation of the options is not possible, and any changes could have unintended consequences. We will keep the law under review and could amend, replace or remove protection in future if the evidence supports it.

For text and data mining, we plan to introduce a new copyright and database exception that allows TDM for any purpose. Rights holders will still have safeguards to protect their content, including a requirement for lawful access.

For AI-devised inventions we plan no change to UK patent law now. Most respondents felt that AI is not yet advanced enough to invent without human intervention. But we will keep this area of law under review to ensure that the UK patent system supports AI innovation and the use of AI in the UK. We will seek to advance AI inventorship discussions internationally to support UK economic interests. There are several important cases ongoing which are important in the context of AI and IP and which are worth mentioning..

Two important judgements handed down in 2025 were *Ayinde v London Borough of Haringey* and *Al-Haroun v Qatar National Bank [2025] EWHC 1383 (Admin)*, in which the Divisional Court issued a powerful warning to legal professionals about the risks of using generative artificial intelligence tools for legal research and drafting, and provided a stark reminder of the severe consequences for both lawyers and litigants who knowingly or inadvertently present 'fake' material to the court.

Getty Images v Stability AI

On 4 November 2025, the High Court's much-awaited judgment was handed down in *Getty Images (US) Inc & Ors v Stability AI Limited [2025] EWHC 2863 (Ch), l*argely dismissing Getty Image's claims for IP infringement despite making some limited findings of trade mark infringement.

Analysis of the judge's reasoning makes clear the need for a modern legislative structure in the UK that supports both AI development and fair compensation and control for creators. The current regime provides adequate support for neither. While this is hardly surprising, given its origins long-predating realistic prospects of usable artificial intelligence, Joanna Smith J's judgement in Getty Images v Stability AI makes plain the need for update, balancing all the interests in play.

****

5. 2

Patents and the Law

The meaning of 'patent'

A patent is a monopoly right. The product or process, which is being patented, must first satisfy the criteria of the Patents Act 1977, which are:

1. There must be an invention, which must be capable of being patented but not an 'as such' invention. Certain inventions are non-patentable. This arises out of the Patents Act 1977 s1 (2) and (3)) The statute does not provide a clear definition of invention but the Patents Act sets out a list of things that are considered to be inventions 'as such': general abstract entities, aesthetic and non-technical things are considered to be excluded. Discoveries, scientific theories and other things such as mathematical methods are not considered to be inventions 'as such'.

One of the most problematic areas to arise out of this definition of things that are not regarded as being true inventions is that of computer programs. Despite not being considered inventions under the PA 1977 it is the case that patents for software related inventions are indeed granted. Software patents are granted when a substantial technical contribution is made, as this is not considered to be a computer program as such.

Emotional Perception AI Ltd v Comptroller General [2026]

The case's key facts-Overview. The UK Supreme Court has handed down a landmark judgment in the case of *Emotional Perception AI Ltd v*

Comptroller General [2026] UKSC 3, significantly reshaping the UK approach to the patentability of software and AI related inventions.

This decision brings the current approach into much closer alignment with the European Patent Office (EPO) and moves away from the long-established Aerotel framework, which had previously restricted many claims relating to computer programs.

This decision is particularly important if people are developing artificial intelligence systems, algorithms, and other software-based technologies. It could make the UK a significantly more attractive jurisdiction for developing technologies of this nature.

Key points from the judgment

1. Artificial Neural Networks (ANNs) are "computer programs", but not necessarily excluded

The Court confirmed that an ANN constitutes a "program for a computer" for the purposes of section 1(2)(c) of the Patents Act 1977. As such, claims involving an ANN engage the statutory exclusion for computer programs "as such". However, crucially, this does not mean such inventions are automatically unpatentable.

2. The Aerotel test is no longer the governing framework

The Court held that the UK should no longer apply the Aerotel four-step test when assessing excluded subject matter. Instead, UKIPO and UK courts must apply an approach aligned with established EPO jurisprudence—particularly the "any hardware" principle and the COMVIK approach (G 1/19). This means the threshold question of whether subject matter is excluded will now be assessed in a more permissive manner.

3. Alignment with EPO approach

Under the EPO framework: *"If a claimed invention involves any technical means (e.g., hardware), it cannot be excluded "as a computer program as such". "*

The question then becomes whether the invention has the required technical character, to be assessed when determining novelty and inventive step. The Supreme Court endorsed this structure and clarified that EPO case law should guide UK practice going forward.

4. Practical effect: A lower bar for AI and software patent eligibility

The outcome of this shift is that many computer-implemented inventions that would previously have been refused at the threshold stage may now be considered patent-eligible. ANNs and other AI systems that run on hardware should now not be dismissed as excluded subject matter simply because they represent "software".

As a result of this decision the UKIPO is expected to follow a more technology-friendly approach consistent with the EPO's examination standards. If you're working in AI, data science, or software development, you'll benefit from a materially more favourable environment for seeking UK patent protection.

However, it remains to be seen how the UKIPO will apply this new guidance will be applied in practice as the matter has now been remitted back to them for reconsideration.

Implications for business

This decision significantly increases the prospects of successfully obtaining UK patents for:

- AI systems and models (including ANN-based technologies)
- Algorithm-driven recommendation engines
- Software-implemented decision-making processes

- Hybrid software–hardware systems
- Computer-implemented inventions that previously risked exclusion under Aerotel

People should still ensure that their claims clearly highlight the technical character of the invention and the specific hardware or technical means involved. However, under the new framework, there is a reduced risk of early rejection on subject-matter grounds. The Supreme Court's ruling is a decisive and positive shift for innovators in the AI and software sectors. By aligning UK law with EPO practice, the Court has broadened the pathway to patent a wide range of computer-implemented inventions.

Technical contribution

One of several approaches is taken when deciding whether there has been a technical contribution:

- The question should be asked whether technical means are used to produce a result or solve a problem
- Does the invention produce a technical result
- Novelty must be present in the product or process which distinguishes it from other products and processes (PA 1977 s.2)
- An inventive step must be present, i.e. the product or process must be seen as containing an clear element of invention (PA 1977 s. 3)
- The invention must be capable of industrial application, i.e., must be of a purpose which can be applied to some form of industry (PA 1977 s.4)

Other areas of enterprise are not patentable 'as such'. Mental acts, schemes, rules playing a game or business methods.

Mental acts. In *Raytheon (1993)* an apparatus and process was claimed for the identification of ships. This involved the digital composition of the silhouette of the unknown ship with silhouettes of known ships, held in a computer memory. The claim was held to be excluded, as it was merely an automation of a method normally carried out by individuals, i.e., a mental act as such. Carrying out the method with a computer did not create a technical effect. Schemes, rules, or methods for playing a game. Innovations in this area do not really amount to a technical contribution.

In relation to business methods. The courts in the UK have always taken a strict approach to the patentability of business methods. Inventions must make a technical contribution but that contribution must not be in an excluded thing (such as a business method) and it is also seen that advances in business methods are not technical.

More recent European patent office developments indicate that a more relaxed approach may be adopted. Whilst process claims to business methods are not inventions, 'as such' product claims may be patentable.

The presentation of information

The Patents Act 1977 s.1 (2)(d) provides that means of presenting information are not inventions 'as such'.

Non-Patentable Inventions

In some cases, rare though they may be, the commercial exploitation of an invention may be contrary to public policy or morality. Such an invention is unpatentable. The European Patent Office in *Harvard/Onco-mouse (1991)* when considering the patentability of a mouse or other non-human mammal genetically engineered so as to be predisposed to develop cancer, suggested that this should be addressed as a balancing exercise. Here the suffering of the mouse and the possible environmental risks were felt to be outweighed by the utility of the invention to humans, hence the Onco-mouse was not immoral.

As public policy and morality objections proved particularly problematic in the field of biotechnology, Directive 09/44/EC on the legal protection of Biological Invention provides further guidance on what is not patentable:

- The formation and development of the human body and mere discoveries of elements of the human body (this includes gene sequences) are not patentable. However, where a technical process is used to isolate or produce elements (including genes) from the human body, this may be patentable.
- Processes for modifying human germ line genetic identity (i.e. genetic changes that can be passed to the next generation.
- Human cloning processes.
- Genetic engineering of animals which is likely to cause the animal to suffer without a substantial medical benefit, either to man or to animals.
- Plant or animal varieties or biological processes for the production of such varieties are not patentable, but inventions concerning plants or animals may be patented where the invention is not confined to a particular variety.
- The concept of novelty

As discussed earlier, an invention must be novel (Patents Act 1977 s.1(1)(a) In UK patent law the terms 'novelty' and 'anticipation' are used interchangeably.

An invention must be new in the sense that it must not previously have been made available to the public. The Patents Act 1977 s.2 (1) provides that an invention is novel where it does not form part of the state of the art. Anticipation is judged by asking 'is the invention part of the state of the art'? Novelty is assessed objectively. In order for an invention to be anticipated, the prior art must either contain an enabling disclosure (in the case of a product patent) or, for process patents, it must give clear and unmistakable directions to do what the applicant has invented.

A key case here is *Lux Traffic Controls Ltd v Pike Signals Ltd (1993)* concerning what use amounts to disclosure to the public. It was claimed that a temporary traffic signal was not 'new' because it had been made available to the public in a paper, by oral disclosure, and by the use of a prototype which had been tested in public in Somerset.

The main principle to emerge from the case was that a prior publication must contain clear and unmistaken directions to do what the patentee claims to have invented: a signpost will not suffice. Where prior use is concerned there is no need for a skilled person to actually examine the invention as long as they were free in law and equity to do so and if a skilled person had seen it they would have been able to understand what the inventive concept was.

State of the art

The Patents Act 1977 s.2 (2) defines the state of the art as comprising all matter made available to the public before the priority date of the invention, this being the date of the first patent application. It therefore comprises all knowledge, global, on the subject matter of the invention. This knowledge can be made available in any way, either written, orally, or by any other means before the priority date.

The state of the art includes matter included in earlier patent applications, including those patent applications that are not yet published. Everything in the state of the art is known as prior art. Novelty destroying prior art could include information that is part of common general knowledge as well as specific pieces of prior art.

In some circumstances, a known invention may still be patented where a new use for that invention can be found, for example first medical use (Patents Act 1977) which provides that the first medical use of a known compound is novel, providing that the medical application of the compound does not itself form part of the state of the art (s.2 (6). Also, second medical use. In Europe a policy has developed of allowing second and subsequent uses of known compounds. Such claims are novel where the second or subsequent medical use does nor form part of the state of the art and provided the patent application takes a very narrow form known as a Swiss Form Claim i.e., the use of medicament X for treatment of disease Y.

The UK courts have sanctioned the use of Swiss Form Claims, but second and subsequent medical uses will only be novel in the UK, where there is a new therapeutic application, discovering information about a medical use is sufficient.

The Inventive step

An invention that is patentable must involve an inventive step. An inventive step is present where an invention would not be obvious to a person skilled in the art. In patent law, the term's 'inventive step' and 'non-obviousness' are used interchangeably.

Inventive steps are assessed from the perspective of the person skilled in the art (PA 1977 s.3), the skilled man. This hypothetical person has certain attributes: he is the average person in the relevant art, possessing the relevant skills, knowledge and qualifications. The statutory test for inventive step is embodied in what is know as the 'windsurfer' test. This test follows the approach set out in *Windsurfer v Tabur Marine (1983)* as modified by *PLG Research Ltd v Ardon International Ltd (1995).* According to the Windsurfer test, to test obviousness the following should be asked:

1. What is the inventive step involved in the patent?
2. At the priority date, what was the state of the art relevant to that test?
3. How does the step differ from the state of the art?
4. Without hindsight, would the taking of the step be obvious to the person skilled in the art?
5. When attempting to obtain a patent, it is important to note that patents are territorial rights, not universal and therefore it is necessary to apply for patents in each jurisdiction for which protection is desired. For example, a UK patent may be obtained from the Intellectual Property Office. Although there is currently no 'European Patent' as such, a so called 'bundle' of patents, national patents, from states that are party to the European Patents Convention 1973 (EPC) may be obtained by a single patent application to the European Patent Office.

The employee inventor – ownership of patents

When a patent is applied for, the basic rules are that a patent must be granted to the following:

1) The inventor or joint inventors i.e., the actual devisor of the invention. (Patent Act 1977 s.7(2) (a)
2) The inventor(s) successors in title
3) The employer of an employee inventor.

Ownership of employee inventions

Inventors have the right to be mentioned as such but the Patent Act 1977 provides that where the inventors are employees their employer will own the invention if:

a) The invention was made in the course of the employee's normal duties or in the course of specially assigned duties, provided that he or she might reasonably be expected to carry out those duties.
b) Where the employee has a special obligation to further the interests of his employer's undertaking. This is related to the duty of fidelity that the employer owes to his or her employer.

Where the invention belongs to the employer, statutory compensation of the employer inventor may be available (PA 1977 s.40) provided that the patent is of outstanding benefit to the employer, the invention is subject of a patent grant and that it is just that compensation should be awarded. There is a very high ceiling for statutory compensation and there has never actually been a reported case where statutory compensation under the 1977 act has been awarded. This is because such disputes tend to be settled out of court.

Patent applications may fail or those that are granted may be withdrawn on the basis of what is known as 'sufficiency'. A patent application consists of a number of components, and the patent specification is a vital part in which the invention is described and defined, it is the source of all the information about the patent that reaches the public domain. The specification must disclose the invention in such a way that the invention could be performed by the person skilled in the art. In other words, the application must contain an enabling disclosure. The patent claim itself determines the scope of the monopoly granted to a patent proprietor.

Claims must be clear and concise, be supported by the description and relate to a single inventive concept.

Infringement of a patent

Certain activities carried out in the United Kingdom without permission of the patent holder constitute infringement (Section 6(1) and (2) of the Patents Act 1977:

1. Primary infringement. This falls into three categories:

i) where a product patent is at issue, making, disposing of, using, importing or keeping the patented product (or disposal or otherwise)

ii) where a process patent is at issue, use of the process with actual or constructive knowledge that non-consensual use constitutes infringement

iii) The use, offer to dispose of, importation or keeping for disposal or otherwise of a product directly obtained from a patented process.

2. Contributory infringement. The supply or offer to supply any of the means that relate to an essential element of the invention, for putting the invention into effect may constitute infringement. This will only be the case where there is actual or constructive knowledge that those means are suitable (and are intended) for putting the invention into effect in the UK.

There are a number of exceptions to patent infringement set out in the Patent Act 1977 s.60 (5)(a)-(i) the main ones being:

- Private and non-commercial use
- Experimental use

The courts have considered whether repairs to patented products constitutes infringement. The position is quite clear, genuine repair of a patented product that has been sold for use does not constitute infringement. Anyone who wishes to attack a patent by claiming for revocation can do so on the grounds that the patent is not a patentable invention 'as such' or the invention is contrary to public policy or morality, the person granted the patent is not the person entitled to the patent, the patent specification does not amount to an enabling disclosure or there has been an impermissible amendment to the patent (PA 1977 s.72).

The Intellectual Property (Unjustified Threats) Act 2017

The Intellectual Property (Unjustified Threats) Act 2017 (the "Act") received Royal Assent on 27 April 2017 and applies from 1 October 2017, making a number of amendments to the Patents Act 1977.

The Act

The Act has three key aims: (i) to protect businesses and individuals against the misuse of threats to intimidate or gain an unfair commercial advantage where there has been no infringement; (ii) to make it easier for those involved in an IP infringement dispute to negotiate a settlement and avoid litigation; and (iii) bring consistency across the law of unjustified threats as it applied to patents, trademarks and designs. There are a number of changes to the law surrounding unjustified threats as a result of the Act, in particular it:

- creates a new statutory test for what is a "threat of infringement proceedings";
- allows for threats to be made by "mass communication" methods;
- creates a new safe harbour for "permitted communications";
- updates the permissible defences, to include situations in which no primary actor in an infringement can be found, despite "reasonable steps" being taken;

- creates an exception for professional advisers, under certain circumstances; and
- creates provisions for unjustified threats in relation to a unitary patent.

Threat Test

The Act modifies the "threat test", introducing an objective, two-step test to determine whether a communication amounts to a "threat of infringement proceedings". This requires that a reasonable person in the position of a recipient of the threat would understand from the communication that:

- a patent exists; and
- a person intends to enforce the patent against another person (in the UK or elsewhere) for an actual or potential infringement in the UK.

Threats need no longer be understood to relate only to bringing infringement proceedings in the UK. As a result, the provisions will apply to the unitary patent and the Act also inserts a new Schedule into the Patents Act 1977 in respect of unitary patents, for when the UPC Agreement comes into force. Furthermore, the new threat test ensures that threats to bring proceedings before the UPC in respect of patents falling within its jurisdiction will, where appropriate, fall within the scope of the threat provisions.

Who may bring an action?

It remains the law that: (i) any person "aggrieved" by a threat may bring an action; and (ii) such a threat is not actionable if it is made in respect of making or importing a product for disposal, or for using a process. In these cases, it is also not actionable to threaten proceedings for any other alleged infringement in respect of the product or process.

The Act also provides protection against threats made through mass communication, such as press releases. Such threats do not have to be directed at a particular individual.

Safe-Harbour

The Act provides a "safe harbour" to allow a patent holder to communicate with someone who might otherwise be entitled to bring an unjustified threats action if threatened. The "permitted communication" must be done for a "permitted purpose". A communication containing a threat of infringement proceedings is a "permitted communication" if:

- the communication is made solely for a "permitted purpose";
- all the information provided is necessary for that purpose; and
- the person making the communication reasonably believes it is true.

Permitted purposes include:

- notifying the recipient that the patent right exists;
- attempting to discover whether and by whom the patent is infringed (by making or importing a product, or using a process); and
- giving notice that a person has a right under a patent where that person's awareness of the patent is relevant to the action that may be taken.

The Act also grants the court the power to treat any other purpose as a "permitted purposes" if it is in the "interests of justice". The aim of this is to provide certainty over what will be considered a permitted purpose, whilst allowing the court the flexibility to take the surrounding circumstances of a case into account. The Act also lists purposes which cannot be considered "permitted purposes".

Defences and Exemptions

The old defence for making threats to secondary actors is retained but reformed to the extent that the threatener must first use reasonable steps to discover the primary actor who is making or importing the product or using the process. The person making the threat must also inform the person threatened either before or at the time of making the threat of the reasonable steps used. It is also a defence to show that the act for which the threat was made is an actual or potential infringement.

Applying for a Patent

The pitfalls of not patenting an invention

The pitfalls of not patenting your invention are immediately obvious. If you choose not to patent your invention, anyone can use, make or sell your invention and you cannot try to stop them. You can attempt to keep your invention secret, but this may not be possible for a product where the technology is on display.

The benefits of applying for protection

Most importantly, a patent gives you the ability to take legal action to try to stop others from copying, manufacturing, selling, and importing your invention without your permission. The existence of your patent may be enough on its own to stop others from trying to exploit your invention. If it does not, the patent gives you the right to take legal action under civil law to try to stop them exploiting your invention.

How much does it cost?

Most people are put off the idea of applying for a patent because of the cost, or potential cost. If you use a patent attorney, then for sure you will pay a lot of money. However, it is relatively inexpensive to apply yourself.

Full and very clear details concerning applying for a patent and the associated costs can be found at:
https://www.gov.uk/patent-your-invention/apply-for-a-patent

****

5.3

Trademarks and the Law

Definition of a trademark

A trademark is a symbol or a sign placed on, or used in relation to, one trader's goods or services to distinguish them from similar goods or services supplied by other traders. Section 1 of the Trade Marks Act 1994, as amended, which is the main legislation covering trade marks, defines a trade mark as any sign capable of being represented graphically which distinguishes the goods or services of one business from those of another.

The enactment of the 1994 Act radically changed the law dealing with registered trademarks. The legislation harmonises the trademark law of the United Kingdom with that of the rest of the European Community and implements the first council directive (89/104/EEC) to approximate the laws of the member states relating to trademarks. The Government also took the opportunity with the 1994 Act to bring the law up to date, as the previous Act, the 1938 Act was inadequate in its scope and coverage.

From 14 January 2019 the long-awaited Trademark Directive (2015/2436) and implemented into Law via the Trademarks Regulations 2018, took effect in the UK, reflecting the UK's continued effort to enhance harmonisation of trademark law across the EU.

However, see below on the effect of BREXIT on trademark legislation.

Brexit & Trademarks

International trademark registrations protected in the EU under the Madrid Protocol will no longer enjoy protection in the UK after 1 January 2021.

Of all the intellectual property rights, trademark practice is likely to be the most impacted by Britain's leaving the EU. The UK's existing trademark law is heavily entwined with EU law – via the EU Trademark Directive. Domestic UK trademarks will be unaffected. EU Trademarks (EUTMs) on the other hand are registered with the EU Intellectual Property Office. Many companies have relied upon EUTMs rather than national trademark registrations for their trademark protection in Europe. The consequences of the UK ceasing to be an EU Member State are therefore of great importance.

International Provisions

There are a number of international conventions and arrangements that give some international recognition to national trademarks. These are the Paris Convention, The Madrid Arrangement and the Protocol to the Madrid arrangement (Madrid Protocol). There is also a Community Trademarks System that creates a trademark that gives rights throughout the European Community and which will be referred to below.

Paris Convention

The Paris Convention came into being in 1883. Its overall purpose was to create recognition between various countries of each other's national intellectual property rights, through the concept of priority.

Priority recognises the first filing date for a particular intellectual property right in any convention country as the filing date for all other convention countries in respect of the same property right. The period of priority differs from intellectual property right to intellectual property right but for trademarks the period is six months. This has given a level of international protection for trademarks because the first to file a trade mark application is, in most countries, the person with better claim to a trade mark. In England, this is not the case because rights in passing off (see later) can be built up through sufficient use of a trademark, without registration, and these rights can act as an obstacle to any subsequent application to register the trademark by a third party.

Another provision of the Paris Convention relevant to trademarks is Article 6, which gives international protection to 'well known' trademarks. A person can own a well-known trademark in registered or unregistered form even in countries where the action of passing off does not exist. Ownership of a well-known mark will prevent a third party from applying to register the same or similar mark in any other convention country that has implemented Article 6 and allows cancellation of an existing registration for such an identical or similar mark during the first five years after registration on the application of the owner of the well-known mark.

The Madrid Agreement

The Madrid Agreement was implemented in 1891 to simplify the procedure for filing trademark registration in many countries. The Madrid Agreement aimed to replace the multiple filing of trademark registrations in (10) individual countries.

The Madrid Agreement allows anyone established or domiciled in an Agreement country, with a trademark registration in his or her country, to file one international application that will cover all Madrid Agreement countries. The central application is filed with the offices of the World Intellectual Property Rights Organisation (WIPO) in Geneva. This is then administered by that office.

England did not sign the Madrid Agreement so this is not available to English trademark owners.

The Madrid Protocol

As a number of key countries did not sign the Madrid Agreement, discussions began in the mid-1980's on how to make the Madrid system more palatable. The result was the Madrid Protocol established in 1989. At the current time there are 42 signatories to the protocol including the UK. Up to date information concerning the countries and the protocol see www. Itma.org.uk

The protocol is based on essentially the same structure as the Madrid Agreement, with a few differences designed to allow more flexibility.

Although classed as an international registration system, the CTM operates differently from either the Madrid Agreement or Madrid Protocol. It is more like the national system (see below) in that it is a means of filing an application for one trademark at one trademark registry to obtain one registration under one set of laws and procedures. The only difference is that the area covered by the registration is a collection of countries within the European Union. The application can be filed in The CTM Office in Alicante Spain or at the National Trademark office in any member country, which passes the application to the CTO Office.

Trademarks and registration of trademarks

As discussed, the function of a trademark is to distinguish between one trader's goods and another trader's goods. The function of an ordinary trademark is to act as an indicator of trade origin, which aids both consumers of branded goods and the trademark proprietor, as follows:

1) The trademark acts as an indicator of quality and reliability, protecting consumers from confusion or deception in the marketplace.

2) The trademark can be enforced to protect the mark's proprietor against certain acts of unfair competition.

Collective marks and certification marks

Although they are rare, such trademarks perform different functions compared to ordinary trademarks. Certification marks (Trademarks Act 1994 s.50) are intended to indicate that goods or services comply with a certain objective standard as to quality, origin, material, the mode of manufacture of goods or the performance of services or other characteristics. Any third party whose goods or services meet the required standards may apply to be an authorised user of a certification mark and the proprietor cannot refuse this request.

Collective marks serve to indicate members of an association. A third party who is not a member of that association does not have the right to use the mark. Collective marks can act as certification marks and vice versa.

Trademark law

As seen, in the UK, trademarks are governed by the 1994 Trademarks Act, as amended by the below:

The Trademarks (EC Measures Relating to Counterfeit Goods) Regulations 1995 (SI 1995/1444) *(1 July 1995);*

Section 13 of the Olympic Symbol etc (Protection) Act 1995 *(21 September 1995);*

Part IV of the Patents and Trademarks (World Trade Organisation) Regulations 1999 (SI 1999/1899) *(29 July 1999)*;

Section 6 of the Copyright, etc. and Trademarks (Offences and Enforcement) Act 2002 *(20 November 2002)*;

The Trademarks (Proof of Use, etc.) Regulations 2004 (SI 2004/946) *(5*

May 2004); $ the Trademarks (International Registrations Designating the European Community, etc.) Regulations 2004 (SI 2004/2332) *(1 October 2004)*;

The Serious Organised Crime and Police Act 2005 (*19 April 2005*); and

The Intellectual Property (Enforcement, etc.) Regulations 2006 (SI 2006/1028) *(29 April 2006).*

The Legal Services Act 2007

The Trademarks (Relative Grounds) Order 2007

The Trademarks (Earlier Trademarks) Regulations 2008 (SI 2008/1067) (10 May 2008)

The Trademark Directive (2015/2436) effective from 14th January 2019)

European Withdrawal Acts 2018/ 2020 and associated Regulations

An application for a national trademark may be made to the Intellectual Property Office (see next chapter). As we have discussed, as a consequence of BREXIT, which became effective on December 31st, 2020, trademarks registered in the European Community, international trademark registrations designated by the European Union Intellectual Property Office (EUIPO) and Community designs, ceased to have effect in the United Kingdom as of January 1st, 2021, keeping their validity in the other 27 member countries of the European Union (EU).

Notwithstanding the foregoing, designs and Community trademarks registered with the EUIPO before December 31st, 2020, shall be automatically cloned in the United Kingdom and assigned a new registration number at the national level, which shall grant their holders the same rights as the pre-existing registrations in the United Kingdom. All dates of the original registration shall be maintained, such as, filing dates, priority and seniority.

Not all marks are capable of being registered as trademarks. Objections to the registration of a mark may be raised, either by the IPO during examination of the mark or by third parties during any opposition actions or proceedings. The grounds for refusing registration are divided into two categories:

1. Absolute grounds for refusal (TMA 1994 s.3 and 4) which are concerned with objections based on the mark itself.
2. Relative grounds for refusal (TMA 1994 s.5) these being concerned with a conflict and third-party rights.

Classification of a trademark

The Nice Agreement for the International Classification of Goods and Services provides that there are thirty-four classes of goods and eight classes of services. Any application for registration must stipulate which classes, or sub-classes, in which registration is sought. Multi-class applications are possible and it would, in theory, be possible to register a mark in respect of all forty-two classes. However, this is very unlikely as applicants must have a bona fide intent to use the marks for the prescribed goods and services (TMA 1994 ss.3 (6) and 32 (3)).

Limited registration for retail service marks is also now possible in class 35. This change follows OHIM's decision in Giacomelli Sports Spa (1999).

Definition of a trademark

The 1994 Trademarks Act s.1(1) provides that a trademark is a sign capable of being represented graphically, capable of distinguishing goods or services of one undertaking, from those of another undertaking. There are a number of elements in the definition:

a) *A 'sign'*. The concept of a sign in UK trademark law is very broad indeed. Although there is no clear definition, signs provided in the UK include works, designs and shapes and also more unconventional marks such as sounds and smells. A sign can be regarded as anything that conveys information (Phillips v Remington (1998) See below.

b) *Graphic representation*. Signs must be represented graphically, i.e. be represented in such a way that third parties may determine and understand what the sign is,. This requirement is normally satisfied by including an image of the mark in the trademark application. However, it has been suggested that provision of an image is not absolutely necessary provided that third parties can clearly identify the mark from the description (Swizzels Matlow Ltds Application (1999). It may be difficult to graphically represent unconventional marks, but practice dictates for example that sound marks are represented by music notation and that for shape marks it is best to submit line drawings or photographs. Applications for colour marks will usually include a representation of the colour and so on.
c) *Capable of distinguishing*. Signs must be capable of distinguishing goods or services of one undertaking from another undertaking. Any sign that has the capacity to distinguish will satisfy this requirement.

Absolute grounds for refusal

The main legislation is Section 3(1)(a-d) Trademarks Act 1994, Art 3 (1) (a-d) Directive on the Legal protection of Trade marks. A sign will not be registered if it falls within one or more of the absolute grounds for refusing registration.

Signs not satisfying the s.1 (1) requirements

Signs which do not meet the definition of 'trademark' provided in the Trademarks act 1994 will not be registered. In addition, it is important for an applicant not to make a mistake as to the graphic representation as the opportunities to correct or amend are very limited (TMA 1994 s.39

prevents the correction of errors in a trademark application that would substantially affect the identity of the trade mark). This is mitigated by the fact that it is IPO practice to examine marks for graphic representation before a filing date is allocated.

Scent marks continue to cause considerable difficulties for graphic representation. John Lewis Application (The scent of Cinnamon) (2001) indicates a description of a scent is unlikely to be precise enough.

Signs must also be capable of distinguishing the goods or services of one undertaking form those of other undertakings. As noted above, this is not a high standard and, in effect, it will only bar those signs that are incapable of functioning as trademarks (e.g. the Philips shaver shape in Philips Electronics v Remington Consumer Products (1999) a case discussed below, was held not to be distinctive in a trade mark sense and thus did not satisfy TMA 1994, s.3 (1)(a)).

Marks devoid of distinctive character or those consisting of exclusively descriptive or generic signs are prohibited unless it can be shown that before the application was made, a mark has acquired a distinctive character as a result of a use made of it. This proviso to the TMA 1994 ss.3 (1)(b)(c) and (d) means that there is no absolute prohibition as a matter of law on non-distinctive, descriptive and generic marks. As recognised in British Sugar v James Robertson (TREAT) 1996, such marks may be registered where they have become factually distinctive upon use despite the provisions stated in the TMA 1994 s.3 (1)(b)-(d). This proviso does not apply to TMA 1994 s.3(1)(a) or any other absolute ground for refusal.

Marks devoid of distinctive character

TMA 1994 s.3 (1)(b) prevents the registration of marks that are not, prima facie, distinctive. An example might include a surname common in the UK. In British Sugar v James Robertson (TREAT) 1996, it was said that a mark is devoid of distinctive character where the sign cannot distinguish the applicants' goods or services without the public being first educated that it is a trademark. The mark at issue in this case, TREAT, for a syrup for pouring on ice cream and desserts, was therefore devoid of distinctive character. Such marks may, nevertheless, benefit from the TMA 1994 s.3 (1)(b) proviso. Therefore, trademarks will only fail where they are not distinctive by nature and have not become distinctive by nurture.

Signs that are exclusively descriptive

For a sign to be open to objection under TMA 1994 s.3 (1)(c) the trademark must consist exclusively of a sign which may be used in trade to describe characteristics of the goods or services. The sub-categories of TMA 1994 s.3 (1)(c) are:

1) Kind. Terms indicating kind or type that should be free for all traders to use, e.g., PERSONAL for computers, are not normally registrable.
2) Quality. Laudatory words, e.g., PERFECTION, are not usually registrable.
3) Quantity. The Trademarks Registry gives the example that 454 would not be registrable for butter, as butter is frequently sold for domestic consumption in 454g (1lb) packs. Where numerical marks are not descriptive or otherwise objectionable, they may be registered.
4) Intended purpose. Generally, words referring to the purpose of goods or services are not registrable.
5) Value. Signs pertaining to the value of goods or services are not normally registrable, e.g., BUY ONE GET TWO FREE.

6) Geographical origin. Geographical names are not usually registrable unless used in specific circumstances.
7) Time of production of goods or the rendering of services. Typically, marks such as SAME DAY DELIVERY for courier services or AUTUMN 2004 for haute couture would not be registrable.
8) Other characteristics of goods and services. For example, a representation of the good or service would not usually be registrable.

Marks falling into any of these categories may still be registrable if they have become distinctive upon use.

Signs that are exclusively generic

TMA 1994 s.3(1)(d) prohibits the registration of signs or indications that have become customary in the current language or in the bone fide and established practices of the trade. An example can be found in JERYL LYNN Trademark (1999) where an application for JERYL LYNN for vaccines was refused as the mark described a strain of vaccine and was not distinctive of the applicant.

Shapes that cannot be registered

Traditionally in the UK, shapes were not registrable. One case highlighting this was Coca-Cola's trademark application (1986).

However, the TMA 1994 makes it very clear that the shapes of goods and their packaging are now registrable (TMA 1994 s.1 (1)), but the TMA 1994 s.3 (2) excludes certain shapes from registration. This is an area of trademark law that has lacked clarity.

ECJ guidance on the registrability of shape marks has clarified matters somewhat. The UK Court of Appeal stayed proceedings in Phillips

Electronics v Remington Consumer products (1999) to allow a preliminary reference to the ECJ in a number of issues, including questions specific to shape marks and this decision has implications for the interpretation of the TMA 1994 s.3 (2). In this case, Philips had been producing a three-headed rotary shaver for a considerable time (the Philishave). When Remington produced a rotary shaver of a similar design Philips sued for infringement of a mark which was the face of the three headed shaver. The TMA 1994 provides that the following shapes are not registrable:

1) Where the shape results from the nature of the goods themselves. Inherent shapes therefore cannot be registered. In the Philips case, The Court of Appeal considered that there would be no objection to Philips three headed shaver shape on this ground as electronic shavers can take other forms.
2) Where the shape of the goods is necessary to achieve a technical result (TMA 1994 s.3 (2)(b). Functional shapes are therefore not registrable. In Philips 1999 case it was considered that the shaver shape was necessary to achieve a technical result, but the ECJ was, nevertheless, asked to adjudicate in the matter, i.e. on the correct approach to functional shapes. They concurred in the matter. They also confirmed that the fact that there may be more than one shape that could achieve the same result is not relevant. Consequently, it appears that only shapes with specifically non-functional aspects are registrable.
3) Where the shapes give substantial value to the goods. In Philips (1999) the Court of Appeal suggested that a valuable shape in this context can be identified where the shape itself adds substantial value, e.g. the shape adds value via eye appeal or functional effectiveness. In contrast, shapes that are valuable because they are 'good trademarks' would not fall foul of the TMA 1994.

Marks likely to give offence or deceive

A mark will not be registered if it is contrary to public policy or accepted principles of morality (TMA 1994 s.3 (3)(a) or is of such a nature that it is likely to deceive the public. For example, as to the nature, quality or origin of the goods or services.

Relatively few marks are deemed to be contrary to public policy or morality. Morality should be considered in the context of current thinking and only where a substantial number of persons would be offended should registration be refused. For example, in BOCM's application, (EUROLAMB) (1997) EUROLAMB was considered to be deceptive if used in relation to non-sheep meat (when used in relation to sheep meat it was descriptive). It is very clear that the test of deception is deceptive and actual evidence of deception must be provided.

Marks prohibited by UK or EC law

The registration of marks whose use would be illegal under UK or Community law is precluded by TMA 1994 s.3(1)(d).

Protected emblems

TMA 1994 s.4 provides details of marks that are considered to fall into the category of specially protected emblems, e.g. marks with Royal connotations, and the Olympic symbol cannot be registered. Marks containing such emblems cannot be registered without consent.

Applications made in bad faith

The key statute here is Section 3(3)(a) and (b) and section 3(6) Trademarks Act 1994, Art 3(1)(f) and (2)(d) Directive on the Legal Protection of Trademarks:

(3) A trademark shall not be registered if it is -
(a) contrary to public policy or accepted principles of morality, or
(b) of such a nature as to deceive the public
(6) A trademark shall not be registered if or to the extent that the application is made in bad faith.

There is no requirement that a mark need be used prior to the application for registration, but the applicant must have a bona fide intention to use the mark and applications may be refused when they are made in bad faith. Therefore, so-called ghost applications should be caught by this section.

Relative grounds for refusal

Section 5(1) Trademarks act 1994, Art 4(1)(a) Directive on the Legal Protection of Trademarks:
(1) A trademark shall not be registered if it is identical with an earlier trademark and the goods or services for which the trademark is applied for are identical with the goods or services for which then earlier trademark is protected.

The applicant must also overcome the relative grounds for refusing registration. These relate to conflict with earlier marks or earlier rights. The 'earlier mark' (TMA 1994 s.6) might be a trademark registered in the UK or under the Madrid Protocol. Alternatively, it might be a CTM or a well-known mark (the latter are entitled to protection as per article 6 of the Paris Convention for the Protection of Industrial Property 1883).

There is no provision for honest concurrent use in the TMA 1994. As it has been made clear that a trademark application must be refused, irrespective of honest concurrent use, if the registered proprietor objects, this provision is of limited value to the applicant. If the proprietor of the registered mark objects, honest concurrent use provides no defence.

Conflict with an earlier mark for identical goods or services

The TMA 1994 s.5 (1) only provides the narrowest relative ground for refusing registration: a mark identical to an earlier trademark and used for identical goods and services will not be registered. The requirement of 'identical goods and services' is sufficiently broad in scope to include cases where the applicants mark is identical to only some of the goods and services for which the earlier mark is registered, but to 'constitute an 'identical mark' a very high level of identity between the marks is required. One such case highlighting this is Origins Natural Resources v Origins Clothing (1995).

The registration of similar marks for the same or similar services is only prohibited where confusion on the part of the public is likely to arise (TMA 1994 s.5 (2). Specifically, what is prohibited is the registration of:

1) Identical marks for similar goods or services or
2) Similar marks for identical/similar goods or services where, because of the identity or similarity, there is a likelihood of confusion on the part of the public, which includes the likelihood of association with the earlier trademark.

What constitutes 'confusing similarity' has been considered at length by the ECJ (Sabel v Puma 1998) and Canon v Metro Goldwyn Meyer (1999). Confusion has to be appreciated globally taking into account all factors relevant to the case.

These factors include:

- The recognition of the earlier trademark on the market
- The association that can be made between the registered mark and the sign
- The degree of similarity between the mark and the sign and the goods and the services, the degree of similarity must be considered in deciding whether the similarity is sufficient so as to lead to a likelihood of confusion

It has also been made clear that 'likelihood of association' is not an alternative to 'likelihood of confusion" but serves to define its scope. This means that if the public merely makes an association between two trademarks, this would not in itself be sufficient for concluding that there would be a likelihood of confusion. There is no likelihood of confusion where the public would not believe that goods or services came from the same undertaking.

Conflict with a mark of repute

A mark that is identical or similar to an earlier mark will be refused registration in respect of dissimilar goods or services where the earlier mark is a mark of repute and the use of the later mark would, without the cause, take unfair advantage of or be detrimental to the reputed mark's distinctiveness or reputation. (TMA 1994 s5 (3).

A mark of repute is a mark with a reputation in the UK (for CTM applications it must have a reputation in the EU). In deciding as to whether a trademark has a reputation, the ECJ has provided some guidance (General Motors Corp v Yplon) (2000). Repute would be judged with reference to the general public or to a specific section of the public, and the mark must be known to a significant portion of that public.

Relevant indicators of the public's knowledge of the mark include the extent and duration of the trademarks use, its market share and the extent to which it has been promoted.

In order for registration to be refused under s.5 (3) use of the applicant's mark will have to take unfair advantage of or be detrimental to the reputed marks distinctiveness or reputation. In OASIS STORES LTD's application (EVEREADY) (1998) it was said that merely being reminded of an opponent's mark did not itself amount to taking unfair advantage. The fact that the applicant did not benefit to any significant extent from their opponent's reputation and the wide divergence between the parties goods was relevant, s.5 (3) could not be intended to prevent the registration of any mark identical or similar to a mark of repute.

Conflict with earlier rights

TMA 1994 s.5 (4) provides that where a mark conflicts with earlier rights, including passing off, design rights and copyright the mark will not be registered.

Surrender, revocation, invalidity, acquiescence and rectification

Surrender. It is possible to surrender a trademark with respect to some or all of the goods or services for which it is registered. Marks may be revoked (removed from the registry on three grounds: non-use because the mark has become generic; or because the mark has become deceptive. A mark will be invalid if it breaches any of the absolute grounds for registration. Where the proprietor of an earlier trademark or other right is aware of the use of a mark subsequently registered in the UK and has, for a continuous period of five years, taken no action regarding that use the proprietor is said to have acquiesced. Where this is the case, the proprietor of the earlier mark or right cannot rely on his right in applying for a declaration of invalidity or in opposing the use of the later mark, unless it is being used in bad faith. Anyone with sufficient interest can apply to rectify an error or omission in the register. Such a rectification must not relate to matters that relate to the validity of the trademark.

Infringement

Section 10(1) Trademarks Act 1994, Art 5 (1)(a) Directive on the Legal Protection of Trademarks:

'A person infringes a registered trademark if he uses in the course of trade a sign which is identical with the trademark in relation to goods or services which are identical with those for which it is registered'.

The proprietor (and any exclusive licensee) has certain rights to a mark (TMA 1994 s.9 (1) which are infringed by certain forms of unauthorised use of the mark in the UK. These rights come into existence from the date of registration, which is the date of filing. All infringement acts require the mark to be used in the UK in the course of trade. What constitutes 'use' of a mark has been the subject matter of some debate and is discussed below.

Use of an identical sign for identical goods or services

Use, in the course of trade, of an identical sign, in respect of goods or services constitutes trademark infringement (TMA 1994 s.10 (1).

Use of an identical or similar sign on identical or similar goods or services

Use, in the course of trade, of an identical sign or similar goods or services (TMA 1994 s.10 (2) (a) or a similar sign on identical goods or services constitutes infringement where the public is likely to be confused as to the origin of goods or services or is likely to assume that there is an association with the registered mark.

Use of a mark similar to a mark of repute for dissimilar goods or services
Registered marks with a 'reputation' are infringed if an identical or similar mark is used for non-similar goods or services, where the use takes unfair advantage of or is detrimental to, the distinctive character or repute of the distinctive mark (TMA 1994 s.10 (3).

Contributory infringement
TMA 1994 s.10 (5) is known as the contributory infringement provision. This provision creates a form of secondary participation where a person who applies a trademark to certain materials has actual or constructive knowledge that the use of the mark is not authorised. This provision extends infringement down the supply chain, but printers, publishers, manufacturers or packaging etc. may avoid a s. 10 (5) liability in practice by inserting suitable contractual forms into their agreement with their clients.

Defences to infringement

a) Comparative advertising. Comparative advertising is allowed under certain circumstances as long as the use is not unfair or detrimental. One such case that highlights this is British Airways PLC v Ryanair Ltd (2001). British Airways had brought an action for infringement against Ryanair for the publication of two Ryanair advertisements comparing fares with BA. The courts found that, in assessing as to whether a mark has been used in accordance with honest practice, the court should view the advertisement as a whole. Although misleading adverts cannot be honest, on the facts, whilst the advertisement at issue may have caused offence it was not dishonest and the price comparisons were not significantly unfair.

b) The use of another registered mark. The use of one registered mark, within the boundaries of the registration, does not infringe another registered mark.
c) Use of own name or address. A person using their own name or address does not infringe a registered mark, providing that the use accord with open honest practice. However, see the note on the Trademark Directive introduced in 2019.
d) Use of certain indications. The use of certain indications (e.g., the intended purpose of the gods or services or their geographical origin) will not constitute infringement where that use accords with appropriate honest practice.
e) The locality defence. Signs applicable to a certain locality whose use predates the registration of a mark may continue to be used in that locality.
f) Exhaustion. Trademark rights are exhausted once the proprietor has consented to the placing of goods bearing the mark on the market within the EEA. For example, once a brand owner consents to a consignment of their goods being marketed in France, trademark rights cannot be used to prevent these goods from being resold in the UK, unless there are legitimate reasons for this. Goods sold in this way are known as 'grey imports' or parallel imports.

****

5.4

Copyright and the Law

Definition of copyright

Copyright is the right to prevent others copying or reproducing an individuals or other's work. *Copyright protects the expression of an idea and not the idea itself.* Only when an idea is committed to paper can it be protected. Others can be directly or indirectly stopped from copying the whole or a substantial part of a copyright work. However, others cannot be stopped from borrowing an idea or producing something very similar.

Copyright is a right that arises automatically upon the creation of a work that qualifies for copyright protection. This means that there is no registration certificate to prove ownership. To claim ownership the author will have to produce original and preferably dated evidence of the creation of the work and proof of authorship. The author will also need to show that he/she is a qualifying person and that the work was produced in a convention country.

To be a qualifying person (s.154 of the Copyright Designs and Patents Act 1988) the author must have been, at the material time, a British Citizen, subject or protected person, a British Dependant territories citizen, a British national (overseas) or a British Overseas Citizen or must have been resident or domiciled in a convention country at the material time, which is when the work was first published. If the author dies before publication the material time is before his death. A convention country is a country that is signatory to the Universal Copyright Convention or the Berne Copyright Convention, which includes most countries in the world.

The works that can qualify for protection are defined in S.1 of the 1988 Act. These are:

2. Original literary, dramatic, musical and artistic works
3. Sound recordings, films, broadcasts and cable programmes
4. Typographical arrangements of published editions

Copyright and the emergence of Artificial Intelligence

As we have seen, since the growth of AI there have been numerous issues about the use of AI content and all aspects of Intellectual Property. The cases against AI companies are growing in number. In one case in particular Getty Images (US) Inc & Ors v Stability AI Limited [2025] EWHC 2863 (Ch) is seen as very important and straddles several areas of Ip law, such as trademarks and copyright.

Copyright – subsistence of copyright

As shown above, copyright is a property right that subsists in certain works. It is a statutory right giving the copyright owner certain exclusive rights in relation to his or her work.

In the 1988 Copyright Designs and Patents Act, as amended, there are nine categories of copyright works:

'Authorial' 'Primary' or 'LDMA' works

1) Literary works
2) Dramatic works
3) Musical works
4) Artistic works

'Entrepreneurial' 'Secondary' or 'Derivative' works

5) Sound recordings
6) Films

7) Broadcasts
8) Cable programmes
9) Typographical arrangements of published editions (the typography right)

Copyright comes into existence or subsists automatically where a qualifying person creates a work that is original and tangible (or fixed).

Qualification

Copyright will not subsist in a work unless:

a) It has been created by a qualifying person
b) It was first published in a qualifying country
c) In the case of literary, dramatic and musical works, the work must be fixed, that is reduced to a material form in writing or oth

Copyright works

The CDPA 1988 defines a literary work as being 'any work written, spoken or sung, other than a dramatic or musical work'. A novel or poem could equally fall into this category. Additionally, the concept of literary works extends to tables (e.g., a rail timetable) compilations such as directories and computer programmes. Databases are also regarded as literary works. In essence, any work that can be expressed in print, irrespective of quality, will be a literary work.

Dramatic works

The CDPA 1988 defines 'dramatic works' as including works of dance or mime. In the case *Norowzian v Arks (1999)* it was stated that these terms should be given their natural and ordinary meaning, the implication being that dramatic works are works of *action.* The courts also recognised in this case that films may be produced as dramatic works, either as dramatic works in themselves and/or as a recording of a dramatic work.

Musical works

A musical work is a work consisting solely of musical notes, any words or actions intended to be sung, spoken, or recorded with the notes are excluded. Therefore, a melody is a musical works with the lyrics being literary.

Artistic works

A wide-ranging definition of artistic works is provided by the CDPA 1988 s.4. Works of architecture are included but focus is usually placed on the remaining artistic works. These fall into two categories:

a)Works protected irrespective of their artistic merit:

i) Graphic works, i.e., paintings, drawings, diagrams, maps, charts, plans, engravings, etchings, lithographs, woodcuts or similar works

ii) Photographs

iii) Sculptures. The protection of functional objects, such as a cast is problematic. In one notable case in *New Zealand Wham-O manufacturing Co v Lincoln Industries Ltd (1985)* a wooden model of a Frisbee was held to be a sculpture. The modern UK position is almost certainly more restrictive, as objects will not now be protected as sculptures where they are not made for the purpose of sculpture.

iv) Collages. Collages are artistic or functional visual arrangements produced by affixing two or more items together. Intrinsically ephemeral arrangements (for example the composition of a photograph) are not collages.

- Artistic works required to be of a certain quality (CDPA 1988 s.4 (1) c i.e., works of artistic craftsmanship. Few works can meet the standard of artistic craftsmanship, as they must be both of artistic quality and the result of craftsmanship. These principles were further developed into a two-part test for artistic craftsmanship in *Merlet v Mothercare (1986).*

First, did the creation of the work involve craftsmanship in the sense that skill and pride was invested in its manufacturer? Second, does the work have aesthetic appeal and did an artist create it?

Sound recordings

A sound recording is a reproducible recording of either:

6. Sounds where there is no underlying copyright work (e.g., birdsong)
7. A recording of the whole or any part of a literary, dramatic, or musical work.

The format of recording is of no relevance.

Film

The CDPA 1988 s.5B (1) provides that a film is a reproducible recording of a moving image on any medium. It is the recording itself that is protected, rather than the subject matter that has been recorded, but it should be borne in mind that a film might also be protected as a dramatic work. Film soundtracks are taken to be part of the film itself.

Broadcasts

Copyright subsists in sounds and visual images that are broadcast CDPA 1988 s.6 (1), a broadcast being defined as a transmission by wireless telegraphy of visual images, sounds or other information. The definition of 'broadcast' therefore encompasses radio and television broadcasts and both terrestrial and satellite broadcasting.

Cable programmes

The transmission of an item that forms part of a cable programme will create separate works that are capable of protection as cable programmes CDPA 1988 s.7. A cable programme service is defined as a service consisting wholly or mainly in sending visual images, sounds or other information via a telecommunications system which may utilise wires or microwave transmission. Items sent via wireless telegraphy are specifically excluded as they are already protected as broadcasts. This means that as well as subscription channels a website on the internet may be a cable programme service.

The typography right

The CDPA 1988 s.8 affords protection to the typography, that is the layout, of published editions of literary, dramatic and musical works. The leading authority on typographical arrangement copyright is *Newspaper Licensing Agency Ltd v Marks and Spencer Plc (2001).*

Copyright works the ideas/expression dichotomy

There is no copyright in ideas. Copyright subsists in the tangible expression of ideas and not the ideas themselves. In America this is referred to as the ideas/expression dichotomy. This principle can be helpful but should not be taken too literally, as whilst it is clear that mere ideas cannot be protected by copyright the following points should be noted:

4) What might be termed 'highly developed ideas', for example an early draft of a textbook, would be protected by copyright, as are preparatory design material for computer programmes.
5) Copyright cannot be circumvented by selectively altering the expression of a copyright work in the process of reproducing it.

Originality

The CDPA 1988 s.1 requires that literary, dramatic, musical and artistic works be 'original'. The originality requirements only apply to LDMA works, there is no such requirement for secondary copyright works, although it is clear that no copyright will subsist in secondary copyright works that merely reproduce secondary works.

LDMA works must be original in the sense that they originate with the author. One such case that highlights this is *University of London Press v University Tutorial Press (1916).* This is a minimal qualitative requirement: original works need not be inventive or original and a wide range of works have been held to be original, from coupons for football pools (*Ladbrokes v William Hill (1964*) to a compilation of broadcasting programmes (*Independent Television Publications Ltd and the BBC v Time Out Ltd (1984).*

Expending skill and judgement in creating an LDMA work usually suffices to deem the work original. Mere copying cannot confer originality. Alternatively, the mere expenditure of effort or labour (the so-called 'sweat of the brow' test for originality) has sometimes been said to be sufficient to confer originality. But in practice some minimum element of originality is required. For example, in *Crump v Smythson (1944)* it was held that the generic nature of commonplace diary material left no room for judgement in selection and arrangement therefore the resultant works were not original. Originality has also been held to be more than 'competent draftsmanship' (*Interlego v Tyon 1988*). Commonly databases and computer programmes were the subject matter of sweat of the brow concerns.

Higher standards of originality: computer/ databases

As a result of two European Directives, The Directive on the Legal Protection of Databases (Directive 96/9/EC) and the Computer Directive (Directive 91/250/EEC) both computer programmes and databases must be original in the sense that they are the author's own intellectual creation. This is a higher standard or originality than that of 'skills, labour and judgement'.

Some databases may not meet the standard of originality to be afforded copyright protection. In this case the database can be protected by virtue of the *sui generis* database right. (See end of chapter and the UK's exit from the EU.)

The Database Directive which was incorporated into UK law by Part 11 of the Copyright and Rights in databases regulations 1997 grant a property right in a database whether or not it qualifies for a copyright work. The definition of database includes:

'a collection of independent works, data or other materials arranged in a systematic or methodical way and individually accessible by electronic or other means'.

A database can also be recognised as a literary work and thus afforded copyright protection. For this the database must be original and the contents and arrangements of the database must be a result of the author's own intellectual creation. In any case, all databases are protected by the new database rights irrespective of whether they qualify for copyright protection or not. To qualify for database rights the data must have been assembled through substantial investment in obtaining, verifying and presenting the contents. One case that illustrates this is *British Horseracing Board Ltd v William Hill Organisation (2001)*).

The duration of the database rights is for 15 years from 1st January of the year following completion of its making, or the first making public of the database within the 15-year period from its making.

Originality and the *de minimis principle*

The question arises, does copyright exist in very short works. The case, *Exxon Corporation v Exxon Ind (1982),* where the invented word Exxon was denied copyright protection, is often cited to support the proposition that a de minimis principle applies in copyright law, i.e. that some things are too small to be deemed copyright works. However, the authority for this is not so clear.

Fixation and tangibility

As we have seen, copyright does not subsist in literary, dramatic, or musical works until they are recorded in writing or otherwise. This pragmatic requirement is known as 'fixation'. Usually, such works will be fixed by the author, but fixation by a third party (with or without the authors permission is also possible.

Other copyright works are not subject to the fixation requirement. This is usually unproblematic as films, sound recordings, broadcasts, cable programmes and typography are inherently tangible works.

Ownership of copyright and the employee

The rule is that the first owner of copyright in a work is the person who created the work, i.e. the author.

A major exception to this rule is CDPA 1988 s.11 (2).

This provides that where a person creates an LDMA work in the course of employment the employer is the first owner of any copyright in the work subject to any agreement to the contrary.

There are special provisions for Crown use, Parliamentary copyright and copyright for certain international organisations (CDPA 1988 s.11 (3).

Authorship, ownership and moral rights

The author is the person who creates the work. Identifying the author is usually a straightforward task. The following is the standard authorship position:

c) Literary work. The writer
d) Dramatic work. The writer
e) Musical work. The composer
f) Artistic work. The artist
g) Computer generated LDMA works. The person operating the computer.
h) Sound recordings. The producer.
i) Films. The producer and principal director.
j) Broadcasts. The broadcaster.
k) Cable programmes. The cable program service provider.
l) Typography right. The publisher.
m) Any work where the identity of the author is unknown. A work of unknown author

Joint authorship

Where more than one person is involved in the creation of a work, careful consideration is needed in determining individual contributions. A person who suggests a subject to a poet is not the author of the poem. Merely supplying ideas is insufficient for joint authorship; an integral role in the expression of ideas is required. Joint authorship arises where the efforts of the two authors is indistinguishable.

BREXIT and changes to copyright law from 1st of January 2021

Copyright is a national right that each country provides separately. However, copyright is largely harmonised internationally by a number of treaties and, in the EU, by a body of EU copyright legislation that builds on the international treaties.

A substantial part of UK copyright law was derived from the EU's legislation when the UK was a member state. Because of this, there are references in UK law to the EU, the EEA, and member states. Some of these are in the UK's implementation of EU cross-border copyright arrangements. These arrangements apply only within the EU and EEA and provide reciprocal protections and benefits between member states.

To address this issue, the Government introduced the Intellectual Property (Copyright and Related Rights) (Amendment) (EU Exit) Regulations 2019 (Intellectual Property (Copyright and Related Rights) (Amendment) (EU Exit) Regulations 2019) under the powers of the European Union (Withdrawal) Act 2018, which came into force on 1 January 2021. These regulations remove or correct references to the EU, EEA, or member states in UK copyright legislation and preserve the effect of UK law where possible. The reciprocal cross-border arrangements will be amended or brought to an end, as appropriate and this outline explains their status from 1 January 2021.

Protection of UK copyright works in the EU

The majority of UK and EU copyright works (such as books, films and music) will still be protected in each other's territories because of their participation in the international treaties on copyright. This applies to works made before and after 1 January 2021.

Copyright clearance in satellite broadcasting

The EU Satellite and Cable Directive provides a country-of-origin principle for licensing of copyright material in cross-border satellite broadcasts. This means that when a satellite broadcaster transmits a copyright work, e.g., a film, from one EEA (European Economic Area) state to another, they are only required to get the copyright holder's permission for the state in which the broadcast originates. This avoids satellite broadcasters having to secure individual licences for every member state in which their broadcasts are received.

Actions for UK satellite broadcasters

UK broadcasters may no longer benefit from the country-of-origin principle for broadcasts into the EEA from 1 January 2021 and might need to get additional right holder permissions covering the EEA states to which they broadcast. This will depend on how the domestic legislation of each EEA member state treats broadcasts originating in non-EEA countries - for example, whether they apply the country-of-origin principle to non-EEA broadcasts, as UK law does. UK broadcasters should:

-check the domestic legislation of each EEA member state into which they broadcast to identify how they treat broadcasts originating in non-EEA countries

-consider whether their licensing arrangements will need to change after 1 January 2021 to allow them to continue to broadcast into the EEA.

Broadcast of works transmitted into the UK

In the UK, the country-of-origin principle will continue to be applied to broadcasts from any country. Legitimate satellite broadcasts of copyright works transmitted into the UK from abroad will not need specific right holder permission for the UK, except where both of the following apply:

2) the broadcast is commissioned or uplinked to a satellite in the UK

3) it originates from a country that provides lower levels of copyright protection.

Sui generis database rights

As we have seen, there are two types of intellectual property protection for databases: sui generis database rights (or just 'database rights') and copyright. Both are automatic, unregistered rights that allow the owner to control certain uses of their database.

Copyright protects the selection or arrangement of material in a database where this is original (i.e., creative). Database rights protect the contents of a database. A database does not have to be original for it to qualify for database rights, but there needs to have been a substantial investment in obtaining, verifying, or presenting the data.

Database rights were introduced by the Database Directive. Eligible databases receive protection in all European Economic Area (EEA) member states. Only databases made by EEA nationals, residents or businesses are eligible.

The UK implemented the directive through the Copyright and Rights in Databases Regulations 1997.

Database rights from 1 January 2021

UK citizens, residents, and businesses will not be eligible to receive or hold database rights in the EEA for databases created on or after 1 January 2021. UK owners of databases created on or after 1 January 2021 will need to consider whether they can rely on alternative means of protection in the EEA – for example licensing agreements or copyright, where applicable.

UK legislation will be amended so that only UK citizens, residents, and businesses are eligible for database rights in the UK for databases created on or after 1 January 2021.

Existing database rights

Database rights that exist in the UK or EEA before 1 January 2021 (whether held by UK or EEA persons or businesses) will continue to exist in the UK and EEA for the rest of their duration. These rights are guaranteed under the Withdrawal Agreement.

Those in the UK who wish to use databases protected by these rights will continue to need the permission of the right holder(s).

Copyright in databases

Copyright protection for databases in the UK and EEA will not change after 1 January 2021. The UK and all EEA member states are members of international treaties on copyright that ensure eligible works (e.g., databases that are original) are protected in all treaty countries. This does not depend on the UK's relationship with the EU or EEA.

Portability of online content services

The EU Portability Regulation allows consumers across the European Economic Area (EEA) to access their online content services (for example, video-on-demand streaming services, such as Netflix and Amazon Prime) as if they are at home when they travel within the EEA. This means that an online service provider must provide customers the same content as in their home state when they are temporarily present in another state. The regulation applies only to travel between EEA member states.

Cross-border portability from 1 January 2021

The EU Portability Regulation ceased to apply to UK-EEA travel from 1 January 2021. In the UK, the regulation will be revoked. Online content service providers will not be required under the regulation to provide content ordinarily available in the UK to a UK customer who is temporarily present in any other EEA Member State. This will not prevent service providers offering cross-border portability to their customers on a voluntary basis, but to do so they will need the permission of the owners of the content they provide.

Changes for UK customers of online content services-UK customers visiting the EEA and EEA customers visiting the UK may see restrictions to the content available to them from 1 January 2021. This will depend on the terms of their services and the licences in place between service providers and right holders.

Orphan works copyright exception

Orphan works are copyright works for which the right holder is not known or cannot be found. Because orphan works are protected by copyright, they cannot be used freely, even though it may be impossible to get the right holder's permission. Under the EU Orphan Works Directive, cultural heritage institutions – e.g. libraries, archives and museums – based in the European Economic Area (EEA) can digitise and make orphan works available online across all EEA member states without the permission of the right holder. Cultural heritage institutions must register orphan works used under the exception on a database maintained by the European Union Intellectual Property Office (EUIPO).

By 1 January 2021 UK cultural heritage institutions will need to:

- remove any orphan works currently placed online under the exception
- consider seeking a licence under the UK's orphan works licensing scheme
- where they have a licence to use the work in the UK, consider limiting online access to users based in the UK to avoid copyright infringement in the EEA.

Changes for UK orphan works scheme licensees

The UK's orphan works licensing scheme allows orphan works to be licensed in the UK for commercial and non-commercial uses, subject to the user paying application and licence fees and completing a diligent search for the right holder. Licensees will no longer need to consult the EUIPO orphan works database as part of the diligent search. No other changes will be made to the diligent search requirements or the licensing scheme in general.

Access for visually impaired people from 1 January 2021

Cross-border exchanges of accessible format works for visually impaired or otherwise print-disabled people may change.

The Marrakesh Treaty to facilitate access to published works for persons who are blind, visually impaired, or otherwise print disabled, is an international agreement to improve the access of visually impaired people to copyright works around the world.

The EU is party to the treaty and has implemented it via a directive and a regulation:

- the directive allows people in the EU with visual impairments and authorised bodies that support them (for example charities) to make or distribute accessible format copies of copyright works. The Regulation allows the import and export of such copies between EU member states and other treaty countries. The UK implemented the directive via the Copyright and Related Rights (Marrakesh Treaty etc.) Regulations 2018.

The Marrakesh Treaty from 1 January 2021

The regulation and the UK's implementation of the directive will be retained in UK law from 1 January 2021. In the UK, people with visual impairment or authorised bodies will still be able to make and distribute accessible format copies of copyright works. However, the cross-border exchange of accessible format copies of works may be affected. The UK has now ratified the Marrakesh Treaty in its own right, the UK's ratification of the treaty came into force on 1 January 2021.

Collective rights management from 1 January 2021

EEA collective management organisations may not automatically represent UK right holders and collective management organisations from 1 January 2021. Collective management organisations (CMOs) are not-for-profit and/or member-governed bodies that license rights on behalf of copyright owners. CMOs in the European Economic Area (EEA) are governed by the Collective Rights Management (CRM) Directive. This includes obligations to represent on request right holders from any EEA member state unless there are objectively justified reasons not to do so. The Directive also requires EEA CMOs that offer multi-territorial licensing of musical works for online services to represent on request the catalogues of other EEA CMOs that do not offer those licences. The UK implemented the CRM Directive via the Collective Management of Copyright (EU Directive) Regulations 2016. The government published guidance on those regulations.

Collective rights management from 1 January 2021

From 1 January 2021, EEA CMOs will not be required by the CRM Directive to represent UK right holders or to represent the catalogues of UK CMOs for online licensing of musical rights. UK right holders and CMOs will still be able to request representation, but EEA CMOs may be free to refuse those requests depending on the law in individual member states. In the UK, existing obligations on UK CMOs will be maintained following 1 January 2021. These include those specific to multi-territorial licensing of musical works for online services.

UK CMOs that offer multi-territorial licensing of online rights in musical works will continue to be required to represent on request the catalogue of other CMOs (UK or EEA) for multi-territorial licensing purposes.

Artist's resale right

The Artist's resale right entitles creators of artistic works to a royalty payment each time their works are sold by an art market professional. The UK implemented the EU's Resale Right Directive through the Artist's Resale Right Regulations 2006. These regulations were amended to reflect the UK's position outside the EU, while continuing to provide the right to foreign nationals on a reciprocal basis.

Nationals of the UK and other countries that provide reciprocal treatment for UK nationals (including EU member states) will continue to receive resale rights in the UK and those countries from 1 January 2021.

This is in accordance with the Berne Convention. No changes are being made to the calculation of royalty payments.

Cable retransmissions of works

When a copyright work is broadcast between EEA member states and retransmitted by cable in the receiving member state, the copyright holder(s) can only exercise their rights through a collective management organisation. The UK applies this rule to cable retransmissions of broadcasts from EEA member states.

From 1 January 2021, member states may no longer apply this rule to broadcasts originating in the UK because it will no longer be a member state.

Copyright holders whose works are broadcast from the UK and retransmitted via cable in the EEA:

- may need to negotiate licences with the cable operator directly
- could see statutory licensing terms imposed on the cable retransmission of their works in certain EEA states.

UK legislation will continue to apply existing rules to cable retransmissions of broadcasts originating in an EEA member state.

Qualification for copyright protection

Works that are currently eligible for copyright protection in the UK will continue to be eligible from 1 January 2021. Works are eligible for copyright protection in the UK if they are:

- made by a national of the UK, EEA or any country that is party to the international copyright treaties or

- first published or transmitted in the UK, EEA or any country that is party to the international copyright treaties.

References to the EEA have been removed from UK law. This will not stop EEA works qualifying for copyright protection in the UK, because all EEA states are party to the international treaties.

Copyright duration

Copyright duration in the UK for works from the UK, EEA, or other countries will not change from 1 January 2021. References to the EEA have been removed from UK law in this area, which means that the duration for EEA works is calculated in the same way as for non-EEA works. However, as copyright duration is equal across the UK and the EEA, there will be no immediate impact on copyright duration in the UK.

Infringement of Copyright

Section 16(1) and (2) Copyright, Designs and Patents Act 1988 states:

"The owner of the copyright in a work has the exclusive right to copy, issue copies of the work, rent, lend, perform, show, play or communicate the work to the public or do any of the above in relation to an adaptation. Copyright in a work is infringed by a person who without the licence of the copyright owner does, or authorises another to do, any of the acts restricted by copyright".

However, the 1988 Act has been significantly amended by a series of Regulations introduced in June 2014 These changes affect infringement of copyright.

Amendments to Copyright Law-Regulations from 2014

The following Regulations were all brought into force from 1st June 2014 and have served to amend the Copyright, Designs and Patents Act 1988.

The Public Administration, Disability, and Research, Education, Libraries and Archives statutory instruments were approved by parliament on 14 May and came into force on 1 June 2014. These instruments, listed below, amended relevant sections of the Copyright, Designs and Patents Act 1988.

- The Copyright and Rights in Performances (Disability) Regulations 2014
- The Copyright and Rights in Performances (Personal Copies for Private Use) Regulations 2014
- The Copyright and Rights in Performances (Research, Education, Libraries and Archives) Regulations 2014
- The Copyright (Public Administrations) Regulations 2014
- The Copyright and Rights in Performances (Quotation and Parody) Regulations 2014

Exceptions to copyright

Copyright protects literary, dramatic, musical and artistic works as well as films, sound recordings, book layouts, and broadcasts. If you want to copy or use a copyright work then you usually have to get permission from the copyright owner, but there are a few exceptions where you can copy or use part or all of a copyright work without permission. Where a work contains a performance, the performance will also have rights over how the work is used. The exceptions to copyright also apply to these related rights.

The law on these exceptions changed in a number of small but important ways, to make the UK copyright system better suited to the digital age. These changes affect how you can use content like books, music, films and photographs.

Personal copies for private use

Copyright law changed to allow you to make personal copies of media (ebooks, digital music, or video files etc) you have bought, for private purposes such as format shifting or backup. Before this change to the law, it was not legal to copy music that you bought on a CD onto your MP3 player.

The changes update copyright law to make this legal, as long as you own what you are copying, e.g., a music album, and the copy you make is for your own private use.

You are also able to copy a book or film you have bought for one of your devices onto another of your devices, without infringing copyright. However, you should note that media, such as DVDs and e-books, can still be protected by technology which physically prevents copying and circumvention of such technology remains illegal. It is still illegal to make copies for friends or family, or to make a copy of something you do not own or have acquired illegally, without the copyright owner's permission. So you cannot make copies of CDs for your friends, copy CDs borrowed from friends, or copy videos illegally downloaded from file-sharing websites.

The law allows you to make personal copies to any device that you own, or a personal online storage medium, such as a private cloud. However, it is illegal to give other people access to the copies you have made, including, for example, by allowing a friend to access your personal cloud storage.

The exception applies to any copies you have bought, other than computer programs. So, for example, it allows you to format shift an ebook you have bought from one device to another for your own private use. However, you should note that media, such as DVDs and e-books, can still be protected by technology which physically prevents copying and circumvention of such technology remains illegal.

Quotation

Previously, it was an infringement of copyright to take a quotation from one work and use it in another without permission from the copyright owner, unless it was done for the purpose of criticism, review or news reporting. Copyright law allows quotations to be used more widely without infringing copyright, as long as the use is fair (in law, the use must be a "fair dealing" see overleaf) and there is a sufficient acknowledgement - which generally means the title and the author's name should be indicated. It is ultimately for the courts to determine whether use of a quotation is fair dealing, which will depend on the facts of any specific case. However, the use of a title and short extract from a book in an academic article discussing the book is likely to be permitted, whereas the copying of a long extract from a book, without it being justified by the context, is unlikely to be permitted. You may benefit from this law if you are an author, academic, or even just a casual blogger.

Caricature, parody or pastiche

Prior to 2014, anyone wishing to use other people's copyright material for the purposes of caricature, parody, or pastiche (such as a parody song or video), required the permission of the rights holder. Copyright law now allows limited uses of copyright material for the purposes of caricature, parody or pastiche, without having to obtain the permission of the rights holder. It is important to ensure you understand the limits if you plan to use other people's material for caricature, parody or pastiche. Only minor uses are permitted and a use must be considered fair and reasonable (in law, the use must be a "fair dealing", see the box below), otherwise you must seek permission from the rights holder.

This exception to copyright has no impact on the law of libel or slander, so you may still be sued if a parody work is defamatory. It also does not affect an author's moral right to object to "derogatory treatment" of their work (as defined in copyright law).

'Fair dealing' is a legal term used to establish whether a use of copyright material is lawful or whether it infringes copyright. There is no statutory definition of fair dealing - it will always be a matter of fact, degree and impression in each case. The question to be asked is: how would a fair-minded and honest person have dealt with the work?

Factors that have been identified by the courts as relevant in determining whether a particular dealing with a work is fair, include:

- Does using the work affect the market for the original work? If a use of a work acts as a substitute for it, causing the owner to lose revenue, then it is not likely to be fair.
- Is the amount of the work taken reasonable and appropriate? Was it necessary to use the amount taken? Usually, only part of a work may be used.

The relative importance of any one factor will vary according to the case in hand and the type of dealing in question.

Education and teaching

After 2014, changes were made to copyright law in order to help teachers to deliver modern multi-media teaching without risk of copyright infringement. The exceptions relating specifically to educational establishments have widened, allowing more extensive use of materials in conjunction with educational licensing schemes.

Another change permits minor acts of copying for teaching purposes, as long as the use is considered fair and reasonable. So, teachers will be able to do things like displaying webpages or quotes on interactive whiteboards, without having to seek additional permission. Education and Teaching

Many schools, colleges and universities copy media which is protected by copyright - for instance photocopying extracts from books for class handouts or recording television programmes to show to a class.

In order to do this, educational establishments hold educational copying licences. So if a school wants to record television broadcasts, it needs a licence from the Educational Recording Agency. If it wants to photocopy extracts from books, it needs a licence from the Copyright Licensing Agency. Most educational establishments already hold these licences.

These licensing schemes are underpinned by copyright exceptions that mean that, where a particular work is not covered by a licence, an educational establishment is still able to copy it. This means that teachers do not have to check the terms of each item they want to copy before they copy it.

The changes to the law apply these exceptions to a wider range of copyright works which were previously not covered - such as artistic works (including photographs), films and sound recordings. They also permit sharing of copies over secure distance learning networks. In order to carry out these activities, schools, colleges and universities simply need to make sure they hold the relevant licences.

Previous to 2014, limited copying of literary, dramatic, musical or artistic works for the purposes of teaching, provided it was not by means of a reprographic process was allowed. This meant copying by hand was permitted, but the use of laptops and interactive whiteboards was not. The previous law was replaced with a general "fair dealing" exception, allowing copying of works in any medium as long as the following conditions apply:

1. the work must be used solely to illustrate a point;
2. the use of the work must not be for commercial purposes;
3. the use must be fair dealing; and
4. it must be accompanied by a sufficient acknowledgement.

This means minor uses, such as displaying a few lines of poetry on an interactive whiteboard, are permitted, but uses which would undermine sales of teaching materials still need a licence.

The new law does not remove the need for educational establishments to hold licences for use that does not fall under the "fair dealing" exception, for instance, photocopying material to distribute to students. Schools, colleges and universities still have to pay for third party teaching materials which are available under licence.

Teaching use which is fair dealing, illustrative and non-commercial is permitted by the exception and uses for exam purposes may fall within these criteria. You may also be able to rely on the new quotation exception, for example where you wish to reproduce a piece of text for analysis in an English exam. This would not extend to the making of a reprographic copy of a musical work for use by an examination candidate when performing the work.

Research

The change in the law meant that for the first time, researchers and students who need to copy parts of sound recordings, films or broadcasts for non-commercial research or private study are allowed to do so. Libraries and archives are also able to make copies of artistic works for researchers and students. Education institutions, libraries, archives and museums are able to offer access to copyright works on their premises by electronic means at dedicated terminals.

Researchers and students were previously allowed to copy limited extracts of literary, dramatic, musical and artistic works for non-commercial research and private study. They are now able to copy a limited amount of a sound recording, film, or broadcast. This amount is restricted by fair dealing, which rules out unfair or unreasonable uses such as copying a whole film for "research" instead of buying the DVD. Any use made of the work must be accompanied by a sufficient acknowledgement.

Quotation

Minor uses of quotations from copyright works could be prevented by copyright owners, unless they fell within fair dealing exceptions for criticism, review, or news reporting. following 2014, the law has been amended to give people greater freedom to quote the works of others for other purposes, as long as this is reasonable and fair ("fair dealing").

Caricature, parody or pastiche

The ability to re-edit copyright works in new and experimental ways is seen as an important learning and teaching exercise for creative skills.

Many works of caricature, parody, or pastiche, involve some level of copying from another work. The law has changed to allow limited uses of other people's copyright material for the purposes of caricature, parody, or pastiche, without first asking for permission.

*

Changes affecting disabled people

Post 2014, the Government made it easier for disabled people to access materials that are protected by copyright. Previously there were exceptions to copyright law that allowed visually impaired people, and organisations acting on their behalf, to make accessible versions (e.g., Braille versions) of certain types of material, such as books. Also, the law allowed certain designated organisations to produce sub-titled copies of broadcasts for people who are deaf or hard of hearing.

However, these exceptions did not apply to other types of impairment, such as dyslexia, and did not apply to all types of copyright work. The law changed so that anyone who has an impairment that prevents them accessing copyright works will now be able to benefit from the exception, not just visually impaired people. The law also allows individuals, educational establishments and not-for-profit organisations to reproduce all types of copyright-protected content in accessible formats.

These changes gave disabled people greater access to creative content, as individuals, educational establishments and charities are allowed to reproduce material without purchasing a licence as long as a copy is not already commercially available in an accessible format.

Also, the law has been simplified so that organisations wishing to produce sub-titled copies of broadcasts on behalf of deaf and other disabled people will be able to do so without going through a bureaucratic designation process.

What's allowed?

The law allows acts such as:

- Making Braille, audio or large-print copies of books, newspapers or magazines for visually impaired people

- Adding audio-description to films or broadcasts for visually impaired people
- Making sub-titled films or broadcasts for deaf or hard of hearing people
- Making accessible copies of books, newspapers, or magazines for dyslexic people.

However, it is only legal to reproduce material if suitable accessible copies are not commercially available. Organisations that make and supply accessible-format copies for disabled people have a duty to keep records of the copies they make and provide them to the copyright owner of the material.

Text and data mining technologies help researchers process large amounts of data.

Copyright law altered to help ensure that if a researcher is carrying out non-commercial research, they will not infringe copyright by copying material for a text and data mining analysis.

Copying works for research and private study

Copyright law recognises that researchers and students may legitimately need to copy limited extracts of copyright works for the purpose of their studies. Therefore, the law already allowed researchers and students to copy limited extracts of some types of copyright works (books, plays and musical scores, picture and photos, literary, dramatic musical and artistic works) as long as they are carrying out non-commercial research or private study. Librarians are permitted to assist researchers and students by providing limited copies of these types of copyright works.

Copyright law changed so that all types of published copyright works are covered by the exception allowing limited copying for the purpose of research. This means that researchers and students (or the librarians and archivists who are assisting them) who need to copy limited parts of sound recordings, films or broadcasts for non-commercial research or private study are allowed to do so. The provisions about only copying a part of a work and sufficiently acknowledging the original work still apply.

Additionally, educational institutions, libraries, archives and museums are permitted to offer access to copyright works on their premises at dedicated electronic terminals for research and private study.

Text and Data Mining for non-commercial research

Text and data mining is the use of automated analytical techniques to analyse text and data for patterns, trends and other useful information. Text and data mining usually requires copying of the work to be analysed. Prior to 2014, researchers using text and data mining in their research risked infringing copyright unless they had specific permission from the copyright owner.

Post 2014, copyright exception allows researchers to make copies of any copyright material for the purpose of computational analysis if they already have the right to read the work (that is, work that they have "lawful access" to). They will be able to do this without having to obtain permission to make copies from the rights holder. This exception only permits the making of copies for the purpose of text and data mining for non-commercial research. Researchers will still have to buy subscriptions to access material; this could be from many sources including academic publishers.

Publishers and content providers are able to apply reasonable measures to maintain their network security or stability so long as these measures do not prevent or unreasonable restrict a researcher's ability to make the copies they need to make for their text and data mining. Contract terms that stop researchers making copies of works to which they have lawful access in order to carry out a text and data mining analysis will be unenforceable.

Copyright material held by public bodies

Some material held by public bodies will have been submitted by third parties, such as by members of the public, businesses or researchers. For example, this could be material submitted to a public body, such as local authority, as part of a duty to capture information required for public register.

Where a public body holds third party material - that is, material in which someone other than the public body owns the copyright - the general position has been that an individual could either view that material in person, or a public body could copy and distribute it on an individual basis. prior to 2014, the law did not generally allow such material to be published online without permission from the rights holders.

Public bodies and keepers of statutory registers can now proactively share copyright material online without seeking permission, as long as it is not commercially available. The same applies to material that is already available for public inspection through some statutory mechanism, such as local planning applications. This change does not permit public bodies to publish material that is commercially available to buy or license (such as academic articles). In these circumstances any public body would still need to seek the permission of the rights holder. Another change in this area applies to certain works that have been communicated to the Crown with the permission of the copyright owner and in the course of public business. This exception applies only to literary, dramatic, musical, or artistic works that have not previously been published. Changes post 2014 make it easier for the public to access information, saving both time and expense for public bodies and individuals.

Libraries, Museums and Archives

Post 2014, the law changed to make it easier and cheaper for cultural institutions like libraries, archives, and museums to use, share and preserve their collections. There are two significant changes which affect libraries, archives and museums. The first relates to making copies of works to preserve them for future generations. The second allows greater freedom to copy works for those carrying out non-commercial research and private study.

Archiving and preservation of resources

Changes to copyright law for archiving and preservation will make it easier to preserve creative content held by libraries, archives and museums. These institutions are now allowed to preserve any type of copyright work that is held in their permanent collection (but not available for loan to the public) and cannot readily be replaced. There is a risk that both the original and the copy of a work may degenerate or corrupt over time. Making a single copy may be insufficient to safeguard a work in the long term.

Copying works for research and private study

Librarians are permitted to assist researchers and students by providing limited copies of books, plays and musical scores, pictures and photos, literary, dramatic, musical and artistic works for non-commercial research and private study.

The amount that can be copied is restricted to a reasonable proportion. This rules out unfair or unreasonable uses such as copying a whole film for "research" instead of buying the DVD and generally means that only a part of a work can be copied. Use made of the work should be accompanied by sufficient acknowledgement (e.g., in a reference or bibliography). The law changed post 2014 so that all types of published copyright works are now covered by the provisions in copyright law allowing limited copying for non-commercial research and private study. The same provisions about only copying a part of a work and sufficiently acknowledging the author still apply.

Educational institutions, libraries, archives and museums are now permitted to offer access to copyright works on their premises at dedicated electronic terminals for research and private study.

A librarian who is supplying a copy of a work will wish to ask a researcher to declare that they are doing non-commercial research, this can now be done electronically`(for example, an electronic copyright declaration form could be signed using a typed signature or checkbox).

What types of libraries are able to provide copies of work?

Publicly accessible libraries and archives, such as those run by universities, schools, local council, government departments and NHS institutions can provide copies of copyright work for non-commercial research and private study, as set out in this guidance. The provisions do not extend to private libraries or archives, such as law firms that run on a commercial basis.

Libraries, archives and museums

How much of a work is a librarian allowed to copy for a student or researcher? The amount you are able to copy of a published work is limited to a reasonable proportion, and a copyright declaration must be provided. This generally means that only a limited part that is necessary for the research project may be copied. However, archivists may supply a single copy of a whole or part of a work provided that the work had not been published or communicated before it was deposited in the library or archive, or the owner of that work has not prohibited the copying of that work. As usual, a copyright declaration must be provided.

Defences to Copyright infringement

There are several defences to infringement:

a) Challenge the existence of copyright or the claimant's ownership of copyright.
b) Deny the infringement.
c) Claim to have been entitled, because of permission granted to do the act in question or argue that it is within one of the statutory fair dealing exemptions or by claiming public interest or EC competition rights.

A claim of ignorance of the law will not work as a defence. Ignorance of subsistence of copyright will, however, have a bearing on any damages awarded. In the case of secondary infringement an element of knowledge is required for the infringement to be actionable in the first place. The infringement only occurs if the person knows that what he or she is dealing with is an infringing copyright work.

If the claimant does own copyright in the work that is allegedly infringed, and facts can be proved, the only defences remaining are:

- that the defendant had permission from the copyright owner to make a copy.
- Provided that the defendant in an infringement action can prove that permission was granted, either in writing, orally or, in certain cases, implied, then the claim of infringement will fail.
- That the act was one of the permitted acts under the 1988 Act, as amended.

The 1988 Act, as amended, contains statutory permissions, or exceptions, to the exclusive rights of the copyright owner. Many of these have come from the results of case decisions over the years that have acknowledged the need for fair exceptions.

These permitted acts are categorised in the Act and comprise:

- Research and private study
- Criticism review and news reporting
- Incidental inclusion of copyright material
- Things done for instruction or examination
- Anthologies for educational use
- Playing, showing or performing in an educational establishment
- Recordings by educational establishments
- Reprographic copying by educational establishments
- Libraries and archives
- Public administration
- Lawful users of computer programs and databases
- Design Typefaces
- Works in electronic form

All the above are categorised in the Act and each case concerning these categories will be on its own merit.

1) That the exercise of the copyright owner's rights to prevent copying would amount to an anti-competitive practice under EC competition law.
2) That the exercise of the copyright owner's rights is against the public interest.

Each one of the above must be proven and each case will be judged on its own merit.

Copyright infringement and the use of artificial intelligence

As we have seen, the use of AI is growing and correspondingly the abuse of copyright, and indeed all other aspects of intellectual property is growing apace. There are numerous court cases ongoing, In particular, the music industry as been up in arms about the use of songs and images without the originators permission.

****

5.5

Design Law

Design law in the UK has been significantly affected as a result of Brexit, as outlined below.

A design patent can protect the visual ornamental characteristics of an article and can be an important part of a company's patent portfolio. Like other patent rights, design patent applications may be filed internationally to expand the number of countries in which a company's designs are protected.

Determining where to obtain protection for a company's designs generally depends on a number of factors, such as where products featuring the designs are being sold, planned to be sold, or likely to be copied, where competitors are located, where products featuring the designs are manufactured, and the local patent requirements. Regardless of these considerations, obtaining protection in Europe and elsewhere can be valuable for a company looking to expand the breadth of protection for its designs.

In the context of intellectual property, the "design" of a product is generally its shape or ornamentation applied to it, although the exact definition varies between different types of protection. Essentially, the design of a product relates to its appearance, rather than to technical principles of its construction or operation.

The effect of Brexit on the EU Community design regime Following the end of the Brexit transition period on 31 December 2020, the Community design regime governed by Commission Regulation

6/2002 (the Community Design Regulation) ceased to apply in the UK. Accordingly, both Registered Community Designs (RCDs) and Unregistered Community Designs (UCDs) ceased to have effect in, provide protection in or be enforceable in the UK from that point (although their force and effect will of course continue in the EU). Instead, design protection in the UK is now solely governed by the UK's domestic design legislation, to which changes have been made to compensate for the loss of Community design protection in the UK.

As mentioned in the introduction, The Design Right, Artist's Resale Right and Copyright (Amendment) Regulations 2023 look to implement some technical changes to IP REUL, amending provisions in four pieces of legislation mainly to make them more relevant to a UK context.

UK registered design law

The main domestic legislation dealing with registered designs in the UK is section 24A (2) of the Registered Designs Act 1949 and The Intellectual Property Act 2014, which made changes to both UK registered and unregistered designs as outlined further on.

What is a UK registered design?

A UK registered design gives a "monopoly" right, i.e., a right to stop anybody else using the registered design irrespective of whether they copied it. A UK registered design gives its proprietor the exclusive right in the United Kingdom to make, use, sell, import and export any product embodying the design, if it is a shape, or bearing the design if it is ornamentation. These rights extend to similar designs which do not produce a substantially different impression on the informed user.

The proprietor can act against any third party who carries out any of the rights exclusive to the proprietor within the United Kingdom without the proprietor's permission, even if they are using a design that they created independently and without copying.

A UK registered design cannot be used to control the movement of goods put on the market in the European Economic Area (EEA) by the proprietor of the design, or with their consent.

What can be protected by registration?

A design may be the appearance of a whole or part of a product (including its inside) and may arise from the lines, contours, colours, shape, texture, material, or ornamentation of the product. The product may even be a graphic symbol, e.g., a computer icon, or a typographical typeface.

The design which is the subject of an application for registration must meet two criteria. It must:

- be novel; and
- possess individual character.

Both these criteria are judged with reference to designs which have been made available to the public before the effective filing date of the application. Designs may be made available by publication, use or any other means.

Grace period

One important exception to the above is that the prior disclosures of a design made by its designer, or in consequence of a disclosure made by the designer, within 12 months before the filing date (or priority date, if applicable) of the application do not count for the determination of Novelty or Individual Character. However, such disclosures may prevent registering the design in foreign countries, especially outside the European

Union, as many countries in the world do not allow such a grace period or allow a shorter period.

This provision *does not* exclude disclosures made independently of the designer during this period, and therefore applications should be filed before the design is disclosed if possible.

Another exception to the above requirements is that prior disclosures which could not have become known before the effective filing date in the EEA in the business sector concerned are disregarded. This provision is thought only to exclude obscure disclosures, whether by virtue of the extent, location, or time of disclosure.

Novelty

For a design to be novel it must differ from prior designs by more than immaterial details.

A key case concerning novelty and individual character is that of *Green Lane Products Ltd v PMS International Group Ltd (2008)*. In this case, a challenge to the validity of the claimant's Community design for spiky laundry balls was based on the defendant's similar shaped spiky balls used for massaging the human body.

It was established in this case that the prior art is not limited to the particular product for which the design was registered, as the scope of infringement is not limited to the product for which it was intended to apply the design. For example, the registration of a design intended for motor cars would protect also against its use for toys. The 'informed user' is not the same as the average consumer of trademark law. The informed user has experience of similar products and will be reasonably discriminatory and able to appreciate sufficient detail to decide whether or not the design under consideration creates a different overall impression. The degree of design freedom is taken into account.

Individual character

For a design to possess individual character, it must produce a different overall impression on the informed user from prior designs. In many cases, the informed user is likely to be the end user of the product.

In fields where the designer has less design freedom, the difference between registrable designs and prior designs will not be as great as where the designer had complete design freedom. This is also reflected in the infringement rights arising from the registration.

A key case concerning individual character and design freedom is that of Pepsico Inc's design (No ICD000000172) OHIM.

The design in question was for a disk having annular rings or corrugations applied to a promotional item for games. There was a challenge to the validity of the design. The design was declared invalid.

The legal principle was that the informed consumer would be familiar with promotional items and would pay more attention to graphical elements rather than minor variations in shape. Furthermore, although there were some constraints to design freedom, these were to do with cost and safety, and, otherwise, there was ample design freedom. Thus, the informed user may focus on certain aspects of a design and design freedom should be looked at in the round and some constraints may be present without significantly reducing the overall design freedom.

Complex products and spare parts

Complex products are defined as products which are composed of two or more replaceable component parts which permit disassembly and reassembly of the product. The designs of component parts of such products can only be registered if the component parts remain visible during normal use of the complex product. Further, the repair of a complex product so as to restore it to its original appearance by the use of a component part does not infringe a design registered for the design of that component part. This is aimed at continuing to permit the manufacture and sale of "non-genuine" car parts, for example, even if such parts are registered.

Excluded features and designs

A design registration cannot protect features of a design which are solely dictated by the product's technical function, or features which are required to permit the product to be connected to or placed in, around or against another product so that either product may perform its function. However, a design which serves the purpose of allowing the assembly of modular products may be registered.

It is not allowable to register designs which incorporate protected emblems which include, for example, the Olympic symbols, Royal arms and national flags. Nor is allowable to incorporate third parties' trademarks or copyright material into a design to be registered.

UK unregistered design right (UK UDR)

The UK Unregistered design right was introduced by the Copyright, Designs and Patents Act 1998, as amended, in an attempt to overcome the problems of protection of functional designs by means of copyright in drawings showing the designs, as highlighted in *British Leyland Motor Corp v Armstrong Patents Co Ltd (1986).*

UK UDR gives its owner the right to prevent unauthorised copying of the design in the UK. In contrast to registered design rights, it is not a monopoly right, in the sense that only if a third party produces an article by copying is design right infringed. The owner may also prevent unauthorised dealing, e.g. by importation, possession, sale, hire, offer to sell or hire, in infringing articles provided the party who does so has knowledge or reason to believe they are dealing in an infringing article. The rights extend to designs which are substantially the same as that which is protected. No formal registration procedure is required (or possible) to obtain UK UDR: it comes into existence automatically upon creation of the relevant design.

Duration of protection

UK UDR protection lasts for a maximum of 15 years from the end of the calendar year in which the design was first recorded in a design document or an article was first made to the design, whichever occurred first. If articles made to the design are put on sale within the first five years of that term, then the design right lasts for only 10 years from the date of first sale. During the last five years of the term of design right its effect is reduced. During that period, the proprietor must, if requested by a third party, grant a licence, the terms of which will be settled by the UK Intellectual Property Office if not agreed by the parties concerned. This means, effectively, that design right cannot be used to stop copying during this period, but it can be used to generate royalties.

What is protected by UK UDR?

Any new design of the whole or part of an article, providing it is not commonplace in the relevant technical field, is protectable by design right. However, there is no UK UDR in:

- a method or principle of construction;
- a feature which is configured for connection to or is arranged to match another article. This exclusion generally applies to spare parts,

excluding them from protection by design right, although registered design protection may be available; and
- surface decoration.

A key case in the area is that of *Dyson Ltd v Qualtex (UK) Ltd (2006)* which concerned various aspects of design rights including the scope of the 'must fit' and 'must match' and surface decoration exclusions.

How does protection arise?

A UK UDR automatically comes into being upon the making of an article to a particular design or by the creation of a "design document" by a "qualified person" (or as a result of employment by or a commission from such a person). A qualified person is a national or resident of the EU or of certain non-EU countries (i.e. those which offer reciprocal rights to UK nationals. The main territories giving reciprocal protection are New Zealand and (Hong Kong). A company may count as a "qualified person". The "design document" must be a record of the design, but it may take any form, e.g., a drawing, photograph, model, prototype, written description, data stored in a computer or on a disc, or even a knitting pattern.

The owner of the design right is the designer (or his or her employer or commissioner, if applicable).

Other Rights

UK semiconductor topography right

Designs which relate to a semiconductor topography (i.e. the layout of a pattern in or on a semiconductor product) are also protected by UK UDR. All the above comments in relation to UK design right also apply to semiconductor topography right, with the exception that as more overseas countries allow protection, qualifying individuals can come from states including Australia, Canada, Japan and the USA.

Design Protection in Europe after Brexit

To obtain protection for designs in Europe, companies generally have two main options: (1) file a Registered Community Design ("RCD"); and (2) file separate design patent applications in individual jurisdictions. RCDs are generally the more popular option due to various advantages, including that they provide a single registration that covers all countries that make up the European Union. With Brexit, however, the protection offered by RCDs has changed. The United Kingdom officially left the European Union as of January 31, 2020 and entered an 11-month transition period that ended on December 31, 2020. Importantly, as of January 1, 2021, RCDs no longer cover the UK. Unfortunately, this means that the costs associated with registering designs across all of Europe, including the UK, will increase for both new filings and for companies that had originally filed only an RCD.

For example, companies looking to protect a design through registration in both Europe and the UK will now need to file both a RCD and a UK design application. As a result, there will be an increased cost to file and obtain protection in both the European Union countries and the UK.

For any RCD that is already registered, the UK Intellectual Property Office ("UKIPO") will automatically create a corresponding "cloned" UK design registration. A cloned UK registration created in this manner keeps the original filing and priority date of the original RCD and forms a fully independent UK design registration that can be challenged, assigned, licensed, or renewed separately from the original RCD. A cloned UK design registration based on a RCD will be allocated a number consisting of the full registration number of the RCD, prefixed with the digit "9."

Although the cloned UK design registration is created at no cost, annuities will be due and payable to the UKIPO to remain in force. If a company already has a UK design registration for the same design, it may choose not to pay the annuities for the cloned UK design registration, resulting in termination of the cloned UK design registration. Companies should carefully consider whether their cloned UK design registrations are identical to their already pending UK design registrations, and whether their cloned UK design registration would add any alternative protection.

While the UKIPO will now create a cloned registration for RCDs that are already registered, the UKIPO will not automatically create a cloned UK design registration for any RCD that is still pending or otherwise not registered as of January 1, 2021. Instead, companies seeking protection in the UK based on a pending RCD are required to re-file the design application with the UKIPO by September 30, 2021. It is important for companies to pay attention to these deadlines to achieve their desired level of protection in Europe.

Applying for a Registered Design-The Practical Process

To apply to register a design you should go to: https://www.gov.uk/apply-register-design

Use this service to register a design with the Intellectual property Office (IPO). You can register more than one design. The site outlines the full process and fees associated with design registration.

****

Chapter 6

Intellectual Property and Computer Software

Computer software and computer designs have pushed the boundaries of intellectual property law. Note in the introduction, the increasing attention to artificial intelligence and concerns about copyright law and protection.

All forms of copyright work can exist in digital form and the Copyright, Designs and Patents Act 1988 acknowledges this, for example, by providing that copying includes copying in electronic form and also extends to transient and temporary copies. protection is also given to technological measures to prevent unauthorised acts in relation to computer programmes (in this case called copy-protection) and other forms of works, including databases, have suitable provisions for this. Of particular interest is the protection of computer programs and databases, which may also be protected by a database right.

Computer programmes and artificial intelligence

As might be expected this is an area now fraught with problems. The relationship between computer programmes and AI and Intellectual property law ids complex and evolving. AI technologies, including neural networks, are often considered computer programmes under patent law, but this does not automatically exclude them from patentability. As we saw earlier, the UK court's recent decision in *Emotional Perception AI Ltd v Comptroller General of patents, Designs and Trademarks (2026)* has opened the door to patent protection for AI inventions, particularly those that contribute to the solution of a technical problem. The UK Intellectual Property Office has updated its guidance to reflect this new understanding, allowing for broader protection of AI inventions.

Computer programs generally

Computer programs and preparatory design material for computer programs are a form of literary work. Section 3(1) Copyright, Designs and Patents Act 1988 states:

...'literary work' means any work, other than a dramatic or musical work, which is written, spoken or sung, and accordingly includes:

(i) a table or compilation (other than a database);(ii) a computer program;

(iii) preparatory design material for a computer program; and

(iv) a database

For the purposes of copyright, a computer programme is original in the sense that it is the author's own intellectual creation. The Act simply requires that a computer program is original, unlike the Directive which uses the above formula.

The basic rules on the restricted acts and infringement apply to computer programs as with other forms of literary work. However, there are some special rules as to what constitutes an adaptation of a compute program and there are some specific permitted acts that apply to computer programs (back-up copies, decompilation, observing, studying and testing and other acts permitted to lawful users). Rules as to ownership are the same as other original works but the nature of the software industry means that many computer programs and other items of software are created by consultants and self-employed persons.

There are no significant issues with respect of duplicate copying of computer programs but non-textual copying can cause problems, such as where an alleged infringer has written a new computer program to emulate the operational and functional aspects of an existing program, sometimes using a completely different computer programming language.

One case that highlights this is *Nova Productions Ltd v Mazooma Games Ltd (2007)* where the defendant created a computer game which had some similar features to the claimant's game such as the 'power cue'. Both games were based on the game of pool with coloured balls and a green baize table with pockets. The main finding here was that there was no infringement. Although there were similarities, there was no allegation of copying the claimant's program source code. Merely emulating an existing program without more does not infringe. The claim was not sufficiently specific to cover copying of the detailed architecture of the claimant's program and merely amounted to a claim to copying general ideas. Jacob LJ said:

'If protection for such general ideas as are relied on here were conferred by the law, copyright would become an instrument of oppression rather than the incentive for creation which it is intended to be. protection would have moved to cover works merely inspired by others, to ideas themselves'.

Databases

It should be noted that although 'computer program' is not defined in the act, there is a definition of 'database' that applies equally to copyright databases and databases protected by the database right even though the two rights are different.

The main definition of a database is that a database is a collection of independent works, data or other materials which are arranged in a systematic or methodical way and are individually accessible by electronic or other means.

Databases can be electronic or other wise. For example, a card index arranged alphabetically would fall within the definition. The contents themselves need not be works of copyright (data or other materials) but if the contents are protected by copyright or other rights, such rights are not prejudiced by the protection of a database as a database.

For the database right to subsist, there must be substantial investment (in terms of human, technical or financial resources) in the obtaining, verification or presentation of the contents of the database. The repeated and systematic extraction and re-utilisation of insubstantial parts of the contents of a database may infringe the database right where, cumulatively. these acts amount to an extraction and/or re-utilisation of a substantial part of the contents of a database measured qualitatively and/ or quantitatively.

Patents and computer software

Certain things are excluded from the meaning of 'invention' for the purposes of patent law. the list of things is not exhaustive, nor is there any deducible common logic between the things excluded. Computer programs, as such, are excluded as are business methods and mental acts. Where there is a 'technical effect' this may overcome the exception but where a computer program only performs other excluded matter, this will not count as a valid technical effect, for example, in the case of a business method implemented by a computer program. The main statute covering this area is Article 52 of the European Patent Convention. This states:

(1) European patents shall be granted for any inventions, in all fields of technology, provided that they are new, involve an inventive step and are susceptible of industrial application.

(2) The following in particular shall not be regarded as inventions within the meaning of paragraph 1:

(a) discoveries, scientific theories and mathematical methods;

(b) aesthetic creations;

(c) schemes, rules and methods for performing mental acts, playing games or doing business, and programs for computers;

(d) presentation of information.

(3) paragraph 2 shall exclude the patentability of the subject matter or activities referred to therein only to the extent to which a European patent application or European patent relates to such subject matter or activities as such.

Design law and computer-generated images

Before the harmonisation of registered design law in Europe and the introduction of the Community design, it was almost impossible to register computer graphics as designs in the UK. The definition of 'design' and 'product' under the harmonising directive and the Community Design Regulation changed this. The key statute here is Article 3 (a) and (b) of the Community Design Regulation (Article (1(a) and (b) of the Directive on the legal protection of designs)

(a) 'design' means the appearance of the whole or a part of a product resulting from the features of, in particular, the lines, contours, colours, shape, texture and/or materials of the product itself and/or its ornamentation;

(b) 'product' means any industrial or handicraft item, including *inter alia* parts intended to be assembled into a complex product, packaging, get up, graphic symbols and typographic typefaces, but excluding computer programs.

Although computer programs are expressly excluded, this does not extend to symbols and images generated by computer programs. Also, fonts, being typographical typefaces, are capable of protection.

Please note the changes to design law and also patents following The UK's departure from the EU, as outlined in the chapter on Design law.

****

Index